STOMP OFF, LET'S GO!

The story of
Bob Crosby's Bob Cats
and Big Band

Other books by John Chilton:

Who's Who of Jazz
Billie's Blues
Teach Yourself Jazz
McKinney's Music
A Jazz Nursery
Louis - The Louis Armstrong Story (with Max Jones)

The Story of

Bob Crosby's Bob Cats & Big Band

JOHN CHILTON

JAZZ BOOK SERVICE
Post Office Box 278
London WC1N 3RD
1983

First published 1983

Copyright © 1983 John Chilton

ISBN 0 950 1290 3 8

Printed by Image Publicity, 2 Northington Street, London WC1N 2JJ Telephone: 01-405 5333

CONTENTS

Grateful acknowledgments to:

Akron Beacon Journal
Van Alexander
Willard Alexander
Richard B. Allen
Mildred Ashcraft
Jeff Atterton
A. Harlow Atwood, Jr.
Harry Avery
Ray Bauduc
Ernani Bernardi
George Bohn
Wilfred Bourgeois
Michael Brooks
Eric J. Brown
Billy Butterfield
Cadence
Capitol News
Pete Carpenter
Lyn Wild Cathcart
Chicago Mercy Hospital
Ron Clough
Coda
Derek Coller
James L. Collier
Ray Conniff
Ian Crosbie
Bob Crosby
Charlie Crump
Tony Dalmado
Stanley Dance
Mel Davis
Bertrand Demeusy
Sophie & Jennie Depew
Dave Dexter
Down Beat
Jack Egan
Scott Ellsworth
Leonard Feather
Gerry Finningley
Footnote
Charles Fox
Steve Giarratano
Bob Goodrich
Sidney Goodsell
Al Governor

Ralph Gulliver
Bob Haggart
John Hammond
Ralph S. Harding
Karl Gert zur Heide
Max Herman
Franz Hoffman
Hollywood Notes
Honolulu Star Bulletin
Dick Hughes
Jimmy Ille
International Musician
Jazz Forum
Jazz Information
Jazz Journal
Jazz Monthly
Jazz Record
Norman Jenkinson
Len Jones
Joseph V. Kearns
Deane Kincaide
Al King
George Koenig
Stan Kuwik
Hilton Lamare
Yank Lawson
Barry Ledingham
Steve Love
John F. Marion
Don Marquis
Lura Matlock
Ray McKinley
Melody Maker
Metronome
Tony Middleton
Eddie Miller
Mississippi Rag
Johnny Mince
Les Muscutt
Music & Rhythm
Alan Newby
New York Times
Frank 'Cork' O'Keefe
Glen Osser
Tony Pearson

Robert Peck
Martin Peel
Brian Peerless
Reg Peerless
Valerie Peerless
Vic Petry
Arthur Pilkington
Bill Priestley
Larry L. Quilligan
Record Changer
Record Research
John Reininger
Rhythm
Isabel Richardson
Rico Corporation
Gertrude Rodin
San Diego Union
Jacob Sciambra
Luke Schiro
Second Line
John Simmen
George T. Simon
Elmer Smithers
Irene & Charles Squires
Jess Stacy
Stephen Stoneburn
Storyville
Swing
Tempo
Frank Tennille
Eric Townley
Tulane University
Blaise Turi
US Marine Corps
Mike Vetrano
David Weinstein
Paul Weston
Jack Whittemore
Bert Whyatt
Rubin Zarchy
Fred Zentner
Dominik Zukowski

*Bob Crosby at the London ▷
Palladium (1958)*
*(photo courtesy of Central Independent
Television)*

6

Johns with the grateful thanks of the "Bob cats" and yours truly Bob Crosby

Chapter 1

Bob Crosby meets the Pollack 'Orphans'

The immaculately dressed silver-haired man raised an arm slowly, held it aloft for a second or two, then emphatically signalled a tempo to the waiting musicians, stroking out each beat with relaxed authority. The small group of musicians circled around the maestro responded to the count-in with precision and spirit, and the inimitable sound of Bob Crosby's Bob Cats began to flow. A succession of perfectly shaped, swinging phrases bubbled from Eddie Miller's tenor saxophone, Yank Lawson's hot trumpet stamped out the melody with zest and rhythmic surety, and Bob Haggart's full-toned doublebass playing underpinned the full blooded sound of the seven piece ensemble with dexterity and vigour.

The year was 1983, and the place New York City, where several of the original Crosby band had assembled for a televised reunion - nearly fifty years after they had first taken the jazz world by storm. But this gathering wasn't simply an exercise in nostalgia, it was a reassembly of superb musicians still at the top of their profession, each following their own individual musical careers, but happy to resume a place in a musical aggregation whose team-spirit and expertise has, for almost half-a-century, remained the envy of countless fellow musicians.

Back in 1935, none of the Crosby "crew", as they were affectionately known, could have forseen that their success would be so enduring; the initial announcement about the band's formation scarcely caused a ripple of interest with the general public, despite the fact that Bob Crosby was the brother of Bing, at that time probably the most famous singing film star in the world.

The first inkling of the remarkable story of Bob Crosby's Band was a simple, and enigmatic, two line item in the August 1935 issue of *Metronome* magazine, which mentioned "a rumour that a well-known warbler is ready to revive the old Ben Pollack Band". A follow-up in the August 1935 issue of the same magazine made things clearer, "The June rumour is reality, Bob Crosby's the boy. From various sources come reports that the band's a sensation, with the young throat husker doing a neat job up-front".

The brevity of these news items wasn't meant as a snub to the new group, it so happened that their formation coincided with the emergence of dozens of other big bands who assembled to meet the growing demand for live music that mushroomed throughout the United States at the end of the Depression. A January 1935 banner headline "Depression over in the Music Industry" helped band-bookers, agents and ballroom owners to gain the confidence to go ahead with various ambitious plans to wipe out all traces of the gloom that had accompanied the years of economic hardship.

During the early months of 1935, the call went out for new bands, and new sounds to bring back music into ballrooms that had been silent for years, hundreds of erstwhile leaders formed up groups to meet the demand. The formation of the Bob Crosby Band had little to do with this stampede, its organisation was entirely different from the usual sequence of events whereby the bandleader recruited individual musicians and moulded them into a band, in Crosby's case the process was reversed, the musicians chose a candidate, then groomed him into being a band-leader. They then set out to play their own highly individual brand of jazz, at a time when jazz was very low in the popularity stakes, to their lasting credit they succeeded triumphantly.

To trace the background of the band's highly unusual course of action we need to delve into the history of Ben Pollack's Band, the group mentioned in the Crosby Band's initial two-line publicity item. Most of the key musicians in Bob Crosby's original band were ex-members of Ben Pollack's group. Pollack, a superb drummer, first became a jazz celebrity as a member of the New Orleans Rhythm Kings, he wasn't from New Orleans, but had joined the band in his home city of Chicago. Pollack's stay with the N.O.R.K., though historic, wasn't lengthy, and he was soon on his way to California, where for almost a year he played in a band led by Harry Bastin. He then returned to Chicago, ostensibly to join his family's thriving fur business, but after working for one day amongst the pelts he quit and made his way to New York to look for musical work. Before he had settled in there he received a cable from California offering the band-leadership that Harry Bastin had just relinquished through ill health. Pollack abandoned his New York plans and moved West to become a bandleader, during the ensuing months he made changes in his personnel, bringing in reed-players Gil Rodin and Benny Goodman, and trombonist Glenn Miller.

Pollack's Band thrived in California until 1925, then a mixture of ambition and home-sickness (most of the musicians were from Illinois) convinced the group that they should try their luck in Chicago. After an uneasy period of three months during which there were virtually no bookings, the Pollack Band got a residency at the Southmoor Hotel. They were heard there by two men who were talent-scouts for the Victor Recording Company, bandleader Jean Goldkette and radio-station director Roy Shield. A recording contract followed, as did lucrative bookings at the Blackhawk Restaurant and the Rendezvous Club.

The Pollack Band's next move took them to New York City, then the mecca of American entertainment, beginning in March 1928 they played a two month residency at 'The Little Club' in Manhattan. When that contract ended the band drifted into a period of unemployment during which time Glenn Miller left to join Paul Ash's Orchestra, his place was taken by one of the greatest of all jazz trombonists, Jack Teagarden. The Pollack Band played some one-night stands in Pennsylvania, then did a six week summer season in Atlantic City before starting a prestigious residency at the Park Central Hotel in New York.

In late 1928, the Pollack Band left New York to play some out-of-town dates with the *Hello Daddy* show, for this production, Pollack decided to stand out front as the band's conductor, to play the drums he had vacated he hired a New Orleanian, Ray Bauduc. When the show reached New York in December 1928, the Pollack Band were able to fulfil the theatre dates and resume their Park Central residency. The band continued their busy doubling schedule for several months, but by the end of summer 1929 several of the musicians who had been with Pollack since California days had left (amongst them, Benny Goodman). Goodman's replacement on clarinet and alto-saxophone was 22 year old, Julian 'Matty' Matlock, who joined Pollack in October 1929. Benny Goodman's brother, Harry remained with the band on string-bass, playing alongside Ray Bauduc on drums, and two new signings, pianist Gil Bowers, and Hilton 'Nappy' Lamare on banjo and guitar. Lamare was from New Orleans, as was another newcomer to the band, tenor saxist and clarinet player Eddie Miller, who joined Pollack's band in the fall of 1930, to begin working in the reed section alongside Matty Matlock and stalwart Gil Rodin.

During his early days as a bandleader, the diminutive Pollack occasionally had stormy scenes with various musicians, and some of the partings were distinctly acrimonious. Subsequently, relations improved between bandleader and sidemen, and even when Pollack deliberately adopted a pugnacious attitude, the evenings ended peacefully. "Ben was basically a good guy" says Eddie Miller, "but when he stuck a cigar in his mouth it was a signal that he was about to undergo a change of personality, and we kept out of his way".

During an early booking at the Silver Slipper in New York, a serious split between leader and sidemen was narrowly averted, Pollack accused the band of going behind his back to offer their services to the management at a cheaper rate, the misunderstanding was soon smoothed out. The next rift developed over Pollack's habit of guesting with other bands on various radio shows. The musicians teased Pollack about the hired chaffeur who had to be on hand to get him from the place of work to the radio studios. One night, the musicians got on the the bandstand emply handed, Pollack, with some agitation in his voice asked "What the hell is going on?", only to be told that the men were waiting for the chaffeur to carry in their instruments. On this occasion laughter saved the day, but nothing could diminish the ill feeling that began to flourish amongst the musicians when Pollack entered into a deep friendship with the band's singer, Doris Robbins, (who later married Pollack).

During the late 1920s and early 1930s, Pollack was amongst the most successful bandleaders in America, and he was particularly popular with the growing number of people who liked to hear jazz soloists featured within the big band arrangements. Eddie Miller, Matty Matlock, and Nappy Lamare were great fans of Pollack's Band from early on, and by joining it they fulfilled an ambition. Another newcomer, trumpeter John 'Yank' Lawson, was a great admirer of the band long before he became a member of it, "As I saw it, Pollack's was the only white band playing jazz, there were jazz musicians in many other bands, Paul Whiteman's for instance, but they never played a number that was jazz from beginning to end".

By 1933, the band's reputation, both with the public and with admiring musicians, was at its highest. Its arrangements (many by Fud Livingston and Deane Kincaide), and its soloists, were acclaimed wherever the band travelled, but by then Pollack had seemingly lost interest in consolidating this considerable success, the musicians felt that all his efforts were directed at furthering the show business career of Doris Robbins, who had formerly been a Ziegfeld showgirl.

Summarising the contretemps between leader and sidemen, Pollack said, "The big disruption came along when Doris joined the band and a love affair sprang up between us. Up to this time I had been palling about with the boys, and spending money as fast, or faster, than I earned it, and now I did not see much of them except on the job".

Unfortunately, jobs became scarcer, because Pollack took the attitude that if a particular booking was not likely to advance Doris Robbins' career he turned it down flat. On engagements he did accept he often argued bitterly with club-owners over the billing for Doris Robbins. The musicians were horrified to see Pollack blatantly destroy prestige that had taken years to build, and none of the onlookers was more upset than the long-serving saxophonist Gil Rodin, even his considerable tact and diplomacy failed to smooth things down between Pollack and angry club owners. Arguments over billing were not the sole problem. Trombonist Jack Teagarden and guitarist Nappy Lamare had worked out some highly engaging vocal duets, and these became a highlight of the band's stage performances. Pollack saw a chance to thrust Doris Robbins into this popular spot, he insisted that the duo should become a trio - the results were disastrous. But worse was to come, as Yank Lawson recalls, "She and Pollack used to sing moist-eyed duets that made the band cringe".

The musicians' morale sank lower as they realised that bookings were becoming scarcer, often they were forced to accept casual musical work to make ends meet, even so, their allegiance to Pollack remained, as soon as he found work the band re-assembled. During one lean spell Jack Teagarden left and was replaced by a fellow Texan, Joe Harris. After a season in Galveston, Texas the band suffered a long lay-off, their reunion took place in California, where Pollack had gained a contract to play a season at the Cotton Club in Culver City, near Hollywood.

Looking back, the survivors of that long trek to the Coast laugh about the countless disappointments they suffered out in California, many of them connected with Pollack's growing habit of promising imaginary radio and recording work to the musicians, simply to bolster up their sagging morale. The chauffeur-driven car again entered the picture, this time the model was even more de luxe, and the driver's livery more resplendent, it was used to take Ben Pollack and Doris Robbins to various booking agencies in the hope that the singer could be shown a route to fame via the movies.

Towards the end of the Cotton Club booking, Pollack told the band that he intended to stay around California for a while, and it was obvious that getting bookings for the band was not his first priority. Matty Matlock, not the most outspoken of men, suggested to Pollack that perhaps too much time was being devoted to furthering Doris Robbins's career, the bandleader's answer astounded all the listening musicians, he said "That girl is this band's meal ticket".

After playing a Thanksgiving booking that seethed with ill will, all of the musicians realised that the band they had nurtured with such pride was about to dissolve. During a band-room discussion it was mutually agreed that the musical rapport that the band had achieved must not be wasted, a new group must be formed. Without a vote being taken it was unanimously decided that Gil Rodin should act as the new band's administrator and manager. After finishing the booking with Pollack, the musicians decided to take home-town vacations before linking up again in New York to seek work there as a co-operative band.

After the final night at the Cotton Club, the musicians drove up to Pollack's home and in dawn-light stacked the band's arrangements up against his front door and left. At first, Pollack was uncertain as to whether the musicians had gone for good, but he soon heard on the grape-vine that his ex-sidemen were moving East, and that some of them had already been offered work on a New York radio show. Realising that he was the victim of a walk-out, Pollack became bitter and said "I never thought this gang of kids, who had never amounted to a thing before, and who were getting damn fine salaries, and who had been working pretty consistently through the Depression, would leave me flat. I do not think I have ever been so hurt in my life".

Pollack's rancour didn't last forever, but it was to be a long time before any of the departing musicians ever entered into easy conversation with their former leader. Pollack, it seems, felt bitterest toward Gil Rodin, who had worked with him for years, and whom he regarded as a close friend and confidante.

The so-called walk out revitalised Pollack's organisational spirit and within weeks he had formed up a new band that was soon to showcase some brilliant young players, such as trumpeter Harry James and clarinetist Irving Fazola. Even Pollack's enemies had to admit that he was a remarkable talent scout, and musicians who worked with him usually agree that he was a superb drummer. None of the men who left Pollack in late 1934 bore him a lasting grudge, in a way they felt sorry for him in allowing his personal life to get so entangled with his work, but they were weary of the continually tense atmosphere. The musicians admitted that they earnt good money when Pollack worked, but there were long periods of unemployment, and above all they felt rancoured that so many golden opportunities had been wantonly wasted. Even those with family commitments didn't hesitate about making the move to New York, all were aware that there were no immediate prospects for the new band.

Gil Rodin, Harry Goodman and trumpeter Charlie Spivak went straight to New York to work as freelance musicians in a band that Benny Goodman was leading on the National Biscuit Company's radio show. Rodin and Harry Goodman did the show for some weeks, but Spivak had a disagreement with Goodman at the onset and took no further part, instead he went off and joined a band led by the Dorsey Brothers.

When the rest of the ex-Pollack musicians reached New York after their vacations, most of them moved into a big apartment block called Electric Court, in Jackson Heights on Long Island, the basement at Electric Court became one of the various rooms in the area that the embryo band used for its initial rehearsals. Almost every day, the conscientious Gil Rodin called in on various agents to try and hustle up work for the band. Rodin, the senior professional in the group, continued to act as their spokesman, administrator and musical director, he was known to the musicians as "Pops".

All of the musicians found freelance work as and when they could. Miller, Matlock, Bowers, Bauduc and Harry Goodman took part in recordings with Wingy Manone soon after they arrived in New York, but this only involved a couple of days' work. Individually the new arrivals played an odd assortment of gigs, all the while fervently hoping that the new band would soon get a break. Immense team spirit pervaded all of the Long Island band rehearsals, and despite the lack of work for the unit as a whole, morale couldn't have been higher.

Incomes increased dramatically when cornetist Red Nichols decided to use most of the band on a regular radio show. Nichols, (temporarily without a band of his own), had secured a contract to provide music for the Kellogg sponsored "College Prom" show, which featured singer Ruth Etting. A booker, Roy Wilson, knew Rodin and had heard from him that the "Pollack Orphans", as the the refugees were then called, were rehearsing hard, and looking for work. The band were offered the job of playing for the show, providing that they had no objection to working under Red Nichol's name, they accepted, and reached an amicable deal whereby Nichols only appeared, each Thursday, on the day of the show, after the band had rehearsed the program.

Unfortunately, Yank Lawson didn't have a New York (Local 802) Musicians' Union card at that time, so he was unable to do the radio show, his place was taken by an old friend of the band's, trumpeter Charlie Teagarden. Charlie's brother Jack was also brought into the "College Prom" band to play alongside Glenn Miller in the trombone section. Ex-Ben Pollack tenor saxophonist and arranger, Deane Kincaide was re-united with the band and added to the ensemble.

The Electric Court rehearsals continued, and several musicians, including trombonists Jack Jenney, Neil Reid and trumpeter Charlie Spivak willingly sat in to try out new arrangements. Glenn Miller frequently appeared with a new arrangement, including an early version of his famous hit *Moonlight Serenade* (then simply called *Miller's Tune*); the band occasionally played the number but felt it was not in the style of music that they were trying to establish, their aim was to transfer the excitement and flexibility of a small jazz group to a big band line-up.

The income of the musicians was further supplemented when Gil Rodin secured a contract to record a series of numbers for Brunswick. The band still hadn't devised an offical name, but for the Brunswick sides made in March 1935 they were billed as the Clark-Randall Orchestra. The name was chosen at random, and as Matty Matlock explained, had no significance, "There was no Clark Randall actually, that was a fictitious name, it was used to cover a partnership agreement, like the Casa Loma Band had". A mistaken idea circulated that Clark Randall was the professional name for singer Frank Tennille, who had worked in Ben Pollack's Band with the musicians, and who had travelled east with them. Tennille himself has put the record straight, "The name Clark Randall was selected as the name of whoever fronted the band". He also said, "The number one priority in my mind is to correct the misconception that I paid for any recording sessions. The early recordings, some of which were made under the Clark Randall name, were arranged by the Irving Mills booking agency".

In all, the band recorded ten titles spread over three sessions in March 1935, none are sensational, but there promising indications of fine things to come, particularly in the brief solos by Yank Lawson and Eddie Miller. Occasionally Matlock's clarinet is heard playing over a scored ensemble, but there is little emphasis on collective improvisation. An augury of later days is Nappy Lamare's light-hearted vocalising on the novelty number *"Here Comes Your Pappy With The Wrong Kind Of Load"*, but the bulk of the singing is done by Frank Tennille whose pleasant tenor voice hits the high ones clear and true. The outline of the band's later style is just discernible, the performances are competent and lively, but no one at the time suspected that the group would become one of the jazz world's lasting successes.

The band continued to strive for individuality, and gradually their efforts paid off, particularly on the arrangements scored by Deane Kincaide and Matty Matlock. One afternoon, music-publisher Jack Bregman attended a rehearsal and was impressed enough to recommend the band to the influential booker Tommy Rockwell, who ran a New York agency in partnership with Frank 'Cork' O'Keefe. Rodin was advised to call at the Rockwell-O'Keefe office to discuss future plans. The powerful Irving Mills agency had shown some interest in the band, and had been responsible for the early recordings, but the strength of the Mills Agency was in booking stage bands, and Rodin, and the rest of the band, wanted to make their initial impact via ballrooms and hotels (which had facilities for broadcasting).

Gil Rodin called at the Rockwell-O'Keefe agency and talked things over with O'Keefe. The agent was impressed by Rodin's optimistic outlook, but according to Rodin, he remained cautious, saying "You boys need a front man, you can't get by on music alone". Rodin was realistic enough to know that he didn't possess the kind of personality needed to front a successful band, he was also aware that in spite of the fact that Frank Tennille had personality, good looks and a pleasing voice, he was virtually unknown. The question of a permanent "front man" had been discussed by the band before Rodin made his trip to the agency, it was originally agreed that Jack Teagarden would be the ideal person, but the idea was aborted by the fact that Teagarden was already under contract to bandleader Paul Whiteman. Nappy Lamare remembers the next step, "Someone suggested Louis Prima, but another voice said 'We don't want more New Orleans guys in the band', so that was out. We figured Frank Tennille would be fine for the band, but then the bookers said the name wasn't strong enough".

In 1983, Cork O'Keefe gave his recollections of the initial discussions with Rodin, "I can clearly remember Gil coming to our office at the RKO Building at 76th and 12th. I mentioned the need for a leader and Gil said, with some spirit, 'We want the right person, and until we get him we can weather the storm'. That's O.K. I said, but meanwhile think about these three names, then I suggested Fred Waring's trumpeter - vocalist Johnny 'Scat' Davis - I had seen him looking after Smith Ballew's Band at the Saratoga Club and he did a good job. Next I mentioned Harry 'Goldie' Goldfield, whom I had first met at High School in Connecticut. Goldie, a trumpeter and comedian, had had a lot of exposure with Paul Whiteman, and he was always telling me he wanted a band of his own. Then I mentioned Bing Crosby's younger brother Bob, we were handling Bing and Bob at that time, and Bob was living up at Tommy Rockwell's summer place in Long Island. I knew he wasn't happy working with the Dorsey Brothers' Band and I felt he'd like the idea".

"Gil Rodin said he wouldn't make any decision there and then, but asked me to draft out my ideas in a letter that he could show to the rest of the band. So the secretary typed out a letter with the names on, I signed it and Gil took it away, but within minutes he was back at the 23rd floor saying he felt certain that the band would chose Bob Crosby, so we arranged a get-together with Bob".

Some months earlier, Gil Rodin had seen Bob Crosby working in a duo with vocaliste Lee Wiley, and had later met him when he went to listen to the Dorsey Brothers' Band, he had been struck by Bob's open friendliness. Cork O'Keefe told Bob Crosby about Rodin's interest, and advised him to go along with the deal, at least for a trial period. Rodin recalled the initial discussions, "Crosby was tickled over the idea of taking the band, and I'll admit I was impressed with Bob's enthusiasm and sincerity. So we closed the deal and Crosby fronted".

At this stage, Gil Rodin was apparently uncertain as to how permanent the arrangement would be, there were rumours that Paramount were preparing to offer a film test, and Cork O'Keefe had mentioned the phrase "trial period". The band's existing front man and singer, Frank Tennille, was told that Bob Crosby was joining the organisation, "I suggested they didn't need me. But Gil asked me to remain a member of the band, saying we would resume our original plans after Bob went on to better things". Gil Rodin, it seems, was living up to his reputation for covering all contingencies.

Rodin thought the original discussions with Crosby took place in a drug store, but Bob himself is uncertain. He has clear recollections of Eddie Miller, Matty Matlock, Yank Lawson and Gil Rodin visiting the Palais Royale on Broadway where he was singing with the Dorsey Brothers Band. He was particularly struck by the friendly way he was greeted by the musicians, "I was delighted with Gil Rodin's invitation, but I think I'd have been pleased to consider anything to get away from working with Tommy Dorsey". It would be fair to say that Bob Crosby detested Tommy Dorsey, and was unenamoured by the co-leading brother, Jimmy. Bob recalls that Tommy Dorsey took the news of his impending departure with impassive joy, "I guess he was almost as happy as I was, but to me he was a totally cold person, so he showed no reaction at all".

Gil Rodin gave Bob some of the Clark Randall recordings, but it wasn't until he heard the band in the flesh that he went overboard. Publicist Jack Egan remembers meeting Bob just after he'd heard his new colleagues "I dropped into the Washington Arms, a roadhouse east of Larchmont, N.Y. When I spotted Bob I joined him at his table. He immediately went into an enthusiastic discourse on the merits of the orchestra he was about to front, exclaiming 'This afternoon I heard the band they're giving me. Wait until you hear it. It's terrific". For Bob, aged 21, whose experience rested on his work with Anson Weeks in California, and the Dorsey Brothers in the East, a great new era was about to start.

Gil Rodin recalled the next moves, "We started rehearsing hard, Cork O'Keefe told us we would start off making good money. But we still had the Kellogg show. All of us couldn't leave at once so we took turns, two at a time giving notice". Mindful of the fact that even during his jazziest period, Ben Pollack had regularly employed string players to placate hotel managers, and customers who only wanted to hear a straight melody, the Rockwell-O'Keefe agency insisted that the new band's penchant for inspired improvising was counter-balanced by the occasional featuring of a couple of violinists.

Gil Rodin acquiesced, "O'Keefe wanted fiddles. We didn't. But he was the boss, and had to sell the band, so we got Eddie Bergman and Charlie Green. We got Phil Hart to take Charlie Spivak's lead trumpet chair, and Joe Harris, one of the Pollack men who stayed on the coast when we all left came East to take Glenn Miller's spot. Those were the only changes, except that Pete Peterson on bass dropped out, and I picked up Bob Haggart, who was working over in Jersey with a little band. Our first date was at the Roseland Ballroom (June 1935). Crosby didn't know how to beat tempo, but we didn't mind. We were started".

Bob Crosby's Orchestra 1935. ▷
Back row: left to right Joe Harris, Charlie Green, Phil Hart, Eddie Bergman, Yank Lawson, Bob Haggart and Deane Kincaide. Ray Bauduc and Bob Crosby within the car.

Front row: left to right Matty Matlock, Gil Bowers, Eddie Miller, Frank Tennille, Gil Rodin and Nappy Lamare.

*Ben Pollack visiting Leon Roppolo
during the 1930s.*

Bob Crosby, c 1933.▷

Ben Pollack

Bob
Crosby

Bob Crosby's Band, Miami, Forida, 1936.
Left to right Joe Baronne, Nappy Lamare, Ward Sillaway, Eddie Miller, Frank Tennille, Artie Foster, Bob Haggart, Dog-track owner, Bob Crosby,
Yank Lawson, Eddie Bergman, Sid Stoneburn, Deane Kincaide, Gil Bowers, Ray Bauduc, Gil Rodin.

22

Chapter 2

The first tour

Bob Crosby has always felt a degree of resentment that most accounts detailing the formation of his band infer that its music was simply a continuance of a style established by Ben Pollack's Band. His chagrin seems justified, none of the band's recorded hits were based on ex-Pollack material. Admittedly some of the Pollack Band's head-arrangements, and musical devices (such as the tenor-saxophone and clarinet unison effect), were retained by the Crosby Band, but the new group rapidly achieved its own identity. Within weeks of the Bob Crosby Band debut, noted critic John Hammond wrote, "The band is infinitely better than at any time Pollack had it".

Bob Crosby's case is that each new sideman who joined gave his band an ensemble sound that moved away from the timbre of Pollack's outfit. By far the most important of these newcomers was bassist Bob Haggart whose arranging proved to be a vital factor in the band's transformation.

Matty Matlock and Deane Kincaide had already begun the process of creating a new style for the band by the time Haggart joined. Haggart was greatly impressed by Kincaide's ability to write counterpoint, and the ease with which he created three different musical lines that flowed simultaneously within an arrangement, an effect Haggart called "the three ring circus". Haggart also admired Matlock's arranging ingenuity and versatility, but his own style of writing owed little to the work of either of his colleagues. Within weeks of joining the band, Haggart was producing scores that were highly original creations, which cleverly captured the spirit of the so-called "Golden Age of Jazz" of a decade earlier but presented it as a contemporary sound. Haggart was a talented arranger and an accomplished bassist by the time he joined the Crosby band, he was soon to reveal that he was also a gifted composer.

But important though good arrangements were to the band, its most appealing ingredients were the swing and inventiveness of Eddie Miller's tenor saxophone playing (and his emotional clarinet work), the exciting drive of Yank Lawson's trumpet, the agility of Matlock's clarinet, and the zest of the rhythm section. All these attributes were skilfully showcased in the arrangements that Kincaide, Matlock and Haggart created. The unwritten law of the band was that every arrangement had to swing, and this policy cut out the pretentious over-writing that made so many other big bands sound stilted.

For want of a better description the Crosby Band let themselves be tagged as a "Dixieland Band" (their advertisements proclaimed that they were "Dixieland Dispensers"), later they came to have misgivings about the billing. Eddie Miller recalled, "We used Dixieland as more or less a trade name, but it wasn't Dixieland, it was just jazz. We certainly didn't play like the Original Dixieland Jazz Band!". Matty Matlock came to rue the stylisation, and used to wince when anyone called him a "Dixieland" musician. The Original Dixieland Jazz Band did not occupy any sort of high placing amongst the band's favourite sounds, collectively, if the band had a particular idol it was Louis Armstrong, a home town favourite with Lamare, Bauduc and Miller, also revered by Lawson, Matlock and Haggart, who it was said could sing note-for-note most of Louis's recorded solos. Two of the Crosby musicians' other favourites were Jack Teagarden and clarinettist Leon Roppolo.

In the recording studio, the band soon learnt that they had to subjugate their love of jazz and concentrate on producing what the company wanted to market. Their first session under Bob Crosby's name took place in New York on June 1st 1935. Ironically, the first title waxed was a vocal by Frank Tennille, *Flowers For Madame,* the plot and performance of which is even more commercial than items made on the Clark Randall sessions that had been recorded two months earlier. In fact, the sweet strains emanating from Eddie Bergman's violin make the whole affair sound very much like hotel dining-room music. However, the next title recorded, *The Dixieland Band* gives a clearer indication of the band's musical intentions. It is a bold and spirited performance of a lively arrangement by Deane Kincaide, Bob Crosby is featured, singing a lighthearted medium-tempo vocal. Trombonist Joe Harris plays a fairly uninspired solo, but the attack displayed during the saxophone-clarinet unison more than compensates.

On the next title recorded, *In a Little Gypsy Tea Room,* Bob Crosby does his best with what was a distinctly ordinary melody, and some unsubtle lyrics, but the wobbly vibrato that was to plague so much of his early ballad work mars the rendering. The session's final item, *Beale Street Blues,* shows that the band sounded much more positive when tackling jazz orientated material. The mood is established by some torrid open trumpet work from Yank Lawson, the piano accompaniment sounds a little contrived but Lamare's guitar rings out an authentic blues timbre. Joe Harris interprets the melody adeptly on trombone, but his vocal is disappointing, particularly when compared to his work with Benny Goodman, but overall the track radiates sturdy sincerity.

For the initial record release Decca decided to cross-back the two ballads on the same disc, following the issue with a coupling of the two "jazz" numbers. At that time the publishers of *In a Little Gypsy Tea Room* had the song on their "plug" list, which meant that their promotional staff were concentrating on getting radio plays for the record. The results of this plugging was that the band's ballad release initially outsold the up-tempo, jazzier, offerings. The record company decided it would be advantageous if the band concentrated on commercially acceptable ballads, as a result the next twenty titles recorded were vocals. Initially singing duties were shared between Bob Crosby and Frank Tennille, later only Crosby was featured.

The arrangements and performances on most of these early titles are unadventurous and tepid, with much useage of the violin, either by Eddie Bergman alone, or sometimes in duo with his colleague Charlie Green. Occasionally, as on *Two Together* and *I'm Sitting High On a Hill Top,* Yank Lawson and Eddie Miller are allocated short solo spots which they fill admirably, and on *And Then Some* Ray Bauduc's drumming launches into some surging rhythmic patterns. On the last chorus of this number Matlock is heard improvising expressively over the ensemble, but excitement is generally in short supply on almost all of the band's 1935 recordings.

Bob Crosby candidly admits that Gil Rodin was speaking the truth when he said that Bob couldn't count the band in properly when he first joined. Crosby reports that drummer Ray Bauduc said to him "You count the band in how you like, but I'll make sure they come in at the right tempo". No trace of this initial problem reached the audience, and the band's initial booking at the Roseland Ballroom in June 1935 was a distinct success. Almost immediately afterwards the band began its first tour by going on a string of one-night stands, most of them in the south. Rodin recalled that initial tour, "We were guaranteed $5,000 in two weeks by Cork O'Keefe, and believe me we earned it. Then came two weeks at Tybee Beach in Savannah, our first location. It was a terrific click, much to our suprise".

Memories of those first engagements stay fresh in the minds of the participating musicians. Nappy Lamare recalls, "Our first job was in Greensborough, North Carolina. You'd ride in the bus and drive right into a tobacco warehouse, take your instruments out and play". Bob Crosby remembers the rural qualities of the bookings, "They'd pull out dozens of ordinary wooden planks, wax them up, then lay them down as the dance floor, in the middle of a warehouse".

Bob Haggart had played away from home on several occasions, but this was his first genuine taste of the wild-and-wooly one-night stand game, "The guys had been cooped up in New York for quite a while, so there was a loud whoop of delight as we booked into the delightfully named Cherry Hotel, in Wilson, North Carolina. We made that our base for jobs in that part of the world, and late at night at the Cherry there were scenes of what might be called wild abandon as the shy local girls, some of them heavily tattoed, came in to say hello to the visiting musicians. I remember trying to break the world record for drinking whisky sours on that trip".

The revelry certainly didn't affect the music-making and the audiences at all of the Crosby Band's early gigs responded to their style with enthusiastic applause. The warm receptions continued when the band began its residency at the Tybisa Pavilion (at Tybee Beach in Georgia), about ten miles from Savannah. The ballroom was owned by Willy Haar and his wife Thelma. Thelma had originally been taught string-bass by the Jean Goldkette star, Steve Brown, and during the late 1920s, as Thelma Terry she had led all-star bands on Chicago recording sessions. As Bob Haggart was unpacking his instrument, Thelma said to him "You'd better be good, because I was a good player myself". She had no complaints, Haggart had settled in well with the band and was playing superbly.

During that tour, the band began playing the first arrangement that Haggart ever wrote for them, *Heebie Jeebies*, "I patterned it on the Louis Armstrong recording, but scored the clarinets low and had the brass playing the after-beats, Eddie Miller played the verse on clarinet. The New Orleans guys responded to the thing instantly, and Eddie and Nappy devised a little shim-sham dance to go with it. Then Fud Livingston, (who was Matty Matlock's idol) came over to Tybee Beach, he was down there visiting relatives nearby. Fud was considered 'King of the arrangers' at that time, but made a special point of saying that he liked the version of *Heebie Jeebies* very much. That sort of set the seal of approval on it, and I was encouraged to write as much as I could for the Crosby Band".

The musical side of things was running smoothly, and so too was the administration, it was handled by Gil Rodin, assisted by Mike Vetrano, (an ex-boxer and footballer) who had been sent on the tour by the Rockwell-O'Keefe office. Vetrano looks back on those days with pleasure, "Bob Crosby's first band tour was also my first tour as a road manager, previously I had been an assistant, learning the business with the Casa Loma Band. I spent two years with them, but on the Crosby tour I was out on my own. I had Joe Kearney (a friend of Bob Crosby's) with me as band-boy, and he too was learning the business, however, it worked out, and everything went smoothly. I got transport organised by going to a bus-hire company in Jersey, who hired out buses to travelling bands for 25 cents a mile. Most of the ballroom operators that we worked for were straight, but on the percentage dates (where the band played for part of the door take) you made it a rule to pick up the money due at the intermission, before the band went back again".

"The band on that tour were wild and happy, but the high spirits were, I think, a way of letting out some of the anxiety that the guys were feeling deep inside. They had all moved to New York, which was where the big radio shows and recordings took place, and they had reasoned, quite rightly, that anything was better than having it rough on the West Coast, with nothing happening, but this tour was a test for them, and they were soon going to need more bookings. But, things turned out swell, Gil Rodin organised everything, business and music, he was a fine gent".

Bob Crosby had settled in well with the band, musically and socially, the unofficial trial period - on both sides - was well and truly over, and there were no more suggestions that he was only with them temporarily. It had always been the intention of the ex-Pollack musicians to form up a co-operative band (similar to the Casa Loma Band, which was also handled by the Rockwell-O'Keefe agency), so, after the return from the southern tour, machinery was set in motion that later made the band into an official corporation. Bob Crosby was allocated a third share, the other two thirds were split between Gil Rodin, Ray Bauduc, Eddie Miller, Yank Lawson, Matty Matlock, Nappy Lamare, Deane Kincaide and Bob Haggart. Haggart, the only non-ex-Pollack man in the corporation, besides Crosby, got a smaller share than the others because he joined later. Haggart and the other two arrangers, Matlock and Kincaide, also lost another fraction because they were promised fees for arranging. The non-corporation musicians were placed on a sliding-scale salary which increased with the number of dates the band played; recording and sponsored radio work was paid as extras. A "holes in the band" policy was incorporated which allowed the entry of new shareholders. Arbitration was left to the Rockwell-O'Keefe agency.

Cork O'Keefe recalls the period, "After the dates down south, things began to look brighter for the band. Ralph Hitz, who ran several hotels was having a fight with MCA (the Music Corporation of America), because they wouldn't give him an exclusive right on the bands he wanted to book, he liked to insist that his hotels were the only place in town where you could hear such-and-such a band. The MCA agency wouldn't go along with the idea, but it suited us fine, and we gave Hitz an exclusive on the Crosby Band for a whole chain of his hotels, including Dallas where he and gambler Sam Macio had most of the entertainment sewn up".

Hitz, an Austrian emigre, then in his early forties, made a point of listening to the Crosby Band when they played the Adolphus Hotel in Dallas in September 1935, he liked what he heard and arranged for them to play other venues in his "chain". Rodin recalled "In Dallas, Ralph Hitz caught us and was enthused. As a result he took us into the Netherlands Plaza in Cincinnati. We found we were using the fiddles very little, so we dropped Charlie Green and hired a second trombone".

On the 19th December 1935, the band began playing a four week season at the big Cincinnati hotel, able to view the coming year with a degree of confidence. Bob Crosby was sounding more relaxed, both in his announcements and in his vocals, Nappy Lamare summarised the feelings that the band had toward their nominal leader "We liked Bob, he was a nice young guy, with a wonderful sense of humour". Earlier in 1935, Bob Crosby had successfully auditioned for a radio show to be sponsored by the Roger and Gallet soap company. It was agreed that the band's move to Cincinnati wouldn't halt the series (which began in October 1935), the broadcasts would take place from wherever the band were appearing.

The weekly Roger and Gallet show went on the air at 7.15 pm, which was a good time for audience ratings. Besides the music, the show also offered prize money and this encouraged the public to tune in. The programme looked like being the big break that the band had been waiting for, but after a bright start, the series went disastrously wrong.

The show's compere, Norman Brokenshire, was having a period of diminishing success, and he was given a spot in the programme in the hope that his comeback would help the ratings. On the night that the sponsors chose to watch the show being transmitted, Brokenshire slipped away for a while and returned in an advanced state of intoxication. His cue to begin speaking on the live show was the sound of Bob Crosby singing the opening phrase of the song *Alone*. Bob sang the required two syllables, and looked over to see a glassy-eyed compere swaying mutely. Crosby tried again, and again, until finally the master of ceremonies realised that something was required of him. It would perhaps have been better if he had remained silent, for once he began talking he couldn't stop, on and on he gabbled, script, timings, and commercial message all went to the wind. Subsequent programmes were cancelled and the series came to an ignominious end.

The disappointment connected with the radio series was counterbalanced for the band by the enthusiastic responses that were being accorded all their live appearances. On the band stand, the group blended ballads, comedy vocals, and burlesque-like routines,with extended arrangements that showcased its array of skilful jazz improvisers. The public loved the mixture, and their particular response to the jazz numbers lead the Decca recording executives to consider allowing the "hot" aspect of the band to be heard on disc.

Gradually the role of the violin in Bob Crosby's band was reduced, its sound was replaced by one of the front-line horns improvising an obbligato. At first these interludes only came in tiny doses, but they were enough to whet the appetite of those record buyers who wanted to hear something that was different from the killer-diller swing routines that spread a carpet of conformity over the big band scene during the mid-1930s. Ray Bauduc was encouraged to play on record as he did on dance dates, and he responded by laying down a strong beat, using all of his drum kit to insert interesting punctuations in the arrangements, and behind an improvising soloist. The band seldom failed to hit a swinging groove when Bauduc emphasised a shuffle rhythm. A more accurate picture of the band's true sound began to come through on record, and the success of the jazz numbers was being reflected in the requests that were shouted up at the bandstand by the dancers.

Most of the band members, particularly those from New Orleans, were delighted with the response the public were giving to the jazz numbers. Each of the men from Louisiana felt considerable pride in their musical heritage, and in a 1936 article Eddie Miller spoke warmly of the pleasure and inspiration he had received by listening to black parade bands in New Orleans during the 1920s. "You know that marching dixieland is still the real swing. It was the stuff they used to parade that really swung. A good drop beat from the drums, and everything played not too fast". Miller went on to list his favourite clarinet-players as Leon Roppolo, Johnny Dodds, and colleague Matty

Matlock. His two choices for drummer were Ray Bauduc and his old leader Ben Pollack.

Early in 1936 the Bob Crosby Band began playing one of the most unusual engagements it ever undertook. The unlikely venue was a dog-track in Miami, Florida, called the Biscayne Kennel Club. The booking was hardly prestigious, the band were hired simply to provide music in between the dog races, but the casual nature of the engagement allowed them opportunity to break-in a whole batch of new numbers. Bob Haggart recalls the engagement, "We hit a cold spell in Florida, and most of the band kept their overcoats on whilst playing the date. I think one or two of the band placed bets just to make things a little more interesting, my lasting memory is of a man bellowing out 'Here Comes the Rabbit' at the start of each and every race".

The band still hadn't settled on a permanent first trumpeter, for reasons outlined by Yank Lawson, "Andy Ferretti, who was a wonderful lead player, did most of our New York dates and the recordings, but I guess he didn't want to travel, so another man came in on trumpet, Joe Barone, and he did the season in Florida and stayed with us for a while". Matty Matlock also stayed in New York whilst the band did the Florida dates, Matty's task was to work steadfastly on new arrangements for the band, clarinettist Sid Stoneburn, (who had worked with a number of name bands) joined the band as a temporary replacement for Matlock.

Deane Kincaide, one of the band's other staff arrangers, has good reasons for remembering the dates in Florida, he still bears faint scars on his face as a testimony of the trip. "There was this willowy-but-drunk female in Miami, Florida, who induced me to come to her apartment after the job, but who kept saying 'No', so I took her for a ride in the car, parked on a dark street away from downtown, got her in the back seat . . . . a milk wagon came alongside the car, a flashlight played in the back seat when I was just about to say, 'the hell with it', and this gorilla burst into the car, pummeled me good. He broke my glasses and pleaded with her to come back to him, (she didn't tell me she left him yesterday), then he apologised to me profusely, took me to the doctor where a giant bandaid was applied. Needless to say, I couldn't read very well for quite a few weeks".

The band's stay in Florida proved to be shorter than they had expected, after only half of the month's booking had been played a shooting occurred at the dog track and the police immediately closed the place down. The band received an unexpected vacation, Bob Haggart seeing how close he was to an old stamping ground of his, Nassau in the Bahamas, spent his holiday there, most of the band drove back to New York. Sid Stoneburn left the band soon after they had re-assembled for the next spate of bookings.

During this period of the band's history road manager Mike Vetrano and his help-mate, band-boy, Joe Kearney travelled separately from the band, transporting the bandstands and heavy equipment in a hired truck. Vetrano said "We usually set out for the next date ahead of the band, the musicians drove their own automobiles, for which they were paid one cent per mile for every member of the band they carried, naturally they didn't get anything for wives, or other passengers. But by 1936 the band was playing lots of location jobs, staying at one place for quite a while, so they had no need of a full-time road manager and a band-boy, once the stands were in place and the drums set up, there was little else to do except lay the music out. I could see that my services weren't going to be required permanently so I decided to leave". Vetrano later worked as a road-manager for Claude Hopkins, Woody Herman and Artie Shaw.

The location jobs that Vetrano mentioned were usually fairly lucrative; in the early months of 1936 the Crosby Band began playing one in the Terrace Room of the Hotel New Yorker (another venue that was part of Ralph Hitz's chain). The band went in on a short, trial booking but they were so well received they were retained for a fourteen week season.

Gil Rodin firmly believed in taking the stealthy, 'softly, softly' approach in hotel ballrooms, and this paid off for the Crosby Band, they had to play for afternoon dances, provide dinner music and get the customers on the dance floor with their lively numbers. The band had to grin and bear the commands of what they called the "Achtung Head Waiters", who were always ordering them to "keep that music down". Eddie Bergman's violin playing again came to the fore during the dinner music sessions, and Eddie Miller's task was to stress the melody on tenor-saxophone, the brass remained muted until the last crumbs had been devoured.

During less busy times in the hotel ballrooms, the band's new trombonist, Ward Sillaway, also contributed to the one-chorus ballad medleys that kept customers contented and allowed individual musicians to play melodies that they liked. Ward's speciality was Ravel's *Pavanne pour une enfant,* he also agreed, after some persuasion, to come out front of the band and sing the one song that he knew all the words of, *There's A Small Hotel,* a contemporary Rodgers and Hart number. The wags in the band arranged with various friendly waiters for a stream of forged requests to reach the bandstand begging that Sillaway be allowed to sing. To say that Ward was staggered by the response would be putting it mildly, but after making three journeys to the front during the same evening, to sing his one song, he happened to glance out of the corner of his eye to see that everyone in the band was convulsed with laughter, thereafter he concentrated on playing the trombone.

Any band playing a hotel residency needed a huge library of material, to bolster its repertoire the Crosby Band began buying scores from outside arrangers, one of them was a young man named Glenn Osser, now an eminent musical director, "I arranged for Bob Crosby's Band from March 1936 thru August 1936, while they were at the Hotel New Yorker (first three months) and then at the Lexington Hotel. I had just arrived in New York City and had a chance to do an arrangement on approval, which they liked, and I continued till they left New York. As you know, they had three great arrangers with the band at that time, Bob Haggart, Deane Kincaide and Matty Matlock, and they were experts in the "Dixie" style that they featured. What I did for them was the current popular ballads"

"The arrangement that I did for the Crosby Band on approval, 'Melody From The Sky' was a current ballad, and in my arrangement, after the orchestra played for first chorus and Frank Tennille sang the second chorus, I then did half a chorus in a swinging style. After they heard the arrangement they said they liked it but I would have to re-do the last part and make it strictly ballad - NO SYNCOPATION. They said that Benny Goodman 'swung' the ballads and they wanted to be different, just as they featured two-beat in the rhythm tunes, as against Benny doing four beat".

The Bob Crosby Band were absolutely determined not to be part of the "swing" craze, which after Benny Goodman's 1935 triumph at the Palomar Ballroom came close to inducing a national hysteria amongst young dancers. The Crosby Band were seeking a discerning section of the public who were looking for individuality, they deliberately eschewed musical devices that made swing bands popular, they were out to create an alternative sound.

Naturally, Decca (in the manner of most record companies) didn't know quite what to do when they had to contend with originality. Two executives of the recording company, Jack Kapp and his brother David, thought it wisest that the Crosby Band establish itself before embarking on a "Dixieland" policy, thus, the Crosby Band were advised to do what lots of other big bands were doing, namely record a version of *Christopher Columbus,* a "swing" hit that had suddenly clicked with ballroom crowds.

The Crosby Band's version of *Christopher Columbus* (arranged by Deane Kincaide), differed from other versions, the usual answering phrases were revamped, new brass figures were added, and a modulation inserted to introduce a bright finale. Everything sounds satisfactory, but only the brief solos by Eddie Miller and Yank Lawson give a clue to the performers' identity, the overall effect is of an anonymous swing band's performance. Bob Haggart summed up the band's attitude by saying, "We always hated riff tunes, and avoided playing them whenever possible". the corporation members of the band let Gil Rodin know, in no uncertain terms, that they felt it near lunacy that they were recording such character-less material, in turn, Rodin argued the case with Jack Kapp.

The record company met the band half-way. The band were due to record a session accompanying vocaliste Connee Boswell during April 1936, if time was available after that task had been completed, then the band could go ahead and record a couple of its jazz numbers. They made sure there was time, and as a result waxed Bob Haggart's arrangements of two jazz classics, *Muskrat Ramble* and *Dixieland Shuffle* (a reworking of King Oliver's *Riverside Blues).* The band didn't shirk their task of recording with Connee Boswell, but the enthusiasm that they felt for the latter part of the session radiates through every phrase. On *Muskrat Ramble* Eddie Miller's tenor saxophone work is a model of buoyancy and inventiveness, stimulated by the lively patterns emanating from Ray Bauduc's woodblocks, Yank Lawson and Matty Matlock also play compelling solos. The last chorus (based on the Louis Armstrong Hot Five recording) sounds a little stiff, but the unsupple phrasing is countered by some warm-toned clarinet playing, and the trombones' final figure creates a sturdy echo of Kid Ory's original coda.

The *Dixieland Shuffle* side is even better. Yank Lawson on trumpet blows a handsome homage to the originators, Oliver and Armstrong, but does so with authoratitive individuality. The clarinet trio sounds superb, Miller's saxophone is both fluent and emotional, and Lamare's graceful guitar provides a satisfying tinge to the sound of the rhythm section. The trombones again have the last word, blowing a series of fruity-sounding final phrases. Slickness forms no part of the performance, instead there is an abundance of feeling, and skill. At last, the band's musical message was getting through on record.

Chapter 3

New York success

After the Crosby Band had completed their 14 week booking at the New Yorker they immediately commenced playing another Hitz hotel residency, this time at the nearby Lexington. This proved to be a happy and eventful engagement for the band, they were pleased with the acoustics of the Lexington's ballroom, and delighted by the favourable reactions to the widely-heard radio shows broadcast from there. In June 1936, Down Beat's radio correspondent, Paul K. Damai, wrote "The most improved band of recent history is Bob Crosby's at the Hotel Lexington in New York, heard over CBS. To our mind Bob has one of the finest on the air these days, and that from a very inauspicious start start not so many months ago. Arrangements that carry ethereally well, and a cohesive style that clicks are the points responsible, with all due respect to the Crosby name and its drawing power".

The last paragraph of that review highlighted a problem that was to be with the band, or rather the bandleader, for a good many years. People with famous relatives often find that the public are slow to take them on their own merits, and they are easily suspected of basking in someone else's glory. Bob Crosby showed a lot of spirit in following in brother Bing's footsteps, for when Bob first began working as a professional vocalist his brother was the megastar of popular singing. In a later chapter, Bob talks about the relationship he had with his elder brother. there is no doubt that 'the brother of Bing' tag assisted Bob's early rise to fame via Anson Weeks' Orchestra and the Dorsey Brothers' Band. The Crosby name also stimulated the Rockwell-O'Keefe agency interest, and even played its part in the ex-Pollack musicians selecting Bob as their leader, but, throughout his career, Bob has steadfastly refused to stress his fraternal links with Bing, and has gone out of his way to stop the fact being automatically mentioned in publicity handouts.

Those who have said that Bob could have avoided a great many problems by working under another name have no idea of the depth of the Crosby family pride.

What is certain is that Bob Crosby never transmitted the vocal 'magic' that Bing created with such ease. It was not simply a question of technique. Bing was a fine singer, but was not technically impeccable, he was, however, a total original. The two brothers shared the same parentage, the same environment and similar educations, it was small wonder that Bob spoke and sang like his brother, particularly as during his formative years the Crosby household was full of the sound of Bing's recordings.

Bob did not consciously copy Bing in the way that a professional impressionist might attempt the task, he simply grew up sounding like his elder brother; some of the early recordings are uncannily like Bing's work. Bob is well aware of the similarities, he is just as aware that a lot of his own ballad work was marred by the sudden instrusion of an uncontrollable vibrato, this incongruous "wobble" cancelled out much of the appeal of Bob's phrasing and enunciation, Bob sometimes made light of his vocal failings by saying that Bing had the better voice, but he (Bob) had the better band, at other times he seemed deeply depressed by his own shortcomings. What has rarely been stressed is that Bob's up-tempo vocals always swing, and they provided a worthwhile ingredient for many recordings by his band.

Bob Crosby could have earnt his living as a singer even if he had not been Bing's brother. As far as the success of his band was concerned, Bob's skills as a compere were just as important as his vocals. After a fairly shaky beginning, his presentation technique developed to the point where he became a superb master of ceremonies, able to showcase the band's music and its musicians with affability, intelligence and personality.

He had to work doubly hard to win the approval of the jazz critics, they didn't enjoy seeing favourite players like Eddie Miller, Yank Lawson, and Matty Matlock playing long notes throughout a commercial vocal, but they had no personal ill feelings toward Bob, they disapproved, just as strongly, of many other vocalists. It took Bob a long time to accept this, despite reassurances from Gil Rodin.

During the band's stay at the Hotel Lexington, a succession of good reviews convinced them that they were on right musical track. Amongst the critics who visited the Lexington was the English-born writer, Leonard Feather. Under the headline "Dixieland Re-born", he wrote in the British *Melody Maker* of October 17th 1936 about his trip to the Lexington.

"At 7.30 dancers almost obscured the view of the boys on the stand, which faced the slightly elevated circular gallery of tables. For a while the band failed to startle me, for the tunes were uninspiring and the brass section seemed to be restraining itself. Then little Eddie Miller came over during an interval and promised something really good in the next set. Bob Crosby, looking more than his twenty-two years, with firm and affable manner, slightly long and tilted nose, and an expression which always seemed to indicate he was just about to bite his lip, added his assurance that towards nine o'clock the place would not be so full of 'ickies', and the boys would be able to 'give out' more freely".

"The promise was not an idle one. Before long, every other number featured the style which had singled out this band as the outstanding new and most original dance orchestra of the year. So co-operative are these boys musically as well as financially, and so well hve their years of collaboration in the old Ben Pollack Band bound most of them together, that the neo-Dixieland style is always perfectly integrated, no matter who does the arrangement and which are the soloists".

Trumpeter Andy Ferretti returned to play lead trumpet with the band during their stay at the Hotel Lexington. Trombonist Artie Foster departed and his place was taken by ex-Fred Waring musician, Mark Bennett. The reed section also had a new look, the band had signed a new lead alto-saxophonist, Ernani 'Noni' Bernardi (who also doubled on flute), Deane Kincaide had temporarily ceased playing tenor sax to devote all his time to arranging, and to fill his place Gil Rodin changed from playing alto sax to tenor.

Whilst at the Lexington the band discarded its signature tune, *With Every Breath I Take*, and replaced it with *Summertime*, which has remained its theme ever since. The exact circumstances of how George Gershwin's song (from *Porgy and Bess*) came to be chosen are vague. The background to the band playing *Bess You Is My Woman*, another song from the same show, is perfectly clear. Pianist Gil Bowers got hold of a copy of the music from the show and wrote out a one chorus version of "Bess. . ." which the band played as dinner music. Subsequently, Deane Kincaide did a full band arrangement of *Summertime*.

Bob Crosby recalled the sequence of events as follows, "We were playing at the Lexington Hotel when George Gershwin, who was a great fan of the band, brought in the manuscript one evening". but Deane Kincaide feels certain that he made the original arrangement from a printed copy of the music, and this ties in with Gil Rodin's account of the events, "We'd been playing the *Porgy and Bess* score, and *Summertime* sounded so beautiful we all thought, 'Wouldn't it make a fantastic theme?'. We got Gershwin to come over and hear us. he was very impressed and gave us permission to use *Summertime* as a theme".

George Gershwin first met several of Bob Crosby's musicians during the time they were working with Ben Pollack at the Casino de Paree on New York's West 54th Street. Three years later, in 1936, he occasionaly dropped in to see them during their Hotel Lexington residency, and both Eddie Miller and Yank Lawson remember him attending one of the Crosby band's after-hours rehearsals that they held in the Lexington's ballroom. It was probably there that Gershwin heard, and approved of, the band's arrangement of his composition. By then the initial production of *Porgy and Bess* had closed, but because of possible copyright complications, Gil Rodin, in his usual thorough way, probably wanted to get official approval before the band adopted *Summertime* as their signature tune.

During the summer of 1936, Decca agreed to record some more of the band's jazz numbers, but on the same condition as before, as part of a session in which the group was booked to accompany a vocaliste. This time the singer was a schoolgirl, who was an unknown quantity as far as the band were concerned, they asked to remain anonymous accompanists, for what was actually a historic recording debut - the girl's name was Judy Garland. Judy sings with a vast amount of style on the two numbers she did with the band, and the musicians give unstinting effort, Matlock and Miller are both in characteristically lively form on *Stompin' At The Savoy*. Both *Stompin'* and the other title with Judy, *Swing, Mr. Charlie* were arranged by Glenn Osser. On that same date, the band recorded a shortened version of one of their "flag wavers", Matlock's arrangement of *Pagan Love Song*. The first soloist, Yank Lawson, demonstrates his adroit use of the plunger-mute in a vigorous solo, then Eddie Miller on tenor-sax plays a chorus that smoulders with intensity. Bob Haggart takes a zestful bass solo then Ray Bauduc is given a chorus in which he plays some "talking drums" in the manner of the great New Orleans percussionists. In his trumpet solo Yank pays indirect homage to the Crescent City by quoting from King Oliver's solo on *Dippermouth Blues*, and the trombones play a series of phrases that would have not sounded out of place in a band marching up Canal Street.

On the next title recorded, *Come Back Sweet Papa*, Matty Matlock pays his respects to past masters by incorporating some Johnny Dodds-like phrases into his solo. Here the ensemble reveals an eager but unflurried approach, every man plays his notes as though he believes in them. Overall, arranger Bob Haggart keeps the plot close to the 1926 Louis Armstrong Hot Five recording. This part of the session ended with another Haggart arrangement, based on Louis Armstrong's 1928 version of *Sugar Foot Strut*. The Crosby Band impart an emphatic two-in-the-bar feel to their version, with Ray Bauduc, in flamboyant mood inserting drop-beats with resourceful aplomb. The ensemble sounds effectively relaxed and the clarinet is left free to improvise freely above the scored band parts. Eddie Miller's vibrant tenor saxophone playing typifies the overall mood.

This trio of June 1936 instrumental recordings underlined the band's intentions of reviving and re-modeling classic jazz numbers from the past, they got inspiration from previous great recordings without ever blatantly copying them. The Decca Recording Company (and the Crosby Band) knew there was only a slight chance that the general public would buy vast quantities of esoteric material like *Come Back Sweet Papa*. Never-the-less the sales response was healthy, and this meant that the band were temporarily allowed to balance their record output between vocal discs aimed at the commercial market, and instrumental recordings that pleased jazz buyers.

The band's next session was a mixture of both approaches. Bob Crosby sang a spirited vocal on a pop song "Guess Who?", on which Lawson, Miller and Matlock created imaginative solos (the arrangement, by Haggart, has an introduction based on the old jazz favourite *Buddy's Habits*). Two other Crosby vocals from this session, *Cross Patch* and *Mary Had a Little Lamb* have their moments, and both have vigorous solos from Matlock, the latter title has some crisp woodblock playing from Ray Bauduc, an anachronistic, but highly effective percussion ploy.

The two instrumentals from this session are in direct contrast, one, a riff number popular at the time, *Big Chief De Soto,* the other a Louis Armstrong success from the late 1920s, *Savoy Blues.* Both have merit, but on *Savoy Blues* the band sounds distinctly more inspired. Yank Lawson's trumpet playing on *De Soto* is full of exhilaration, and Matlock's clarinet is eloquent enough, despite some intonation blemishes, but somehow the identity of the Crosby Band gets lost, whereas on *Savoy Blues* they produce a performance that no other big band of the period could have conceived. Haggart's arrangement is again inspired by a Hot Five recording. Matlock and Lawson share the melody, backed by a deliberately prominent guitar, then Lamare is overtly featured, and nicely captures the spirit of Johnny St. Cyr's work on the original. But as if to emphasise that this version has its own life to lead, Yank Lawson's playing in the last chorus, and the sign-off coda, take nothing directly from the Armstrong version, Yank creates a pleasing mixture of subtle half-valving and bold, triumphantly individual articulations.

At the band's next recording session, two months later, they continued their inspired revivalism by recording a slowish, almost elegant, version of *Royal Garden Blues,* scored by Deane Kincaide with Bix Beiderbecke's version in mind. Jazz fans could hardly believe their ears when they first heard these early Crosby releases, tributes to Louis Armstrong, and now a salute to the memory of Bix, led them to think that perhaps a mighty renaissance of jazz was about to take place. Their enthusiasm wasn't diminished by the band's recording of the slow and sombre *Woman On My Weary Mind,* a composition by Matlock and Rodin, which had been part of the Ben Pollack repertoire. The performance of the clarinet trio, who answer the crisply phrased muted trumpets, is superb, and the trombones, given more prominence that usual, make the most of the limelight.

However, the other tunes recorded at this session would have jolted even the most perversely romantic jazz fan back to reality. *My Kingdom For a Kiss,* is a positive hark-back to the sedate ballads that the Crosby Band had recorded a year earlier. Eddie Bergman's violin re-surfaces during the opening bars, and Bob Crosby gives a wavering delivery to a maudlin tune. Some of the ballads allocated to Bob during this era were real "dogs", with indifferent lyrics and forgettable melodies. In consequence it was difficult, both for Bob and for the arrangers, to muster enthusiasm about their presentation, as a result, insufficient care was taken by all concerned. In several instances, the key of the song is pitched too low for Bob to project the melody effectively. *Through The Courtesy Of Love* is a typical example of these failings, the treatment afforded the piece could politely be described as "commercial tango", it serves to accompany a Crosby vocal that radiates the discomfort he's having in trying to pitch notes that are below his normal working range. Alongside violinist Eddie Bergman is heard gently sawing-off strips of a particularly trite melody.

Fortunately, most of these commercially-slanted discs were soon forgotten and were not brought up as evidence against the band at a later date. The

August 1936 session was Bergman's last recording with the Crosby Band, even though he remained with the band until the following summer.

Whilst playing their residency at the Hotel Lexington, the band also briefly doubled at the Paramount Theatre, dashing to and from their hotel gig to share billing with (and accompany) vocaliste Mildred Bailey. Both Mildred and the Crosby Band got excellent reviews, and one of the hits of the show was the "fan-dance" routine that Eddie Miller, Nappy Lamare and Bob Haggart performed with great success.

Miller and Lamare had first seen the routine being performed by a burlesque troupe who shared the bill for a while with Ben Pollack's Band. The musicians never failed to laugh at the risqué impersonation of a line of careless fan-dancers, and conceived the idea that they would make a party piece of the sketch. They asked the troupe if they objected, but were told "Go ahead, have fun".

At first, a trio consisting of Miller, Lamare and Frank Tennille, (whose place was later taken by Bob Haggart) did the routine for private amusement, but they soon realised that it would make an effective comedy interlude for the Crosby Band's stage shows. Thus, the "Debutramps", as the act was originally called, began wowing audiences, the presentation became so popular, and received so much publicity, the originators seriously considered taking legal action to establish the exclusive use of the idea. The routine was consistently requested and retained its popularity for years, even in Boston where the local dignitaries insisted that the act be played wordless.

In preparation for the routine the three musicians rolled their trouser-legs up and grasped a fan in each hand. As an introduction the band played a "cod" version of an old ballad, usually *By The Sea,* or *Beautiful Lady,* on cue the three troupers took the centre of the stage, the two short figures of Miller and Lamare standing each side of the lofty Haggart. With backs to the audience at the start, they slowly turned around and in doing so gracefully covered themselves with the fans, in the manner of elegant strippers. Nappy Lamare immediately pretends to spot an old friend in the audience and lifts his fan to wave, his modest companions attempt to cover him with their fans, and so the fun begins. The fairly innocuous "script" containing such items as Haggart saying "Now you see it, now you don't", took on bold meanings when actions were added, and Eddie Miller demonstrating his advice to "Try it the hard way", usually had the women in the audience falling out of their seats, helpless with laughter.

The "fan" presentation fitted in with the band's general concepts that musicians were entertainers, a belief strongly held by the New Orleans contingent, besides their "fan dance" routine, Eddie and Nappy did a shim-sham dance. Ray Bauduc had his own front-of-stage solo spot in which he performed a remarkably lithe "snake-dance" that he had originally seen performed in Mardi Gras parades back home. This routine gave Bob Crosby the opportunity to keep time on the cymbals, which was officially quite in order as his Musicians' Union card listed him as a drummer. During the summer of 1936 the band were forced to make a change in the vocal department. After the briefest of romances Frank Tennille married Alice Foy, the hat-check girl at New York's Onyx Club. Frank's family in Montgomery, Alabama, apparently disapproved strongly of the marriage. All this made good copy for the New York tabloids. To avoid the limelight Frank and his new bride made for Armonk, New York, incognito, but the story of the elopement was splashed across news-stands. Tennille soon made tracks for his hometown, alone, and the marriage was annulled.

The treatment that the press gave to the affair certainly hastened Tennille's departure, but it is doubtful whether he would have chosen to stay with the band much longer anyway. Frank realised that he would never become the "front man" of the band, as had originally been envisaged by Gil Rodin, he wrote recently, "After a couple of years it became obvious that our 'dream' would never come true so I left". There was no open hostility between Frank and Bob, but the long-time members of the band came to realise that the two vocalists could never be totally happy working alongside each other. Deane Kincaide summarises the situation "It can't be said there was any real friction between the two. Just a singer's natural animosity toward other singers".

During the mid-1930s almost every big band except Bob Crosby's featured a girl singer. Frank Tennille's departure gave an opportunity to remedy that situation, however, the memories of the Doris Robbins-Ben Pollack saga were still so painful the band made no effort to recruit a female vocaliste. When Tennille left, in came another male singer to work alongside Bob Crosby. He was Bob Wacker, a 6ft 3 inches vocalist who had worked regularly on NBC, and also appeared in a Ziegfeld Follies production. The towering singer joined the band at the Hotel Lexington and was billed as Bob Walker.

Walker did his job well enough, but the band, under pressure, finally acknowledged that a good percentage of the current popular songs were better suited to female interpretation. Walker left, and Gil Rodin (on Bob Crosby's recommendation) sent for Kay Weber, who was then working in California with Jimmy Dorsey's Band. Kay, who had worked with Bob Crosby in the Dorsey Brothers Orchestra soon settled in and with a Snow White-like charm became good friends with everyone in the band. Yank Lawson said "Kay was a true professional, but she had a nice 'non-show business' attitude". Most of the singing was done by Bob and Kay, but occasionally Nappy Lamare was featured on a light-hearted comedy song, and sometimes Eddie Miller got up and sang some effective, and well-received, blues lyrics.

Pianist Gil Bowers, who had been with the Crosby Band since its inception (and with Pollack before that) decided to leave the band in the summer of 1936. Bowers, from Des Moines, Iowa, was an ex-Drake University student, he had been unsettled for some months, and let it be known that he was not happy about the structuring of the co-operative band. He had been particularly aggrieved to discover that the handsome moroccan leather toilet cases that had been given to each founder-member, had actually been paid for out of the band's earnings. Bowers left and worked in New York, before moving to Hollywood where he enjoyed considerable success for several years. Things were financially tight, during Bowers' days with the band, and for a long time Gil Rodin was unable to pay the staff arrangers the money that was due to them for their writing.

The Crosby Band were unanimous that the piano vacancy should first be offered to the Chicagoan pianist, Joe Sullivan. Sullivan, who was then working in California, immediately accepted the band's offer and in late August 1936 caught a cross-country train to New York. Sullivan's playing immediately gave the rhythm section a fuller sound, and his playing of the blues sounded so much more authentic than Gil Bowers' concepts, though in general all of the band were satisfied with Bowers all-round playing.

When Sullivan first joined the Crosby Band only a few of the arrangements featured piano solos, things gradually changed, but from the start Sullivan was always featured extensively on the band's head arrangements. On September 12th 1936, soon after Sullivan had joined, *Metronome* reviewed the Crosby Band at the Earle Theatre in Philadelphia, and noted, on *Pagan Love Song,* "Joe Sullivan was given his first and only chance to display his swing proclivities, he set to work with gusto and his three choruses were about the best part of the entire program. Joe displayed terrific swing and highly original licks in his brief appearance". A local critic, on the *Philadelphia Evening Bulletin,* reviewing the same date, found proceedigs too hectic, and wrote "The Crosby swing music is indeed jazz at about its lowest level, with none of the later Paul Whiteman refinements". The Bulletin's words were just what the band wanted to read, and they set out in high spirits for a wide ranging odyssey that took them to Pittsburgh, Carrolltown, Greensburg, Minneapolis, Minnesota, St. Louis, Houston, Memphis and Dallas.

The engagement in Pittsburgh proved to be a happy one for Matty Matlock who was feted by ex-colleagues with whom he had previously worked in that city, but in general Matty wasn't finding much time to enjoy himself at all. He was playing clarinet and saxophone with the band and was then staying up most of the night in order to keep the band supplied with new arrangements. After a meeting with Gil Rodin, it was agreed that Matty return to New York if a suitable replacement could be found, thus Matlock could be near his wife and two small children, and be able to devote time to regular arranging. He contacted Johnny Mince, who like many of the Crosby Band, dwelt in the Electric Court apartments in Jackson Heights; the two clarinettists worked out a deal whereby they temporarily swopped jobs, Mince joined Crosby and Matlock began working in New York, at the Rainbow Grill with Ray Noble's Orchestra.

In late 1936, Johnny Mince joined the Crosby Band at the Adolphus Hotel

40

in Dallas, Texas, no sooner had he arrived than one of the band's biggest dramas occurred. Joe Sullivan hurt his shoulder in a fall and went to the doctor, the resultant x-rays revealed a much more serious problem - pulmonary tuberculosis. Amidst sad farewells, Sullivan left to recuperate in the Dore Sanitarium in Monravia, California. His loss was keenly felt, and the prospect of finding a suitable replacement quickly seemed impossible, however, saxophonist Noni Bernardi warmly recommended the talents of a pianist he had often heard in Detroit, his name was Bob Zurke. Zurke was contacted and immediately accepted the offer. It was arranged that he fly to Dallas to join the band as soon as his air fare was cabled to him.

A delegation from the band met Zurke at the airport, the new pianist stepped briskly down from the plane dressed in a tuxedo that Eddie Miller had described as "crumpled and green with age", beneath this shapeless, heavily stained suite, Zurke wore an ancient, tattered shirt. When Zurke was asked if he needed a hand with his luggage he looked amazed, "Luggage? this is all the luggage I've got" he said, smoothing down the lapels of his weary old coat with a certain air of delicacy. His next gesture consisted of emptying his pockets dramatically to prove to the onlookers that he wasn't kidding when he said he only had 87 cents in the world. Turning to Eddie Miller, he confided "A five dollar loan would make the world of difference to my circumstances, friend". Miller reluctantly obliged, correctly surmising that he would never get the money back.

The band soon realised that they had taken on a full-blown eccentric, a superb musician who showed little interest in clean clothes or creature comforts. A man whose first thoughts rested on playing the piano and drinking hard liquor, whose next pleasure came from having female company and doing a little pool hustling. The entire Crosby travelling ensemble soon grasped the fact that in Zurke's mind the words "loan" and "gift" were interchangeable. No employee, even the humblest band-boy, was by-passed when the new pianist was questing for funds, but, Zurke (whose real name was Zukowski), did everything with a smile.

Washing was low on Zurke's priority list, and during the band bus trips lots were drawn before each long journey; the loser sat next to Zurke, and took in the strong aroma oozing both from Zurke and from the large Polish sausages that he liked to munch en route. After the gig was over, Zurke loved to unwind by topping up his already considerable intake of alcohol, and sauntering off into the night looking for places to sit-in on piano.

But all of Zurke's social failings were forgotten the instance he sat down to play piano. His technique was enviable, despite the fact that his fingers were short and stubby. He greatly admired, and was extremely conversant with, the works of J.S. Bach, Zurke's colleagues felt that the ingenious bass lines that the squat fingers created with such skill were inspired by the work of the great master. Zurke quickly learnt all of the features that Joe Sullivan had been playing, and added some of his own to the repertoire, with the result that he was soon one of the band's most applauded players. The favourable responses weren't limited to members of the audiences, and before long none other than Jelly Roll Morton singled Zurke out for praise.

From Dallas, the band made its way to New Orleans where they played a residency in the Blue Room of the Hotel Roosevelt. For several of the band it was literally home town week, and after the night's work was over they left to go to their relatives. As visitors, Johnny Mince and Ward Sillaway wanted to see as much of the city as possible, but no matter how fast or how far they travelled in their search for late-night music spots they always found that Zurke had arrived ahead of them and was already seated at the piano keyboard. Eventually Mince and Sillaway, feeling tired, would return to their hotel. Not Zurke, he'd hang on for as long as any club would have him. Mince recalls, "Zurke would stay up all night, every night, he'd get back next morning, fall into the 'bag' until it was time to play, then he'd start the same routine all over again".

Whilst at the Hotel Roosevelt, Gil Rodin was faced with the task of severely disciplining a particular member of the band, violinist Eddie Bergman. Eddie, a very popular member of the band, had a life-long passion for gambling, and as the local racetrack was close by it meant that Bergman lost his money even more quickly than usual. Each day he felt certain that he was going to get even with the bookmakers, and he began "subbing" the hotel, on behalf of the band, for extra funds.

Gil Rodin and Bob Crosby soon became aware of the heavy bills that were mounting daily, they established who the culprit was then called the band committee together for a meeting to decide on a course of action. There was no question of legal action, or of dismissal. Eddie's part on the band's recordings was non-existent but on hotel jobs he still played many regular feature numbers. It was decided to play a king-size practical joke on him, one that was large enough to shock him into repaying the loan and never repeating the manoeuvre again.

Eddie Miller's cousin was in the local police force, which in those immediate post-Huey Long days was not in a state of the highest formal organisation. It was arranged that several uniformed policeman were to rush on stage during the band's performance and haul Bergman away for alleged non-payment of debts. Seymour Weiss, who ran the Blue Room, was let in on the stunt.

That evening when the police arrived and arrested a terrified Bergman, the other musicians looked on with fake horror. A couple of hours later, after they had finished work, the band turned up at the Police station complete with their instruments; during the interim, Bergman had been held incommunicado in a small cell. The band quietly set up their instruments within the jail, and as Bergman was brought out, supposedly to be charged, they struck up with *Come Back Sweet Papa.*

Bergman, a natty Mischa-Auer like figure, attempted a somersault of joy as he realised that he's been the victim of a giant hoax. However, he made - and kept - a promise to mend his ways. The night ended on a happy note, and a wild one at that. The band had brought along girls and crates of booze, there was drink enough for everyone but there weren't enough girls to partner all the police staff. This proved to be only a fleeting disappointment, one of the jailers took his keys and let out a dozen detainees of a large cell known as "Faggot's Corner", and soon everyone had a dance partner.

Chapter 4

The birth of the Bob Cats

After their successful stay in New Orleans had ended, the band began to wend their way back north, but travel plans were severely disrupted by the devastating floods that swept through the south in late January 1937. Ray Bauduc remembers the journey, "We had just played a one niter in Nashville, Tennessee and had a few days off to make the Towers Theatre, Kansas City for a one week engagement. The floods came and we had to go south to Memphis, Tennessee, then cross the Mississippi to get to Little Rock, Arkansas, before going north to Kansas City, but we got flooded in at Harrison, Arkansas for a few days. So they had to show movies till the band got there".

The band, most of whom were travelling in their own automobiles, arrived in Kansas City in relays, but eventually the whole crew assembled to finish out the date and resume the trek north. One of the band's first important dates in the north was a Junior Prom at Cornell University in Ithaca, New York. On the same bill were the Will Hudson-Eddie De Lange Band and Jimmie Lunceford's Orchestra. About four thousand people turned up to hear the three groups battle against each other over a period of five hours.

Though a contemporary report put the honours even, saying the Crosby Band "matched the terrific ensemble arrangements of Lunceford with equally terrific individual exhibitions", most of the Crosby Band felt that it was one of the few occasions on which they were positively "cut" by another band. Over forty years later, several of them could recall the encounter clearly, Nappy Lamare said "Hudson-De Lange played *Bugle Call Rag,* and we followed with our version, a head arrangement that lasted for about ten minutes, then Lunceford stormed in with his version, and he cut us, no doubt about that". Yank Lawson and Eddie Miller think that the intensity of the Lunceford onslaught was stirred by the fact that they were under the impression that the Hudson-De Lange deliberately played a Lunceford speciality, thinking that the band had already packed all their arrangements in preparation for an imminent trip to Europe. Whatever the reason, all hell was let loose on the Lunceford bandstand.

The encounter at Cornell highlighted the fact that in the "cutting contests" that were so popular at the time, the Crosby Band were relying too heavily on head arrangements, there was a need for a big array of powerful numbers that were exclusively associated with them. Via the imaginative work of Haggart, Matlock and Kincaide, good orchestrations were regularly being added to the band's repertoire, but there was still a shortage of notably original "flag wavers". Unfortunately, much of the three staff arrangers' time was taken up with writing commercial scores that were being featured on the band's growing number of radio programmes.

The shortage of new arrangements became acute after Gil Rodin called a meeting of the "committee" to discuss the premise that some of Deane Kincaide's more recent arrangements were too complicated to be effective. Deane, later to be regarded as one of America's finest arrangers, was reluctant to amend what he had written, he explains the aftermath, "I was asked to take a leave of absence, due to a meeting the Crosby Band had in getting to the bottom of my intractibility regarding editing of my arrangements - the bottom turned out to be Gil Rodin's conclusion that I needed help. That remark led me to believe that my bickering over money was getting too close to the truth of the matter, and I think he thought I was going to close in on him. I cried bitter tears over that, but left and went with Lennie Hayton".

Deane's instrumental versatility had been very useful to the band, in emergencies he could play all the saxophones, clarinet and flute. He could also double effectively on trombone, and Bob Haggart still remembers the eerie timbre of a low note that Deane played on trombone to end the band's version of *Old Man Mose,* "It was more a death rattle than a musical note, but it was highly effective". But Dean's most important role for the band was as an arranger, his departure was a blow because so few "outside" arrangers were able to grasp exactly what the Crosby Band required. Several of the leading arrangers of the day including Fud Livingston, Mary Lou Williams, Joe Lippman and Frank Marks, submitted arrangements to the Bob Crosby Band, they were usually accepted but follow-ups were rarely commissioned because the scores never sounded "tailor-made" for them, the charts made their music resemble the output of other swing bands of the period.

It was agreed by the band that if a suitable clarinettist could be found Matty Matlock could quit the reed section to concentrate exclusively on arranging. The problem (as in the search for arrangers) was in finding a clarinettist who really understood, and was capable of playing, what the Crosby Band wanted. The recent formation of a small band within the Crosby Band added to the dilemma, because the clarinet played a vital role in the four strong front-line, trumpet, trombone, tenor saxophone and clarinet. Originally these four instrumentalist had stood up in the ride-out choruses of a big band jazz number, but more recently they had been featured as a separate unit on occasional feature numbers.

Matlock's playing on the band's February 1937 recording session conveyed the sort of individuality that the Crosby Band required. Matty's clarinet improvising over the last ensemble on *The Old Spinning Wheel* was in a style that few "swing era" reed players could capture. Yank Lawson's half chorus on the same record has the same qualities of involved sincerity, and no other white drummer of the period seemed capable of getting such an authentic variety of sounds from his drum kit as Bauduc. Those who suggest that Bob Zurke simply copied other people's solos would do well to listen to the originality, and amazingly dexterous left-hand patterns that the pianist played on this number, which marked his recording debut with the band.

On the same session, Zurke also imparts his own stamp on Joe Sullivan's *Gin Mill Blues,* and is equally brilliant on the bouncy *If I Had You* (a Kincaide arrangement). Bob Crosby's vocal on this title is appealingly jaunty, marred only by some slack phrasing in the last eight bars. Yank Lawson's continual improvement is made obvious by the powerful way he plays the opening and closing melody statements. The final title of the session, *Between the Devil & The Deep Blue Sea,* is one of Bob Haggart's most ingenious arrangements. It bristles with witty modulations, and was just the sort of musical armour that was needed to triumph over any rival group that was attempting to challenge the Crosby Band. The opening theme is played by muted brass, alongside them the reeds play a counterpoint that is striking enough to make attention flit from original line to accompaniment. Lawson, Miller and Matlock solo engagingly before handing over the final chorus to the rhythm section. The recording of this arrangements caused all those who had written the Crosby Band off as nostalgic recreators to start looking for a much larger pigeon-hole.

Soon after these four sides were cut in February 1937, the band solved a long-standing problem by finding a permanent lead trumpeter. The newcomer was Rubin "Zeke" Zarchy, who contrary to existing discographical details, was about to play with the Crosby Band for the very first time. He is emphatic on this point, "I did not record with the band in 1936. I joined the band in February 1937, replacing my friend Andy Ferretti. I had just returned from Dallas after the break-up of Artie Shaw's first band. That night I went to the Pennsylvania Hotel where Benny Goodman was playing. During one of the intermissions, Benny asked me to meet some people. He took me to a table and introduced me to six guys who turned out to be part of the Bob Crosby Band. One of them (I later remembered as Gil Rodin) asked me if I would like to come with the band, and I said 'Sure'. The next morning we left town". Another change was imminent in the brass section, Warren Smith on trombone was soon to replace Mark Bennett.

The Crosby Band's growing reputation was reflected by the size of the audiences that paid to hear them at the Hippodrome in Baltimore and at Nixon's Grand in Philadelphia during February 1937. These dates led-up to another of the band's "turning-point" engagements, which was soon to begin in Chicago, (at a hotel that Ralph Hitz had bought the previous September). Gil Rodin recalled, "We went into the Congress in Chicago, where we got our best air time and started to click for sure. That was the turning point. From then on we were better off financially, and our records began to sell".

During their residency at the Congress Hotel's Casino Room, the band (together with *Down Beat* magazine) organised a benefit for the ailing Joe

Sullivan (who was still recuperating on the West Coast). The show, which was held on a Sunday afternoon (18th April 1937) ran for over three hours; 877 people paid the dollar and fifty cents admission charge. Sharing the bill with the Crosby Band was a group co-led by the legendary Dodds Brothers, Johnny on clarinet and Baby on drums, (their quartet included Natty Dominique on trumpet and Leo Montgomery on piano). There was also a trio consisting of Roy Eldridge on trumpet, Teddy Wilson on piano and Zutty Singleton on drums; ten year old Bobby Short also played three numbers on piano. Red Nichols was in the audience, as were Jimmy Durante and Ethel Merman, altogether the sum of 1550 dollars was raised for Joe Sullivan and later presented to him in the form of a spectacular two foot long cheque.

From 2 pm until 2.30 pm the National Broadcasting Company transmitted (coast to coast) an excerpt from the show. It was one of the first occasions, if not the first, that a jazz concert had been thus organised, and the announcer, adopting a tone suitable for such a momentous transmission made a preliminary announcement that attempted to tell the waiting listeners what was about to happen. The net result was about as effective as an Englishman trying to explain the game of cricket in two sentences, he said:

"The National Broadcasting Company brings you something new and truly unusual in musical broadcasting. . . . a Swing Concert. This differs from the usual jazz band numbers usually heard, in that the musicians, being specialist on the instruments they play, are permitted to improvise as they play, the result will be swing with unexpected hot breaks and arrangements that become genuine swing tunes".

Undeterred by this fatuous preliminary talk, the Crosby Band launched into a session of inspired playing. After a formidable *In a Minor Mood*, (based on an early Joe Sullivan solo recording that blended Fats Waller's *"Zonky"* with Rachmaninoff's Prelude in C sharp minor), the band performed a sublime version of Bob Haggart's recently composed opus *Dogtown Blues* (dedicated to Bob's home town, Douglastown, L.I.). The insertion of this piece in the coast-to-coast broadcast emphasised the Crosby Band's dedication to their jazz beliefs, they could have inserted two popular songs in the time (over six minutes) that they allocated to what is virtually a blues tone poem, Another Haggart arrangement followed (*Between The Devil & The Deep Blue Sea*), then another, *South Rampart Street Parade* (a lively Haggart and Bauduc co-composition). The broadcast ended with Bob Zurke being featured on Joe Sullivan's *Gin Mill Blues.*

Throughout the transmission the audience made history by clapping individual solos. It was a historic occasion in more ways than one, because for the first time, the small band within the Crosby band received its own formal billing. In the concert's printed programme it was announced that in the second-half THE BOB CATS would be heard playing *Tin Roof* (sic) and *Driving Me Crazy* (sic).

Amazingly, no one quite remembers who first had the brilliant idea of calling the small group by such an appropriate name. As Bob Crosby points out, it was just perfect, a combination of his own first name and the current slang for a jazz fan, but even Bob is unsure as to who originally suggested the name that was soon to become synonymous with the best of small group jazz.

After the successful booking at the Casino Congress had ended on May 15th 1937, the band moved on to play in Atlantic City, before taking up a July residency at the Ritz-Carlton Hotel in Boston, Mass. En route the band called into New York where Kay Weber made her recording debut with the band. Kay's voice was not particularly strong or unusual, but she enunciated lyrics clearly and had a good sense of pitch. Kay sang two on the session, as did Bob, it was an all vocal occasion because Decca wanted to issue recordings of material that was being featured in currently successful films. Kay and Bob each sang a song from the *Artists and Models* movie, then Kay sang *You Can't Have Everything* from Alice Faye's film of the same name. Bob's remaining vocal, *The Loveliness of You* was praised at the time of release as being his best effort.

A new spirit had entered the band's backing of vocals, less emphasis was placed on a sedate "hotel" approach, instead the group swung their way into each tune as though they were out to enjoy themselves come what may. Several good solos are sprinkled throughout these July 1937 vocals, and the ensemble on *You Can't Have Everything* has all the vim and panache of a street parade band, with Bauduc's snares setting a lively pace.

Whilst at the Ritz-Carlton, the Crosby band took a whole page advertisement in the July 1937 issue of *Down Beat* congratulating the magazine on its third anniversary. The full band personnel was listed:
Bob Crosby,
Gil Rodin, Eddie Miller, Matty Matlock and Noni Bernardi.
Yank Lawson, Zeke Zarchy,
Ward Sillaway, Warren Smith,
Ray Bauduc, Nappy Lamare, Bob Haggart and Bub Zurke,
plus Kay Weber.

Violinist Eddie Bergman's name was conspicious by its absence. After steadfastly retaining the "fiddle" for two years, as part of its ballroom presentations, the band finally decided that it didn't suit their image, so reluctantly they parted with Bergman. There were no ill feelings, and Bergman kept in regular touch with all his friends in the band throughout the years he spent as a musical director for leading hotels, he never once forgot to send Yank Lawson an "Ace of Spades" playing card at Christmas as a reminder of the many card games that they had shared. Early that same summer (1937), another change took place in the band, Noni Bernardi was taken ill and returned to his home in Detroit to recuperate, his place was taken by a young ex-Benny Goodman saxophonist, from Pittsburgh, Billy Depew.

In the August 1937 *Down Beat*, George Frazier, one of the most celebrated jazz writers of the 1930s, made some interesting comparisons between Bob Crosby's Band and the hugely successful orchestra led by Benny Goodman. In a long article headed "Does Goodman or Crosby Play Best White Man's Swing?", Frazier compared the merits of each band, both of which he had heard recently at the Ritz-Carlton Hotel,:

"In its best moments, the Crosby band is a thing of sheer magnificence. It is, I think, a large band packing the irresistible thrill of a small jam combination. You can't say as much for Benny. Both rhythm sections are obviously close to perfection, and whatever slight edge there may be must go to Bob Crosby by virtue of Bobby Haggart's superlative bass. But jazz is essentially an affair of improvisation, and therein lies a significant and oft-obscured point. The Crosby band allows plenty of solo room, in it best moments and in its best vehicles, far more than Benny's".

At the Ritz Carlton, which had what was described as "one of the swankiest roof gardens in New England", the Crosby band played some rousing jazz sessions, but Gil Rodin was also mindful that some ballroom dancers only feel at ease when they can hear the melody. A happy medium was achieved by blending the commercial vocals (by Kay and Bob) with high spirited versions of *There'll Be Some Changes Made, Come Back Sweet Papa* and other jazz favourites. It was the stomping numbers that produced a reaction that was described at the time in *Metronome* magazine as "howling and cheering". The elite crowd who frequented the plush ballroom, which maintained a high 3 dollars 50 cents cover charge, obviously felt they were getting value for their money.

The band always enjoyed its forays into New England, they felt extra happy during their 1937 visit to Boston and one reason for their contentment was that they were continually feted by a lady who they came to regard as the band's Number One Fan. The newcomer's name was Mrs. Celeste Le Brosi, a widow in what might be called the prime of life. Mrs. Le Brosi was one of the three daughters of Doctor Murphy, a Chicago physician who had invented a 'drip device' that was much used following operations for appendicitis. The patent produced royalties that allowed his immediate family to live luxuriously, but Mrs. Le Brosi felt a need to share her good fortune, and after hearing the Crosby band play in Chicago she was struck by the charm of the musicians and particularly Gil Rodin. She resolved to make sure that some of the luxuries of life reached the musicians, and for a while in the late 1930s she carried out her plan with a kindness and abandon that was remarkable. In Boston for instance, she took an entire floor of the Ritz Carlton and arranged that tables were laden with the choicest delicacies for the Crosby band, no drink was too exotic or expensive for them to order on her tab. Not that she was foolish with her money, for one feast she had the plumpest turkeys flown in, but on being told that local Boston lettuces were fetching 75 cents apiece she refused the quote.

The band were close to being overwhelmed by a surfeit of kindness. If anyone casually mentioned cashmere he could well find that he was presented with an expensive sweater, a musician without a pen was given the latest gold-plated model. For a time, Mrs. Le Brosi's Cadillac flowed along in convoy with the less salubrious automobiles belonging to the band, her teenage son's La Salle also joined the travelling line. Jim, who was popular with all of the band, was fascinated by the touring musicians' life, and asked his mother if he could join the Crosby band in some official capacity. Mrs. Le Brosi and Gil Rodin came to an arrangement whereby James was appointed as the band's librarian, whose task was to keep the music parts in order and to generally assist the recently promoted road manager, Joe Kearney. He did the job for about a year at no expense to the band, his wages being paid for out of the Le Brosi family funds.

The band concluded its residency in Boston in August 1937, and left to play dates in Cleveland and Detroit. Whilst the band were appearing at the Aquacade in Cleveland they augmented the trumpet section to a three piece unit by signing a brilliant teenager to share duties with Yank Lawson and Zeke Zarchy. The newcomer was Billy Butterfield, who developed into one of the world's most versatile trumpet soloists. Billy had been on the band's "recommended list" for some while, ever since Bob Haggart had heard him playing with a local band at the Joyland Park in Lexington, Kentucky in the summer of 1936. At that time there was no money available to increase the band's complement of musicians, but by mid-1937 the economic outlook was brighter and after Haggart and Matlock had heard the young trumpeter playing on an Austin Wylie band broadcast they recommended that Gil Rodin make Butterfield an offer, post haste. A telegram of invitation was duly despatched and acceptance immediately confirmed.

During the late 1930s, most travelling bands had their own softball teams, and the Crosby group was no exception. For some bands preparation for the ball game became an affair of deadly seriousness, but the Crosby team never became desperately anxious about their results, never-the-less they usually put up commendable performances, and in the fall of 1937 whilst playing some return dates in Chicago they scored a notable victory over Red Nichols' Band.

Billy Butterfield usually remained a spectator at these sporting fixtures, but he settled in easily with his new companions, all of whom were impressed by his musicianship. An arranger, Bob Pearce, had been paid to write out the new third trumpet parts, but they did not blend easily, and Butterfield's excellent ear allowed him to find a much more effective harmony. One thing that his friends in the band forgot to warn Billy about was Zurke's borrowing habit. On an early date with the band, Billy found himself seated next to Zurke in a coffee shop. "Why my young friend, look what I have here" said Zurke, smacking an envelope and returning it hastily to his pocket. "It's a request for photographs of my hands, would you believe? Some publicity idea I guess". Billy was suitable impressed and waved to the lively pianist as he hurried off. Zurke was back in a trice, looking ashen-faced he said "Good God! I've left my wallet in the hotel room. . . and this thing is so urgent . . . do you think you could loan me ten dollars to prevent a calamity?". Billy willingly advanced the money, but a week later he had still not been reimbursed, thereafter whenever he raised the subject Zurke either looked totally blank about the transaction or smacked Butterfield on the back and said "People will do the craziest things for publicity, won't they?".

Billy bore no lasting grudge, and he and Zurke often defeated travel tiredness by having a friendly drink together. After a humdinger of an itinerary had taken the band from Houston, Texas to Memphis, Tennessee and then on to Lexington, Kentucky prior to playing Columbus, Ohio, the band reached Akron, Ohio on September 22nd 1937 to play a date at the Summit Beach Park. On the day after this gig, Butterfield, Zurke and Bob Haggart went for a few drinks together in the Merry-Go-Round Bar in Akron. After a good few rounds the trio left the bar in a state of some merriness, and on the sidewalk Zurke was suddenly taken with a desire to demonstrate an intricate dance that had been practiced by his Polish ancestors. Haggart recalls the scene, "Zurke started waving his arms, and doing a sort of heel-and-toe step, but he forgot about the edge of the sidewalk and fell crashing to the ground. We couldn't stop laughing, but he started groaning and saying he'd broken his leg".

When the laughing stopped, Zurke's colleagues lifted him into a nearby taxi and he was taken to St. Thomas's Hospital on Main Street where x-rays revealed that the self-diagnosis was only half right, Zurke had actually broken his leg in two places. He was forced to rest up in hospital in plaster, but impatiently discharged himself on October 8th so that he could travel west to rejoin the band in time for their Californian debut at the Palomar ballroom in Los Angeles. During Zurke's brief absence the band used two deputy pianists, Harry Walton of Pittsburgh (who later worked with Dick Stabile) and Lester Ludke (who had been with Ray Noble and Nye Mayhew).

Earlier on the same tour, before Zurke had his accident, there had been other personnel changes in the band. Saxophonist Billy Depew left to return to Pittsburgh and his place was taken by Joe Kearns. Gil Rodin maintained a close friendship with his ex-Ben Pollack colleague, Glenn Miller, and it was through Miller that Kearns came to join the Crosby Band, "In late 1937 I received a 'phone call from Glenn Miller (this was before he made it big). He had heard me on the air (with Jan Savitt's Band) and asked me to consider going with the Crosby Band who were looking for a lead alto and were good friends of his". Another change saw Deane Kincaide resuming his place as staff arranger, he rejoined the band in Detroit at the start of the Crosby Band's long journey west.

The Crosby band's booking at the Palomar was the group's first booking (as a unit) in California. The venue was the one that had been the site of Benny Goodman's first big success two years earlier, but despite some monumental performances there by the Crosby Band there wasn't a similar explosion of public interest. Business was steady throughout the booking, and whilst they were in Los Angeles the band were able to undertake four recording sessions (in November 1937) which further increased their growing reputation. From the Palomar the band did regular widely heard radio programmes via stations KEHE, KNX AND KECA.

The band's first-ever Californian record date was a mainly commercial affair, but the first two titles cut featured material that was markedly superior to the run-of-the-mill "pop" song. *Nice Work If You Can Get It* (sung by Bob Crosby) and *A Foggy Day in London Town* (a vocal by Kay Weber), justifiably became evergreen songs. On the session they were followed by an evenescent movie tune called *I've Hitched My Wagon To A Star*, a song of true indifference, whose sole point of interest today is that it demonstrated that Bob Crosby could comfortably hit a high 'C'; in retrospect it seems a pity that more of Bob's backing arrangements didn't take him up to this pleasant sounding register. Kay Weber sang a light, musical-comedy type number *This Never Happened Before*, then the stage was set for two fine instrumentals.

The new three man trumpet team (Zarchy, Lawson and Butterfield) were in excellent form throughout the session, continually imparting a cohesive flare to their phrasing, clearly apparent on Matty Matlock's arrangement of *Nice Work. . .*, but particularly noticeable on the instrumental numbers, where the rapport of the whole brass section is truly impressive. On the piano feature, *Little Rock Getaway*, Bob Zurke (with leg still in plaster), pays sincere homage to the tune's composer, Joe Sullivan, but still imparts his own concepts of phrasing and chord-voicing. Eddie Miller is the only other soloist, playing as ever with elan and invention, creating a succession of lyrical phrases mainly in the middle register of the tenor sax. The same two musicians are satisfyingly featured on *Squeeze Me*, an effective Bob Haggart arrangement which ends some intriguing bass-register scoring.

On the next recording session, a few days later, the band ably backed four Bob Crosby vocals, the one instrumental recorded was based on the quaint Corsican melody *Vieni Vieni*. Arranger Haggart does a workmanlike job on the busy, almost fussy, tune, but despite the stirring rapport between Miller's tenor and Bauduc's drumming things never consistently swing. Matlock and Lawson sound a little tense in their solos, and a similar jerky quality mars Warren Smith's 16 bar solo. Smith's apprehension is perhaps understandable as this was one of the first solos he had recorded with the band, but the real culprit is probably the unsuitable material.

In November 1937, whilst they were on the coast, a contingent from the band were due to take part in a recorded re-union with Connee Boswell. One of the resultant recordings, *Martha* became a big seller, but in terms of musical significance *Martha* was of secondary importance, the vital part of the session, as far as the Crosby jazzmen were concerned, was that it marked the recording debut of the Bob Cats. In swift time, the eight piece contingent made an indelible mark on jazz history by recording their first six titles, *Stumbling, Who's Sorry Now, Coquette, Fidgety Feet, You're Driving Me Crazy* and *Can't We Be Friends?*.

The Bob Cats were certainly not the first 'band within a band'. The strategy of featuring a small jazz group selected from a full ensemble had been employed previously by other leaders, notably Tommy Dorsey, whose *Clambake Seven* had first recorded in 1935. But none of the earlier experiments ever graduated beyond a tiny interlude within a main programme, whereas the Bob Cats' features soon became the most talked about part of the Crosby Band's output. The Bob Cats played a style of music that appealed not only to jazz fans (young and old) but also to the general public, who responded to the infectious sincerity and abundant skills that hallmarked every one of their performances.

Zez Confrey's old favourite *Stumbling* got the Bob Cats off to a great start. Everyone sounds relaxed, and the bouncy tempo seems perfect. The opening ensemble is warm and invigorating and the interplay between the front-line instrumentalists is interesting and cohesive. Eddie Miller solos admirably, both on tenor and clarinet, (Matlock is left to concentrate on an ensemble role); when asked about this allocation of solos, Miller explained, "When there was something with a New Orleans taste, they'd usually call me out front". Bob Zurke's excellent 16 bar solos seems to successfully blend two disparate styles - barrelhouse and conservatoire - during the piano solo, double-bass and guitar drop out leaving Bauduc on drums to supply the accompaniment. In the final chorus Miller's tenor sax creates an emphatic counter-melody to Yank Lawson's succinct lead, Miller's "weaving" not only creates interesting counterpoint it also causes the trombonist to avoid routine, tailgate fill-ins. Thus the overall sound of a Bob Cats' ensemble was not of players simply going through the motions of recreation, but rather of eager jazz spirits seeking new ways to express themselves within a tradition that they revered.

Who's Sorry Now (with a crisp introduction devised by Matty Matlock) again features Miller and Zurke, both of whom are allocated full 32 bar choruses. Miller, first up, concentrates on embellishing the melody for the first half of his solo, before developing some ingenious arpeggic ideas. Zurke's outing is fairly staid, except for a burst in his second eight bars which highlights his interesting use of left handed counter rhythms. The full ensemble return and nattily paraphrase the melody (with Bauduc's drum phrasing fitting in crisply), this leads on to brief solos by Matlock on clarinet and Smith on trombone, both sound lively and unfettered. During the final surge of the ensemble, Matlock counters Lawson's long, commanding note with a perfectly conceived phrase, that garlands and enhances the trumpeter's idea.

The ensembles intertwining of musical creativities also figures strongly in *Coquette*. After a smoothly harmonised opening chorus, the old 1920s hit becomes a vehicle for joyous solos from Miller on tenor and Lawson on trumpet. Matlock, superbly backed by Haggart's bass playing, creates some reflective lines, then trombonist Warren Smith, not ideally placed as far as balance, blows a robust half-chorus before the horns re-gather for a final ensemble that epitomises the Bobcats' relaxed drive - so different from the antics of many other dixieland-orientated bands of the period.

The New Orleans contingent in the Bobcats made sure that every individual in the group gave as much thought to their work in the ensembles as they did to their solo playing. This care for tradition is clearly shown in *Fidgety Feet*. It seems obvious that all of the group were familiar with *The Wolverines'* recording, but none are content to be copy-cats, the Miller clarinet solo is pure delight, and the timely splash of Baucuc's cymbals and his lively drum breaks are a triumph, unfortunately Lamare's brief guitar solo is poorly recorded.

The liveliness of the Bobcats is emphasised in their version of *You're Driving Me Crazy*. Drop beats from Bauduc abound in the opening chorus then the patterns change as Miller and Matlock solo elegantly, before giving way to the robust brass team of Lawson and Smith. The ride-out chorus rolls inexorably on, it is packed with stimulating counter-rhythms much like the final part of a recording by King Oliver's Creole Jazz Band. The last title of the day, *Can't We Be Friends?*, shows the Bobcats in an entirely different mood, they interpret a slow ballad in a way that is full of expression, but devoid of schmaltz. Eddie Miller is featured, and shows even in these early days that he was one of the finest of all ballad interpreters, everyone of his inflections are guaranteed to add to the original melody. Bob Zurke's 16 bar solo sounds distinctly less committed, but contains some ruminative ideas. Matlock conceives a poised 8 bar solo, then a block-harmonised ensemble concludes the piece with 8 bars of unruffled melody. Throughout the session the group had proved that they were an expressive coterie of jazz talents who could cover many areas of jazz with admirable sensitivity.

The full Crosby band also achieved a first on the 13th November 1937, when they took part in the initial West Coast transmission of CBS's popular radio show *Saturday Night Swing Session*, by then there had been a change in the trumpet section, Charlie Spivak (who had been part of Ben Pollack's Band) arrived from the East to replace Zeke Zarchy. A few days later, the full band recorded an historic session. After accompanying three ordinary vocal numbers the band stormed into Bob Haggart's marvellous arrangement of *South Rampart Street Parade*.

This tune had started life as a series of phrases that Ray Bauduc had hummed to Haggart after the band had finished a session at a hotel in New York. Bauduc called Haggart over to an empty table and began softly humming the outlines of a new tune, accompanying himself by thwacking his hands on his knees. Haggart immediately saw the potential of the ideas and began scribbling down the melody on a table cloth. He later realised that his only hope of making sense of the pencilled outlines was to take the table-cloth home and study it in daylight. He did this, and thus the embryo version of *South Rampart Street Parade* was preserved and nurtured. At first the tune was called *Bulls On Parade*, in honour of an old New Orleans organisation "The Bulls' Society, Aid and Pleasure Club" which Bauduc had seen marching years before in his home city but under its new title it became one of the band's biggest successes.

The stark call of the trumpets, with drum accompaniment, announces in New Orleans fashion that things are about to get under way. The opening figure leads into a strongly syncopated melody, over which a liquid-toned clarinet roams free, a marching anthem follows - complete with percussive piano interjections. Then a long, dramatic bridge passage, with trombones well to the fore, precedes Miller's eloquent low-register clarinet solo (which is elegantly trimmed by the sound of Bauduc's woodblocks). In the next, loosely arranged section, Yank Lawson's sparse but scintillating lead lifts the band in preparation for the ensueing, climactic ending. In the finale, a brass-led figure is countered by an ingenious sax phrase, the clarinet swoops and soars before joining the saxophones, then together they create the perfect answer to the brass's concluding statement.

The arrangement of *South Rampart Street Parade* is masterful, but not more so than its session mate *Dogtown Blues*, arranged and composed by Bob Haggart. It is one of the finest of orchestrated blues, and worthy, both in form and content of a score by one of Haggart's supreme musical heroes, Duke Ellington.

The piece opens with Yank Lawson on trumpet playing a sombre theme, accompanied by a mellow clarinet trio, scored over fruity-sounding low notes on the trombones. The reeds assume prominence, and develop a secondary theme, which is countered by a strong motif from the trombones. The piano enters to share the limelight then Lawson takes a dramatic stop-time solo leading-into Eddie Miller's two clarinet chroruses, which must rank high amongst his many praise-worthy solos. The full band re-enter to play a brooding melody which builds cohesively over two choruses and emerges as an almost jubilant finale.

Amazingly, the band were able to quickly don their commercial hat to record a medium-tempoed Kay Weber vocal, *Sweet Someone*, which offers a brief round of subdued solos and a nicely scored blending of the trombones and the two tenor saxophones. The band then waxed *Just Strolling*, a Bob Haggart arrangement which allocates most of the opening work to Zurke's piano playing and an agile reed section. Nappy Lamare's brief guitar solo is charming, and the band again nods in Louis Armstrong's direction by playing a riff based on his recording of *Gully Low Blues*.

The last tunes recorded on the band's 1937 West Coast sojourn were also commendable, the first a Matty Matlock arrangement of *Panama*, which has lilting ensembles either side of Miller's graceful tenor sax solo, and some vigorous improvisations from Warren Smith. The final title features a vocal from Nappy Lamare, the first apart from his words on *Come Back Sweet Papa* that he had recorded with the Crosby Band. The vehicle is the old favourite, *When My Dreamboat Comes In,* but it was sub-titled *Big Apple Calls,* because Lamare takes on the role of caller, and shouts instructions to an imaginary audience. The opening chorus has some deft Zurke piano fill-ins, and Lamare's lively vocal is enhanced by Miller's tenor-sax obligato and Matlock's clarinet work, the band climaxes the piece with a blazing last chorus, scored by Bob Haggart on phrases suggested to him by Eddie Miller.

Ordinarily, these last two sides, Panama and . . . Dreamboat, would have been prize items from any Crosby Band session, but they were dwarfed on the occasion by the superlative *South Rampart Street Parade* and *Dogtown Blues* coupling. The arrangements of both masterpieces were soon on the market as printed orchestrations, and so, for years afterwards, ballrooms throughout the world echoed with the sounds of Haggart's superb scoring as countless bands attempted to recreate the magic of that November 1937 Californian recording session.

Chapter 5
Enter Fazola

After playing a December residency at the Rice Hotel in Houston, Texas, the Bob Crosby band moved back to the east coast to begin a booking at New York's Hotel Pennsylvania on the 17th January 1938. For a complicated variety of reasons, the band's opening there was virtually devoid of publicity. The ballroom they moved into was one in which Benny Goodman had recently enjoyed an overwhelming success, the so-called 'swing era' was at its zenith, and most of the Hotel Penn crowd were devotees of Goodman's band, which meant that applause for the Crosby band's subtle moments was often sparse.

An onlooker, the eminent jazz writer, George T. Simon, regarded the Hotel Pennsylvania booking as one of the low spots in the history of the Crosby band. Summarising the affair (in 1941), he wrote, "Why the guys, especially the astute Gil Rodin, were ever foolish enough to consent to a thing like this, nobody to this day can explain". The Crosby band continued to play its usual repertoire at the Hotel Pennsylvania, undaunted by the occasional indifference of the audience, if anything the booking strengthened their resolve to avoid becoming another swing band. Asked about the band's attitude in a contemporary interview, Bob Crosby replied, somewhat acidly, "We play jazz, not swing. Maybe that's harder to do, but we like it a lot better". In discussing the 1938 Hotel Penn booking with the musicians involved, one is struck by the fact that none of the participants were at all dismayed by events there, but in retrospect it seems likely that most of them had their minds on a problem that was looming large at that particular time.

The problem that faced the band as it began its stay at the hotel concerned its dealing with the Rockwell-O'Keefe agency. Throughout 1937 the band had become progressively disenchanted by the way their business affairs were being handled. There were particularly disgruntled that a representative of the agency was invested with the power to spend unrestricted amounts in connection with expenses incurred in administering the band. The band felt that any outlay should be under the strict jurisdiction of their own corporation.

The agency's argument was that a good deal of the money spent on building up the Crosby band was used on establishing goodwill; by entertaining the press and possible bookers. They pointed out that if an agency man took a two thousand mile trip to try and finalise the contract for a week's band booking, there was no certainty that his mission would be successful, and whatever the outcome, the expenses were the same. The Crosby band corporation could see the logic there, but pointed out that the journey might not have been undertaken exclusively on their behalf, several of the other bands that the agency handled might have also benefitted from such a trip. Neither side was willing to give ground, and in the late stages of this long-standing dispute considerable pettiness developed. Things even got to the stage where the agency presented the band (to their great annoyance) with a demand for part of the office's electricity bill.

All of the issues in dispute would probably have been resolved eventually if the band had been totally happy about the way their bookings were being organised, and if they had been content that the money spent on their behalf for buying radio-time had been used to best advantage. The agency-band relationship gradually turned sour, a fact that was openly discussed amongst other band bookers; almost everyone in the music profession got to hear about the agency mistakenly sending a telegram to the Crosby band addressed to a venue they had left months before. The powerful MCA agency learnt of the band's discontent, and let Gil Rodin know that if the band decided to leave Rockwell-O'Keefe, they would be pleased to represent them. By coincidence, Bing Crosby also ceased to be represented by Rockwell-O'Keefe from late 1937.

Gil Rodin, determined to break the deadlock that had developed between the band and its agency, decided to force the issue into the open by accepting a contract to play at the Hotel Pennsylvania (whose bookings were then handled by MCA). The *Melody Maker* explained the lack of publicity concerning the band's opening "The band feared they would be served an injunction restraining them from opening, as a result of a recent altercation with its former booking office".

In January 1938, Bernard Miller, the Rockwell O'Keefe agency's lawyer prepared to sue the Crosby band corporation for 4,000 dollars, allegedly for past services. O'Keefe himself claimed he was owed 8,000 dollars - money he said he had advanced to launch the band. The band bitterly disputed these issues, and asked for detailed accounts to be submitted. Joseph Weber, then President of the American Federation of Musicians, explained to both parties that he was powerless to intervene as the dispute did not concern individual musicians, it was officially a battle between a corporation and an agency.

In order to break their contract, which O'Keefe said was for five years beginning in September 1935, the original band corporation was dissolved, to be immediately replaced by an almost identical set-up-one that was able to negotiate officially with MCA.

The Rockwell-O'Keefe office issued a rancorous statement saying, "Another office comes along just at the time the boys are ready to make some real dough, makes them lots of promises and they leave us and sign. So, after we build them to a state in which they can make a lot of money they jump their contract and leave us holding the empty bag". An un-named "important member" of the Crosby band, (sounding very much like Gil Rodin), countered this with a statement, "There has been mismanagement of us on the part of the Rockwell-O'Keefe office, and moreover a lack of harmony between them and us makes the future look decidedly black. MCA offers us a marvellous contract, and, what's more, seems to be 100% behind the band. Since we are still building, we need that kind of co-operation".

None of the storm waves emanating from the dispute were allowed to move the band off its musical course, and during the spring of 1938 both the full band and the Bob Cats carried out recording commitments. The first session of 1938 (on February 3rd) was devoted to vocal numbers from Kay Weber and Bob Crosby.

Despite the acclaim that the Crosby band's instrumentals were getting, Decca still had high hopes of achieving big sales figures for the vocals, which is why they actively encouraged the recordings of the latest tunes. Unfortunately only a small part of the arranging ingenuity that was a feature of the Bob Crosby band's instrumentals found its way into its vocal backings. There is nothing unprofessional, or unmusicianly, about these items, but by 1938 the band's lack of keeness to play accompaniments often made itself apparent. Bob Crosby himself has said that every time he sang a ballad Ray Bauduc started tuning up his drums, and Bob Haggart readily admits that he and Matty Matlock worked on some vocal arrangements in much the same way as they might do a crossword together, when one was stuck for an idea he passed the score over to the other, and sometimes it went back and forth until it was completed.

When I asked Bob Haggart about the seemingly unadventurous approach to writing vocal arrangements, he said "Gil Rodin never liked to disturb anything that was working smoothly. His motto was 'carry on as before'. The vocal arrangements had never been complex, so they stayed that way. The lack of alto-saxophone solos within any of the arrangements was also an example of this thinking. Gil Rodin thought back to the Pollack days, they rarely featured alto-sax solos, so Gil saw no reason for us to use them either".

Both Bob and Matty Matlock admitted to me that they often availed themselves of a "special fee" offered by various publishers to arrangers who could get their songs played on the radio, this became known as "the quick route". Bob Haggart fills in the details, "After a gig was over, Gil Rodin used to sit down with a table full of music-business executives and song pluggers, they'd be trying to persuade him to play this or that song on the air. Gil would call Matty and myself over and say to the publishers and pluggers, "You'll have to see if these guys like the look of your songs". So they'd pass us a batch of song copies, and inside the ones they really wanted to plug they would tuck 35 bucks - that was the going rate for doing an arrangement that the band would use on radio - we took the cash and made the arrangement. Gil Rodin looked on, quite aware of what was going on. The same deal was happening with every band that broadcast".

Gil Rodin was glad to see his arranging staff were happy, because he was in a long-standing dispute with them over payments for the arrangements they did for the Crosby Band. It was this issue which caused Deane Kincaide to leave the band for a second, and final, time. He said, "In March of 1938, after much agonising I told Gil I was through for good, not having the temerity of saying why I thought I was being had, pecuniary-wise".. Haggart says, "We just couldn't nail Gil Rodin down to a system of payments, but actually I didn't mind, believe it or not, I was so happy it just didn't seem to matter".

During this period, Bob Crosby, despite being the figurehead of the band, was rarely given a vocal feature, where he sang at the beginning and the end of the recording, he was invariably simply allocated the middle chorus, with few build-up finales. In fairness, it seems that anyone with a flair for arranging would have been daunted by some of the material allocated to Bob, one from February 1938, *In the Shade of the New Apple Tree* was bound to thwart any fruitful endeavours.

One of the band's more unusual instrumental recordings was made at this time, it is called *Grand Terrace Rhythm* but is actually Fletcher Henderson's *D Natural Blues*, Gil Rodin had bought the arrangement from Henderson whilst the band were working in Chicago. The band give the piece a satisfactory reading, but it was certainly not appropriate fuel for the trail that the Crosby group were blazing. One riff follows another, and Bauduc's drumming, which usually sounds admirably appropriate, seems incongruous, the saving grace is Yank Lawson's torrid 16 bar trumpet solo. The very next number recorded brings the band fully back to life, it is a superb Matty Matlock arrangement of *Wolverine Blues*. It sounds as though every man jack in the band is raring to go, and the playing of the verse is particularly lively. The trombones pump out the main theme with exhilarating gusto, whilst the superbly-phrased clarinet trio play an attractive counter melody, then Eddie Miller takes a ravishing solo on clarinet. The band articulate a series of exciting shot-notes that punctuate Bauduc's highly entertaining solo, then the percussionist moves into the background again as the arrangement surges to a climax.

A month later (in March 1938), the Crosby group re-entered the studio to work on a batch of fifteen numbers, that were to occupy three recording sessions. These recordings, by the full band and the Bobcats, mark the beginning of a new era for the band, and the central reason for the transformation was the arrival of a new clarinettist, Irving Prestopnick, known to one and all by his nickname, Fazola Fazola's contribution to various recordings by the Bob Crosby Band and the Bobcats strengthened a widely held viewpoint that he was one of the greatest jazz clarinet players of all time.

The New Orleans contingent within the Crosby band had long raved about the jazz talents of the plump young clarinettist that they had all grown up with. The rest of the band were slightly sceptical, not quite believing that anyone could be as good as the Louisianians were making out, however, as Bob

Haggart says, "When we heard the recording of *Jimtown Blues* that Faz had made with Ben Pollack's Band we knew that he was the man we needed on clarinet".

Gil Rodin joined in the general approbation, and began what turned out to be a series of attempts to sign Fazola for the band, but Faz was very much his own man, and if he was enjoying himself in one particular locale, wild horses wouldn't get him to move. Originally, back in 1936, Rodin thought he had his man, then working with Ben Pollack's Band, but Faz upped and joined Gus Arnheim, a year later Rodin was certain he'd made the catch and actually told *Down Beat* magazine that Fazola was about to become a member of the Crosby Band, but this time the elusive clarinettist went off and joined Glenn Miller's Orchestra.

These disappointments made Rodin all the more keen to sign Fazola, and he pursued his quarry with increased fervour. He was stimulated by the knowledge that several critics thought that Fazola was a superior jazz clarinettist to Benny Goodman. Rodin and Goodman had been firm friends for years, in fact it has been suggested that no other musician ever got closer to Goodman than Rodin, never-the-less, Gil felt competitive towards Goodman when it came to band business, so it gave him immense pleasure when Fazola eventually joined the Bob Crosby band in March 1938.

Just before Fazola joined, the band made a movie short (with Matlock on clarinet) in which they performed two lively numbers, *South Rampart Street Parade* and *Pagan Love Song.* With Matlock, the band also did a transatlantic broadcast in January 1938, which CBS relayed to the British Broadcasting Corporation from the bandstand of the Hotel Pennsylvania. The band used this important outlet to again stress their musical intentions, all of the band's offerings, except for *Beale Street Blues,* were instrumentals. The programme consisted of: *Summertime, South Rampart Street Parade, Squeeze Me, Old Spinning Wheel, Gin Mill Blues, Muskrat Ramble, Beale Street Blues, Dixieland Shuffle* and *Pagan Love Song.* Despite atmospheric interference, the broadcast was a huge success with British listeners, and led a *Melody Maker* critic to report "Bob Crosby's Band is all, and more than, its records have led us to believe".

One of the band's recordings from this period featured an arrangement by Glenn Miller of *Do Ye Ken John Peel?,* which despite its pedigree never became a favourite with the Crosby band's audiences. Nappy Lamare took an infectious vocal on that number, and on the same session Bob Crosby sang an effective medium-slow version of the minor-keyed *Jezebel.* This March 1938 session marked a seven month pause in Bob's recording activities. The moguls at Decca decided that the time was ripe for the band to concentrate on instrumentals, so Bob wasn't heard on the following 22 titles recorded either by the band or the Bob Cats. At the time, the strategy didn't cause a sales stampede, but over the years it paid off handsomely, Demand for a March 1938 vocal coupling (one side by Bob, *How Can You Forget?* and one by

Nappy, *There's A Boy In Harlem*) was negligible, and as a result the record was only accorded its initial release (on Decca 1732). However, two instrumentals recorded on the following day, *Yancey Special* and *At The Jazzband Ball* are still being issued over and over again throughout the world, over forty years after they were first released.

Yancey Special is an unashamed tribute to two great black pianists Meade Lux Lewis (the tune's composer) and Jimmy Yancey. Zurke pays devout homage to the originators without ever seeming obsequious, and the full band strengthen the tribute by capturing the delicacy of Meade Lux's trills. Haggart's arrangement of *At The Jazzband Ball* was inspired by Bix Beiderbecke and his Gang's 1927 recording. Again, clever scoring plus the band's understanding of the original recording allow the full band to transmit the feel and the elan of the smaller "Gang".

On *Louise, Louise* Eddie Miller is featured, with success, as a vocalist. On live appearances Eddie's occasional vocals always got favourable response from the audience, he didn't possess a great voice as far as tone and range, but he looked, and sounded, sincere when he sang the blues and this authenticity transferred to the listeners. Nappy Lamare also had his own quaint way of singing the blues, and technical limitations seldom restricted his expressiveness. He is featured on *Milk Cow Blues,* which also contains two momentuous choruses by the newly arrived Fazola. Faz begins his first 12 bars in the chalameau register then ascends majestically to show that his tone was superbly broad in every register of his instrument. The next item recorded, *Tea For Two* was a memento of Bob Zurke's period hors de combat; he wrote the arrangement whilst in his hospital bed. After a widely voiced ensemble introduction the pianist gives a dynamic interpretation of the melody, aided by some staccatoed brass phrasing. Eddie Miller takes a tenor-sax solo that deliberately hugs the melody, then Zurke re-enters to swop exciting phrases with the full band. The pianist reveals his adventurous spirit, expressing boldly rhythmic ideas, couching them in a sophisticated harmonic vocabulary. Both the performance and the arrangement are scintillating, and Zurke's high register scoring for the brass section allows them to display the full tonal brightness of their upper ranges.

On March 14th 1938, the Bobcats were allocated a full recording session instead of being a subsidiary part of a studio date. Bob Haggart is missing from the session, having taken leave of absence to marry Helen Frey (a relative of Mrs. Celeste Le Brosi), on that very day in Philadelphia. Bob's replacement on the recording was bassist Haig Stephens, brother of Decca's recording manager, Bob Stephens. A month before his marriage, Bob Haggart had also taken a leave from the band to undergo a nose operation for the relief of a deviated septum, his deputy on that occasion was the Texan bassist, John "Haynie" Gilliland.

The Bobcats began their session by recording a tune based on the old folk theme *Tannenbaum* (known principally in the United States as *Maryland,*

My Maryland). Decca chief executive, Jack Kapp, happened to hear the band preparing the number, and said, in no uncertain terms, that he didn't approve of the group sacreligiously "jazzing" a much respected tune. Accordingly Yank created some new variations to disguise the original intention, and these formed the basis of *March Of The Bob Cats,* (however, on the original label the composition was credited to "The Bob Cats", as a group). Bauduc's crisp and incisive snare-drum playing lays the foundation of a forceful performance. Fazola is featured first, playing a solo that is a satisfying melange of his own extemporised ideas and some of the test-piece phrases so beloved by New Orleans jazz clarinettists. Yank Lawson and Eddie Miller take brief engaging solos, then the band dips its volume to play a soft penultimate chorus followed by a crescendo that announces a vigorously swinging finale.

On this series of recordings the limelight dwells in turn on each of the Bob Cats, and all of them seem to be in exemplary form. Nappy Lamare is featured singing *Palesteena* (aided by some powerfully played piano fill ins), after the humorous vocal, Eddie Miller on tenor-sax produces a marvellously emphatic chorus. Eddie's feature is *Slow Mood,* on which he gets ample opportunity to demonstrate his masterful ballad playing. The tune (later given lyrics by Johnny Mercer and re-named *Love's Got Me in a Lazy Mood*) became a constant part of the Bob Cats' repertoire. The main theme was composed by Eddie Miller, but on the original recording a 16 bar middle section was devised by Yank Lawson. Even before it was called *Slow Mood* the tune was known as *Tenormental,* written by Eddie whilst the Crosby band were in Defiance, Ohio. Their engagement was in a cold school gymnasium; the band arrived early, and in order to keep warm Eddie started blowing his tenor, Haggart joined him on piano, and in no time the marvellous composition had fallen into shape under Eddie's fingers.

Bob Zurke's feature is *Big Foot Jump,* a tribute to the extended time that his broken leg had been swathed in plaster. At the start, Zurke sounds more Fats Wallerish than usual, but he quickly moves on to create a chorus that examplifies his own highly individual approach to stride piano playing. On Bauduc's feature *Big Crash From China,* the drummer demonstrates the many varying tone colours that he was able, in the manner of the revered New Orleans percussionists, to get from his drum kit. He produces an amazing array of differing sounds by using his snare drum, bass drum, tom-toms, skulls, cowbell and woodblocks. The rest of the Bobcats play a subsidiary role which is restricted to the performance of a short *Copenhagen* like interlude between various segments of Bauduc's tour-de-force.

Yank Lawson's *Five Point Blues* (which he composed as a tribute to a locale in his home town of Trenton, Missouri) is an arresting trumpet feature, which became an all-time favourite with fans of the Bobcats. Yank sounds plaintive during the attractive opening theme, he follows on by constructing a well-shaped solo which is devoid of superfluities, the half-valved crying effect sounds particularly expressive. The trumpeter's heartfelt performance seems to inspire the rest of the group and they respond by producing one of their most satisfying ensembles. The whole performance made a worthy finale to the Bob Cats' first full recording session. The small group were soon to play these numbers in front of ecstatic crowds at their next important port-of-call, Chicago.

In late March 1938, at Chicago's Blackhawk Restaurant on North Wabash and Randolph, the Bob Crosby band began one of its most memorable residencies. There they caught the whole nation's attention via eleven coast-to-coast radio shows each week, and their growing fame was reflected in countless magazine features, including big spreads in *Life* and in *Collier's*.

The long narrow room at the Blackhawk (which had been a stamping ground for the early Ben Pollack band) seemed on first appearances to be hide-bound in formality. The heavy velvet drapes around the bandstand, the vast, gleaming tureens, and the near-ceremonial way that each portion of its celebrated roast-beef was carved, all strengthened the impression of staidness. But, within the Blackhawk's audiences there had always been a hot-bed of liveliness usually ignited by the regular visits of local college students. The owner Otto Roth, unlike many hoteliers, welcomed displays of spirit, and encouraged every band he booked to emphasise their own identity. The booking was a fertile opportunity, and the Crosby band made the most of it.

△ *Nappy Lamare and Eddie Miller*

Eddie Miller c 1926 ▷

Eddie Miller, Frank Tennille and Nappy Lamare do the 'Fan Dance'.

Billy Butterfield, Yank Lawson and Zeke Zarchy at the Palomar, Los Angeles, November 1937.

New York's Hickory House, February 1938. The Bob Cats in action. Yank Lawson thought it was an informal jam session and left his tuxedo at home.

Sterling Bose

Bob Zurke

Charlie Spivak

Joe Kearns

Bob Crosby, Len Esterdahl, Bing Crosby and Ray Bauduc, 1937 rehearsal.

A benefit cheque for Joe Sullivan, 1937.

Bob Crosby and Marion Mann, 1938. (Ray Bauduc in background).

Chapter 6

Big Noise hits Chicago

Most of the Crosby band agree that their initial booking at the Blackhawk in Chicago was a high point in the group's history, and the majority of critics concur. During the early part of their stay at the Blackhawk, George T. Simon gave the band a glowing 'A' review in *Metronome,* he began by saying, "As dixieland dispensers the Crosby crew is greater than ever. Credit goes, in the first instance to the entire band, for probably more than any dance orchestra in the business, this outfit feels and plays as one complete unit. They're all thoroughly convinced that they're producing the best swing has to offer, not conceitedly mind you, but rather sincere belief in their work. To them, the New Orleans type of music, the blues and the two-to-a-bar rhythm is the ultimate in dance music".

In discussing the band's repertoire, Simon said "Whether any other band could make those arrangements sound so good is quite problematical. The Crosbyians are blessed not only with the necessary 'feel' but also with certain key-men who help greatly to carry out the intended spirit of the manuscript". The key men especially praised were Bauduc, Miller, Zurke, Fazola, Haggart and Yank Lawson, about whom Simon wrote, "his rhythmic attack, choice of phrases, and inflection make him one of the very greatest hot trumpeters of all time". There was also lavish praise for Lawson's colleagues in the brass section, Billy Butterfield and Charlie Spivak, but Simon detected that the band took a casual approach to performing "commercial" material. "There's no getting away from the fact that if the band were to beautify their ballads even more in an effort to impress a mood upon the dancers, that both their sweet and their swing would benefit - the latter if only in contrast with the former".

Simon was perceptive, not only in noting the Crosby band's approach to ballads, but also in acknowledging the undiminished pride that the band felt towards its own style of music, nothing had shaken their belief that jazz should form the basis of their popularity. Warren Scholl, an American correspondent for the *Melody Maker,* emphasised the individuality of the Crosby band's approach when he commented, "Those who throw up their hands in horror at the degradation of hot jazz in America still turn as a last resort to Bob Crosby's swell outfit heard nightly via WOR or WABC". Soon afterwards, Leonard Feather also stressed the important part that the Crosby band was playing in jazz by developing its own unique style, "If white jazz is to become an entity, let the Crosby band formulate it". No less a talent than Duke

Ellington added his thoughts by saying that the Crosby band had become, "a truly gutbucket band with a strong blues influence". With such encouragement the Crosby band saw no reason to change their basic concepts, and stimulated by such praise the Bob Cats went to their self-appointed task of reviving an interest in traditional jazz.

It was at the Blackhawk, more than at any other venue, that the Bob Cats really came into their own. On Sunday afternoons, the small band was given a session all to itself, the resultant interest was so overwhelming that it was decided to start a Bob Cats' Club, which, within weeks had attracted over a thousand members. This was the era of the "jitterbug" dance, and on each Bob Cats' session the Blackhawk's wooden dance floor "sprang" like a slack trampoline as the dancers' gyrations became wilder. The unrestrained reactions of the crowd helped give birth to intriguing novelty instrumental duet, performed by Bob Haggart on string-bass and Ray Bauduc on drums.

Ray Bauduc recalls the first performance of *Big Noise from Winnetka*, "The place was jammed, including kids from the 'New Trier High School', in Winnetka, Illinois, a suburb of Chicago. As usual we played a few dance sets, we did our regular floor show, then we brought out a small piano on the dance floor together with the 'Bob Cat' drums, which I had placed on a rubber carpet so that they wouldn't slide when if was playing on them. Well as we did that the kids came out and sat down in front of the piano and drums on the dance floor".

"We played about 8 or 10 tunes, featuring each of the Bob Cats, finishing with *Big Crash From China,* the kids went wild and wouldn't stop yelling for more. As the band boys took the piano off the kids grabbed the drums and wouldn't let them off the dance floor..It was a cold day in Chicago that Sunday afternoon. Back in those days, drum heads were made of calf skins, and in dry weather the skins would tighten up, so as we played with the Bob Cats I used to kid with Haggart by slapping the bass strings with my stick for a laugh, and saying 'Wake Up', 'Let's Go', 'Make It Walk'. As I did this I noticed a similar sound of the 'G' string on the bass and my big floor tom-tom - being tight (with the cold) it was pretty close".

"Years before, I used to play with my sticks on Nappy Lamare's banjo, and he would finger the chords and melodies of some tunes for a gag. This all seemed to come back to both Hagg and I, as I had talked about this many times before. Bob Crosby came down to the microphone and announced that we were going to do a special broadcast he said, 'We still have a few minutes before we go on the air, so we'll let Bob Haggart and Ray Bauduc play for you'."

"So the kids screamed and yelled as Haggart and I started fooling around. Hagg would take four bars, and I would take four bars, then we would play eight or 16 bars together. Finally I started beating on the big floor tom-tom and I started vamping with one stick on the 'G' string keeping one stick on the tom-tom. Then I looked up at Hagg and he got the cue, I kept vamping and he got to the microphone and started whistling through his teeth. He whistled a few tunes, then he went into the theme we had been fooling around with backstage. Then he started arpeggioing up and down the G minor scale and I started playing on my cymbals, wood block, cow bell, rims on the drums, tom-toms, etc. Finally I got back to the big floor tom-tom, then I started playing with both sticks on the 'G' string, then Hagg started to finger up and down on the 'G' string as I was playing on it with my sticks".

"After playing a while we both looked up at Crosby to see how much time we had, he gave us the cut signal so I went into the vamp on the 'G' string, and the big floor tom-tom, and Hagg went into the theme, whistling like he did before, we went out and the kids screamed and yelled".

As Bauduc's co-partner in the creation, Bob Haggart says "It created a very different sound, like a strange new technique. As for the breathy whistling, that seemed to be the only thing to do to fill out the time. The inspiration for the whistling came from a waiter who worked in New York. After we'd finished our New York gig we'd drop into the Hotel President to visit the basement club where Putney Dandridge sang and played the piano. A waiter who worked there used to whistle through his teeth as he dashed through the crowd, all the while twirling his tray high in the air. I was fascinated by his style of whistling and I started to try it out for myself".

Big Noise From Winnetka became one of the band's biggest sellers, and on its initial release picked up a considerable number of radio plays, one station played it 22 times during the course of a single day. The Crosby band's 1938 stay in Chicago also saw the birth of another Haggart song hit. This one took shape at the Evanston, Illinois home of a jazz-loving attorney, Edwin Ashcraft III, Squirrel (as he was nick-named) had played alongside several jazz greats during his student days at Princeton, and had never lost touch with the jazz fraternity. For years his spacious home was a meeting place, and a musical workshop, for many famous jazz musicians. Bob Haggart, Billy Butterfield, and Bob Zurke often went out to Squirrel's house on their night-off from the Blackhawk.

Haggart recalls, "We'd drive out there and listen to records, talk about music, and hold very informal jam sessions. Squirrel had a recording machine and after the wives had had their fun singing into it we'd record some numbers on tiny discs that had to be played with a cactus needle. On one occasion whilst Billy Butterfield played trumpet I accompanied him on piano, and I began plotting a series of chord changes that eventually became the basis of *What's New?*".

At first, Haggart's composition (which was subsequently recorded by innumerable other musicians and singers) was called *I'm Free,* but after lyrics were added by Johnny Burke it became known as *What's New?.* Under its original title it became a popular instrumental in the Crosby band's library, but the original distribution of the band parts caused a big problem. Billy Butterfield's early role within the Crosby trumpet section stretched across a wide stylistic area. He could play jazz and ballads with equal ease, but usually Yank Lawson took most of the hot trumpet solos, and Charlie Spivak was featured playing melodic songs. Bob Haggart felt that *I'm Free* was a natural feature for Butterfield's sensitive playing so when he allocated the various band parts, the one marked "Billy" carried the melody.

Spivak and Butterfield did not enjoy the smoothest of relationships, Billy says candidly 'I didn't get on with him at all". Spivak, who had something of a reputation for petulance, looked down at the part he had received from Haggart, and saw instantly that he was not going to be featured. He looked along the row and then took the melody part off of Butterfield's music stand, Billy gave him a hard look, held out his hand and asked "Is your name Billy?'". Spivak reluctantly handed back the music, and that was the last time the two trumpeters ever engaged in conversation. Thereafter Yank Lawson acted as a go-between, Spivak would turn to him and say, "Will you let the third trumpeter know we're using cup mutes on this number".

This curious practice didn't last too long, because in August 1938 Spivak and Lawson created a sensation within the American music profession by both leaving Bob Crosby to join Tommy Dorsey's Orchestra. But the previous contretemps between Butterfield and Spivak had nothing to do with the move. Spivak was never as closely involved in the progress of the Bob Crosby band as were the rest of the ex-Pollack musicians. When the original 'orphans' had moved to the East coast, most of them felt that Charlie only made the trip because he wanted to be with his wife who was expecting a child. When Charlie finally linked up with the band in late 1937 he got on well enough with most of its members, but several of them particularly those in the brass section felt that Zeke Zarchy was a superior lead trumpeter. Yank Lawson gave his views, "Gil Rodin wanted the same type of broad sounding lead that had been part of the Pollack's Band appeal and he figured Charlie would give that sound to the Crosby band, but although Charlie had a good big tone, and was renowned as a first trumpeter, he wasn't a fast reader, and Zeke phrased better anyway".

Tommy Dorsey had a high opinion of both Lawson and Spivak's playing, and felt that signing them in tandem would greatly strenghthen his brass section. Money was no object to Dorsey, who was then riding on the crest of a financial wave, but he wanted to ensure that his initial offers to the two Crosby men were kept secret from Gil Rodin. After a preliminary meeting with the two musicians in Chicago, Dorsey moved on with his band to California, but confirmed his offer via a cable marked "Identification of addressee must be assured for delivery". Yank Lawson stalled for a while but when Dorsey returned to Chicago and told him he could write out his own pay check, Yank succumbed to the offer, as did Charlie Spivak.

The band were able to take Spivak's departure with equanimity, it simply meant that they had to look for another lead trumpeter, but Yank's individualism had been a key factor in the band's growing success, the audience responded to his playing, more importantly, his positive approach to leading a jazz ensemble emphatically melded the rhythm section and the front line. Both Haggart and Eddie Miller have never forgotten the stunned suprise with which they heard the news, Gil Rodin was quoted as saying he couldn't help feeling disappointed.

To this day, Yank says he has never regretted making the move, "Tommy Dorsey was generous to me in a thousand ways, and my family were able to live like millionaires. I found the 'team spirit' within Dorsey's band to be just as good as that of the Crosby band, and I was free of all the corporation problems". This last comment refers to the long drawn-out wrangle with the Rockwell-O'Keefe office, which had not been resolved by the summer of 1938, on several occasions during the Blackhawk residency Gil Rodin flew to New York for negotiations.

Despite the universal acclaim that the Crosby band were enjoying, their financial situation had still not reached a comfortable level of stability. The non-shareholders in the band (or non-corp men as they became known) received their full wages come what may, but the share-holders (or corp-men) often had to forgo their full salaries because of impending expenses. Yank, together with other corp-men, had a growing family, and felt dissatisfied that things had not improved financially during 1938. When Yank attempted to raise the problem with Gil Rodin he says he was always answered "with much talk about re-investing in the company". Tommy Dorsey's offer reached Yank after one such discussion with Rodin, so the trumpeter decided to better himself.

The other corporation men were dismayed by Yank's departure, but there was some sympathy for his action, as Eddie Miller recalls, "Gil Rodin made the decision, and he felt we should be building a pot, so went along with that, some more reluctantly than others". In those days, the term "pot" related to a fund of money, certainly as far as the Crosby band were concerned, there was hardly any marihuana smoking within its ranks. The Crosby gang were much more into booze. In 1933, when Yank Lawson had first joined the Ben Pollack band he had just finished working with Wingy Mannone (a devotee of hash), and to be sociable toward his new companions Yank arrived with a small cardboard box full of good quality marihuana. He offered some to Matty Matlock who declined with a look that suggested he had been asked to swallow a dung fritter, Yank found similar responses came from the rest of the Pollack Band and eventually discarded the box and its contents.

By a twist of fate, Yank was replaced in the Crosby Band by Sterling Bose, the musician whose place he had taken in the 1933 Ben Pollack Band. An abundance of anecdotes about Bose gathered during the 1930s, he was what might be called "a character", one who usually engaged in a daily battle with the bottle. He was a small man, once described by Pee Wee Russell (no heavyweight himself) as "weighing less than a sparrow", Bose was not a powerhouse player but he had a lot of feeling for jazz, and up until the moment that alcohol applied the knock-out punch he could create serene phrases that were enhanced by his attractive, cloudy-sounding tone.

The ex-Pollack musicians within the Crosby band awaited Bose's arrival with an apprehension unconnected with his musical prowess. His first day with Pollack's band was still all too fresh in their minds. Bose attended his first Pollack rehearsal carrying a full pint of whisky. Noting the alarm on the assembled faces, he said "Look fellows, the last band I worked with gave me this as a leaving present, but it's no use to me, I don't drink". Greatly reassured, the band quickly swigged the pint, but as Miller recalls, "Bose sure was kidding, by the end of the first night he was too drunk to talk or walk, never mind about play".

Fortunately, no such disaster overtook Bose's initiation into the Crosby band's ranks, the only oddity was a sartorial one. Yank Lawson had left his band jacket behind for whoever took his place, but as there was nearly a foot's difference in Bose's height he was never able to wear the jacket, he sent a good humoured rejection note to Lawson which read "Thanks, I would have worn it but for the puke stains".

A veteran of several big bands, Tommy Di Carlos worked briefly as lead trumpet with Crosby's band until Zeke Zarchy arrived to resume the position he had relinquished to Spivak nine months earlier. Other personnel changes took place at the Blackhawk, at the onset of the run, Marion Mann, (who had formerly worked as Alice Marion with Richard Himber), replaced Kay Weber, however the band didn't lose touch with Kay, in June 1938 she married trombonist Ward Sillaway. Two of the band's stalwarts spent time in Chicago hospitals whilst the band were at the Blackhawk, in late October 1938 Gil Rodin underwent a nasal operation (his place was taken temporarily by reed-player Drew Paige), and Nappy Lamare had an appendectomy (whilst he was away Len Esterdahl, one of the band's music copyist, played guitar with the band).

Len Esterdahl and an ex-saxophone player from Texas, Henry Nelson "Hix" Blewett, did most of the copying out of the arrangements that Bob Haggart and Matty Matlock devised (Matlock now worked full-time, writing arrangements). Blewett who also assisted Joe Kearney with the road-management chores, was probably the most popular individual in the Crosby organisation, Eddie Miller said of him "He was a wonderful character and humorist. We all loved him". Blewett's natural sense of fun expressed itself mainly in a style of droll philosophing, he also vied with Bob Haggart for the position of "band cartoonist", both men were continually amusing the band with their humorous drawings. Blewett who had led his own band around Texas during the 1920s, was the senior member of the Crosby party, having been born in 1901. He was not only a quick and accurate copyist he was also an arranger in his own right, and orchestrated several numbers for the Crosby band including, *Mama's Gone Goodby, Boo-Hoo,* and *Lulu's Back In Town.* To cap it all he was something of a poet whose work was occasionally published in *Down Beat.*

Usually the Crosby band's night off from the Blackhawk was on a Tuesday, and as most other bands took their rest night on Mondays, the Crosby musicians had plenty to listen to in Chicago. On his night off, Irving Fazola sometimes called in to hear another band, if there were any musicians from New Orleans in it, but usually he made his way to Paul Mares's Barbecue at 935 N. State Street, There, at the rib-bar run by the former New Orleans Rhythm Kings' trumpet player, Fazola would satisfy his gargantuan appetite, then to aid his digestion he'd play clarinet until dawn.

In the late summer of 1938, John Hammond, in his role as music critic, paid a visit to Chicago and summarised his findings for *Down Beat* magazine. John had mixed reactions to the Crosby band's music:

"Bob Crosby's band is the smash hit of the town these days, having revived the ailing Blackhawk Restaurant. It would be stupid to deny that the band has many virtues (any band with such solo talent as Billy Butterfield, Fazola, Sterling Bose, Eddie Miller and Ward Sillaway must be good) but the rhythm section leaves me absolutely frigid.

Once in a while the band forgets itself, relaxes and more than lives up to its reputation, but I'm afraid I'll never be able to respond to the Bob Cats, even though they are one of the most popular features of the band. I don't feel like a viper in saying all this, for it is only fair to say that I am hopelessly in the minority when I express even the slightest criticism of the band. If all goes well in the managerial end it should be a safe phophecy that Crosby's will be one of the top 5 bands in 1939"

The Crosby band (after a gap of 8 months) resumed their recording activities in October 1938. The first waxing was by the "new look" Bob Cats (with Butterfield and Bose sharing trumpet duties), neither man had much to do on the two sides recorded except to play written parts in accompaniment to a vocal by Marion Mann. Fazola's rendering of the melody of *Speak To Me of Love* and Miller's playing on the same piece, are the musical highspots of the date, though Marion Mann shows finesse and style in her singing. Both Fazola and Miller were superb interpreters of melody, each was wonderfully adept at applying skilful cross-etchings to the composer's original work.

The other side of the Bob Cats's issue, *The Big Bass Viol* is a feature for Bob Haggart, who bows and plucks his way through an indifferent novelty song with skill and aplomb. Bob had much more chance to display his all-round talent on the next three titles recorded. The first coupling was by a group billed as "Four of the Bob Cats" (being Miller, Haggart, Zurke and Bauduc). This talented quartet waited for the recording engineer's signal then waxed two bursts inspired improvisations, one on the changes of *Lady Be Good* was issued as *I Hear You Talking;* the other, on the harmonies of *Honeysuckle Rose,* was entitled *Call Me a Taxi.* The two items, which have been re-issued countless times over the years, are superb demonstrations of joyous, impromptu jazz. Eddie Miller is the inventive star of the proceedings, but the skills of all four musicians come through with crystal clarity.

To conclude the day's recordings, Haggart and Bauduc recorded the sensational duet which was proving to be a show-stopper at the Blackhawk, *Big Noise From Winnetka* remains one of the most extraordinary duets ever recorded, the mixture of drums, double-bass and eerie whistling might not seem perfect ingredients for musical success, but the ingenuity and verve of the two performers made the piece into a triumph.

A few days after the *Winnetka* recording, the full band began a series of recordings, 14 titles spread over a three day period. The first title *Swinging At The Sugar Bowl,* a four man collaboration, (Crosby/Rodin/Haggart/Lamare), paid tribute to a venue regularly mentioned in the band's favourite comic strip, drawn by Carl Ed. The tune itself is a run-of-the-mill swing opus, but the overall zest of the performance makes up for the indifference of the theme. Lamare's humorous vocal contains reference to the strip's main character, (Harold Teen). Miller's 32 bar solo is exhilarating throughout, Bauduc's off-beat cymbal accompaniment tends to be over-emphatic, but even this underlines the enthusiasm of the overall performance.

The next item, *I'm Prayin' Humble* was based on a Negro spiritual and arranged by Bob Haggart as a feature for plunger-muted trumpet. The inspiration for Haggart's imaginative restructuring came from an old 78 record that he found whilst the Crosby Band were in Chicago. Zeke Zarchy supplied the details of the find "One day Bob Haggart and myself took a walk down State Street, a few blocks from where we lived, and we wandered into this second hand shop. They had old shellac records a nickel apiece, and we started browsing. I found one by Paul Whiteman called *When,* and Haggart bought one by a Southern Gospel group called the Mitchell Christian Singers. Now I was the only one in the band with a record player - a portable Emerson I carried with me on the road - so anyone who had a record would come to my room and play it. Haggart played this record and it was *I'm Prayin' Humble,* and he wrote that arrangement based on it".

Haggart captures the fervour and rhythm of the gospel singers and cleverly transfers it to the muted trumpet part, he says of his score, "It was originally conceived as a feature for Yank Lawson's plunger playing. Yank was a specialist with that mute, but Bose wasn't. He did his best, but Yank would have done an even better job of it". Bose certainly performs satisfactorily, crying out his phrases over the catchy eight-in-a-bar feel established by the rhythm section.

Next it was Billy Butterfield's turn to be featured on Haggart's recently composed *I'm Free.* He gives an illustrious interpretation of a superior melody, playing with poise and feeling within a gem of an arrangement. Eddie Miller enters the picture briefly, then Butterfield, displaying admirable clarity of tone shapes a wistful, supremely satisfying finale. Matty Matlock's arrangement of Meade Lux Lewis's composition, *Honky Tonk Train Blues* came next, it featured Bob Zurke, amidst a few incidental band drapes. Zurke excelled at this type of recreation, but it seems a pity that he wasn't allowed to play more of his own features on the recording sessions. The individualism and flair that his colleagues heard on the bandstand (and at late night jam sessions) was unintentionally kept under wraps in the studio.

Marion Mann's skilful interpretation of the pleasant Robin-Rainger ballad, *What Have You Got That Gets Me* underlines both her technique and her powers of expression. Most of the band liked her singing, and one of them even went as far as to say, "she was the only half-way decent singer we ever had". The long session concluded with Haggart arrangement that Bob himself was pleased with, *Diga Diga Doo*. The time offered by the double-sided 78 rpm version allows us to appreciate Haggart's sense of thematic development. The trombones bark out the verse energetically, then Zurke plays a high-spirited chorus, Fazola emerges from a series of tension-building riffs and plays an 8 bar solo which is an appetiser for the magnificent full chorus he plays later - rarely has the beauty of his tone been so faithfully captured. Eddie Miller competitively creates a piquant solo, then the bass and drums share a well-integrated duet. A new series of interesting riffs bring the arrangement to an exciting conclusion.

The final two days of recording were mostly taken up with the task of replenishing the reservoir of vocal numbers. Marion Mann and Bob Crosby do a commendable job duetting *Two Sleepy People*, the singing is enhanced by a brief, tender solo from Billy Butterfield's trumpet, but the most interesting aspect of the arrangement is noting how much Fazola's huge clarinet tone had improved the overall sound of the reed section. Faz established the melody of *Wait Until My Heart Finds Out* with admirable finesse, Bob sings the lyrics, Eddie Miller solos briefly on tenor - and another transient recording is created.

The highspot of this recording session was Haggart composition, *My Inspiration* which had originally been conceived as a trumpet feature for Billy Butterfield, as the trumpeter had alreay been showcased on *I'm Free* the number was recast for Fazola's clarinet playing. He makes the most of the opportunity, giving an inspired performance in which his articulation, intonation and expression are all magnificent. Mid-way through Haggart's supremely thoughtful score Bauduc takes a double-time drum break which introduces a bright new tempo. Fazola sounds just as relaxed and eloquent at the new speed. Like most of the band's instrumentals this one too began life under a different title, it was originally called *Fat Mouth*, which was Fazola's name for his favourite drink, gin.

Fazola was already a star within the Crosby band, and was featured extensively on most of the arrangements, sharing the position of premier soloist with Eddie Miller. Miller was neither fazed nor anxious about the competition, his playing, which never lacked feeling, seems positively inspired by Fazola's presence. The only disappointment for listeners is that Miller rarely played clarinet solos with the band after Fazola joined. During this period it seemed as though Faz soloed on almost everyone of the band's recordings, there were less outlets for Billy Butterfield's subtle versatility, but his day would come.

It was Sterling Bose who was featured on the final Bob Cats' recording of 1938, which was a Nappy Lamare composition *Loopin' The Loop* - dedicated to a Chicago landmark. The small group achieves a bright, free-wheeling ensemble sound and makes the best of indifferent material, Bose's lead is relaxed but confident. For once Fazola sounds almost too relaxed, Eddie Miller takes a non-feverish solo, which is interspersed with some twangy blues sounds from the guitarist-composer. Warren Smith contributes a brief, earnest solo, then the full ensemble move with power and grace to the finale, Bose's acrid tone stimulating the action throughout.

The full band's final contribution to the session was a recording of their signature tune, *Summertime.* It seems that copyright restrictions had delayed an earlier plan to record the theme, but as the tune was being heard so regularly on the band's broadcasts it seemed a wise strategy to put a recording on the market. The Deane Kincaide arrangement is a beauty, demonstrating his gift for creating strong counter melodies, and showing the skill with which he blended orchestral timbre. Unfortunately, the performance sounds as though it suffered from repetition fatigue, the trombones seem undetermined thoughout, but overall the superior score is full of merit. A few years later a V-Disc issue of this recording brought much pleasure to countless servicemen.

As the band made plans to leave the Blackhawk, alto saxophonist Joe Kearns (not to be confused with the band's road manager, Joe Kearney), decided he did not want to go touring again, he moved back to his home town of Philadelphia and his place was taken by Jack Ferrier. Despite the problems caused by the loss of musicians from both the brass and reed section the band finished its season at the Blackhawk in triumph. The year had been a momentous one for Bob Crosby, for on the 22nd September he married June Audrey Kuhn. They had first met in Chicago whilst the band were appearing at the Congress Casino; their marriage took place in Bob's home-town Spokane, Washington. Brother Bing couldn't attend the ceremony, but he and Bob had a reunion a fortnight later when the Crosby band accompanied Bing on a recording session in Chicago, where Bing stopped off en route from Los Angeles to a Bermuda vacation.

The publicity gained during the Blackhawk residency, and the combined effect of radio exposure and record sales had turned the Crosby band into an excellent box-office draw. In November 1938, following their long stay in Chicago, the band played to huge crowds in Colomo, Michigan, and Peoria, Illinois, climaxing the short burst of three one-nighters by playing for 5,300 dancers at the Coliseum in Cedar Rapids, Iowa, during the three bookings the band grossed 8,200 dollars. It looked as though John Hammond's forecast that Bob Crosby's band would become one of the "Top Five of 1939" was about to come true.

Chapter 7

Zurke's mournful tale

After playing a series of far-flung one-night stands which took them from Kansas City up into Canada, the Crosby band began 1939 at the Stanley Theatre in Pittsburgh, where they learnt, to their delight, they had gained third place in the big band section of the annual popularity poll organised by *Down Beat* magazine. Artie Shaw's band was first, and Benny Goodman's second. Individually the band's star performers were all well placed in the poll, Bob Haggart easily won the bass category, Zurke was runner-up on piano, as was Bauduc on drums. Eddie Miller, Fazola, and Nappy Lamare all took third places in their instrumental sections.

Four of the band also did very well in a similar poll organised by *Metronome*, as a result, Miller, Haggart, Zurke and Bauduc, took part in an All Star recording session held in New York during the early hours of January 12th 1939. In order to do so they dashed from the band's gig at a Philadelphia theatre to catch the 11.30 pm train to New York. Unfortunately, the train was held up, but Miller Haggart and Bauduc finally clocked into the studio at 2am, followed some twenty minutes later by Bob Zurke, who had been taken by an exasperating whim to call in at Nick's Club first. After the *Metronome All Stars* date (which featured Bunny Berigan, Benny Goodman, Jack Teagarden and others) was over, the Crosby contingent caught a dawn train back to Philadelphia in order to be ready for the Crosby band's first theatre show, which began at 10.30am.

Six shows a day was not an unusual schedule for a band working in theatres during that era, but the rewards could be high, particularly if the band was on a percentage of the door take. Crosby's band grossed 28,000 dollars for their January 1939 week at the Stanley in Pittsburgh, and then, with the union approval of Local 60, they went out and joined in a jam session by way of celebration. It was during the band's stay in Pittsburgh that they took on a new trombonist, Jimmy Emert. Emert replaced the long-serving Ward Sillaway who departed to join his good friend Yank Lawson in Tommy Dorsey's band.

The Crosby band's next big theatre date was in New York, where they were booked to play at the Paramount for a fortnight beginning January 27th. The band didn't quite top the business that Benny Goodman achieved during the previous week, but they scored a distinct hit with the audiences. *Big Noise From Winnetka* was a notable success there, as was Bob Haggart's comedy routine on *The Whistler and his Dog House,* which, according to one contemporary report, "had them rolling in the aisles". The bill at the

Paramount was a double-headed Crosby presentation - the film showing in between the band's sets was Bing's *Paris Honeymoon*.

Not all of the band's theatre bookings were as glamorous as their engagements at the Paramount. Mention of the Adams in Newark (whose 8 shows a day began at 7.30 am), and the Pitkin in Brooklyn are guaranteed to bring a wry smile from the Crosby sidemen. A regular at the Adams' early morning shows never failed to shout at the stage demanding to see the performers' genitalia, and the Pitkin crowd made a point of aiming rubbish across the footlights, even at acts they enjoyed.

Whilst in New York the band completed another series of recordings, the first of these was a brilliant Bob Haggart arrangement of Waldteufel's *Les Patineurs*, re-titled, *The Skater's Waltz - In Swingtime*. Both the scoring and the performance are admirably accomplished, Fazola's introduction sets the pace, then the warm-sounding brass, phrasing as one, play the rapturous melody, in the background Zurke's piano playing complements things perfectly, then the reed section establish some effective counterpoint which leads into a telling low-register clarinet solo. The combined tenor saxes and trombones re-establish the melody which is answered by the trumpets, Eddie Miller floats in for eight glorious bars, prior to an exchange between trumpets and reeds. The band modulates, then a melange of arranging ingenuity moves to an emphatic, off-beat laden, climax.

Haggart's arrangement of *Stomp Off (and) Let's Go* was based on a recording that Louis Armstrong had made with Erskine Tate in 1926. Nappy Lamare shouts an initial command and the band respond by stomping their way through an exuberant ensemble. Bauduc's drum breaks precede a brilliant interlude from Fazola's clarinet, then a clarinet-led passage recreates the spirit of early jazz very effectively, with the trombones playing a solid "tailgate" role. Miller's tenor sax and Bauduc's drums combine effectively for a chorus, with Miller responding to the drummer's flamboyant woodblock patterns. The brass emphasis the phrasing of Louis Armstrong's work on the original and the momentum of this achieves an unfettered swing.

The next item the band recorded was Ray Bauduc's composition *Smokey Mary* (dedicated to an old New Orleans steam train), it is one of the fastest pieces the band ever recorded. After a rather tense first chorus, Fazola brings an aura of relaxation by emphasising his rhythmic surety, and his gift of skilful note placement. Trumpet, tenor and trombone have brief solo rides aboard the old locomotive, then the composer takes over, playing a vigorous drum solo that threatens to arrive ahead of the timetable, but all ends happily with a series of firm ensemble phrases. A remake of *South Rampart Street Parade* came next, which featured a truncated version of the previous band recording, which had been issued on a 12 inch disc. This time Fazola's superbly played clarinet graces the piece. Then Bob Zurke is featured on Neil Moret's *Song of the Wanderer*, his opening chorus, accompanied only by Bauduc's drumming, is superb, and there are also absorbing solos from Sterling Bose (in particularly good form), Eddie Miller and Fazola. The final ensembles pack a creditable punch.

This January 1939 session was primarily convened to record instrumental numbers, but Nappy Lamare's voice is featured on Don Redman's delightful tune *Cherry*. Usually Lamare's vocals were restrictd to humorous material, but on this standard song he produces one of his best vocals. A barrelhouse piano intro launches the piece which begins with a whole chorus of ensemble melody, nicely supported by Haggart's vigorous bass playing. The saxophones are a model of co-ordination as they back Nappy's vocal. Eddie Miller improvises a sublime half-chorus, then the band move into a new key to produce some clever variations which are superbly answered by Fazola's clarinet. Matty Matlock's arrangement allows the band to drop into a swinging groove from start to finish.

The final item from this studio date was another feature for Zurke, this time on a number he and Matlock co-composed, entitled *Eye Opener*. The piano sounds a little fastidious throughout the proceedings, but there are bonuses in the shape of fine blues choruses, two from Butterfield's trumpet and two from Miller's tenor sax. Miller has always set great store on a player's ability to play the blues; his own talent in that direction is superfine.

This January 1939 series of big band recordings produced several items that were hailed as being amongst the group's very best work. On most of them, less emphasis was placed on the roving role of the clarinet and jammed ensembles, instead the arrangements had taken a more ingenious turn, dwelling on lustrous block-scoring, blending of tone colours and the use of more advanced chords in the subtle voicings. The resultant sounds were still unmistakeably the Crosby Band, but the identity took on a broader spectrum. The free-wheeling ensembles were much more the province of the Bob Cats.

In February 1939, the Bob Cats (with Butterfield on trumpet) went to the studios ostensibly to accompany the Andrews Sisters (then rapidly gaining international fame). On *Begin The Beguine* the small band merely provides a scored background, but on *Long Time No See,* the arrangement is much looser, and Miller, Fazola and Zurke all get the chance to solo. To make up the session quota of four tunes the band recorded two instrumentals. On *Hindustan,* Fazola again plays the early card, then a succinctly led ensemble launches an Eddie Miller solo, soon followed by half choruses from Warren Smith, Butterfield and Fazola. The bass and drums duet just keeps this side of gimmickry, but the final ensemble never takes off. However, all of the ensembles on *Mournin' Blues* are imbued with a lovely amalgam of spirit and skill. Unusually, Warren Smith is given the first solo spot, he responds with more vigour than invention, but there is a lot of imaginative work from his soloing colleagues.

The full Crosby band rarely featured long trombone solos, the instrument played a subsidiary role in most of the band's arrangements. Unlike the band's persistent neglect of the alto saxophone, this had nothing to do with the Pollack band's tradition - Jack Teagarden was the star soloist in Pollack's group. Perhaps it was a yearning for Jack's amazing jazz prowess by the band's arrangers that kept the Crosby trombonists virtually in the background. When the band first heard Warren Smith he seemed to be just the player the band needed, but thereafter he never quite lived up to their first impressions. Bob Haggart summarises, "Wingy Mannone came to us and said 'You gotta hear this guy Smitty play the trombone, he's sensational'. So Gil Rodin sent for him to come and audition and he travelled overnight on a bus from Chicago to meet up with us at a theatre in Indianapolis. When we had finished work we took our instruments into a basement under the theatre and jammed with Smitty. We couldn't believe our ears, despite having gone without sleep Smitty played marvellously well. Even Gil Rodin, usually cautious, agreed it sounded great. So it was arranged that when a vacancy occurred we would get Smitty. This was 1936, and Gil Rodin didn't want to fire the man who already had the job, despite the fact that he played a 'silent part' that nobody could hear. Eventually Smitty joined us, but unfortunately he never played as well again as he did during the audition in Indianapolis. It wasn't for want of trying, it was just like a hunter who gets 'buck fever' and can't pull the trigger, somehow Smitty never seemed able thereafter to let his phrases flow out as we knew he could".

Soon after the Bob Cats' February 1939 New York session the entire band wended its way to Chicago in order to begin a new season at the Blackhawk starting February 10th. For a brief while at this time the Crosby band featured two girl singers. Marion Mann, and a newcomer, Dorothy Claire, a 20 year old from La Porte, Indiana, who after working with her sisters in a vocal group had sung solo with Joachim Grill's Band in Philadelphia. Gil Rodin heard Dorothy sing and saw her dance and was greatly impressed by her vivacious stage personality, he reasoned that her versatility would be a big asset to the Crosby band and signed her up. Dorothy Claire proved to be a sensation at the Blackhawk, she not only outdanced everyone in sight, she also put over her vocals with a zany liveliness that the young crowd liked. Whilst performing a song, Dorothy would happily descend to the dance floor and move out to the arc of tables to emphasise a point, then she would race across the dance floor and leap acrobatically back on stage to finish the number in spectacularly energetic style. At the time a critic remarked, "by comparison, Betty Hutton was a slumber singer".

For a brief while it seemed as though there would be romance within the band. Writer George T. Simon observed that Dorothy Claire was very keen on Gil Rodin, though Rodin himself seemed unaware of the affection. Simon put Rodin wise, and therafter Gil began swopping love-lorn looks with the new singer. The situation greatly amused some of the Crosby sidemen, and inspired Bob Haggart to draw a lively cartoon depicting Gil Rodin making sheep's eyes at Dorothy, but no serious romance developed between the two, and Rodin steadfastly maintained his bachelor status.

Alto-saxophonist, Joe Kearns, was persuaded to rejoin the band in Philadelphia, resuming the place temporarily filled by Jack Ferrier. Kearns said "I went back on the road mainly because I liked the music they played. The dedication to the classic Dixieland style, which can thru in most of the arrangements. There was an avoidance of tricky effects, and any hint of 'Mickey Mouse' music. The band was gifted with many great soloists, who were neither 'corny' or too 'far out'. All this contrasted with those bands which tried hard to be commercial".

Another change saw the departure of Sterling Bose, replaced by Bill Graham. Bose drifted into the precarious New York club scene, leaving behind no ill fellings. The late stages of his stay with the band brought forth an anecdote from Matty Matlock, which somehow highlights Bose's penchant for getting into losing situations. Matlock, standing by a hotel elevator, saw Bose tottering along the corridor obviously having just woken up from a long, deep sleep. Bozo (as he was known) asked Matty if there was any news. Matty replied "Well, there's been quite a bit of action", then truthfully recounted details of a remarkable visitor to the hotel, "Seems a gal came visiting some of the fellows, said she'd give them a good time providing they bought a pair of new socks from her, she was a travelling hosiery saleswoman. I heard all the guys were well satisfied with the deal". A grim look came on Bose's face and he began kicking the hotel wall. "Gee, Bozo don't get so sore, I think it only amounted to a head job" said Matlock consolingly. Bose turned on Matty and said, with immense feeling, "But you don't understand, I really need a new pair of socks".

The Crosby band's return to the Blackhawk proved to be a huge success, and Otto Roth, the manager there, soon offered the band an extension of its contract. Gil Rodin gladly accepted and the Chicago engagement stretched into the middle of May 1939. This long stay at one venue enabled the Crosby band to undertake another long series of recordings. The Decca recording company had again rethought their policy toward the Crosby band, and again decided to concentrate on vocal numbers, during a three week period a total of 21 new recordings were made, most of the vocals. Quantity did not mean quality, and some real 'dogs' were waxed, once again, indifferent material is the root problem.

Marion Mann does well on *Don't Worry 'Bout Me*, and Bob Crosby performs satisfactorily on *If I Didn't Care* (nicely aided by cup-muted obbligato from Billy Butterfield). Butterfield's playing provides much of the lasting worth from these dates, and his ending to *What Goes Up Must Come Down* is positively Bixian, Fazola and Eddie Miller have attractive, fleeting solos. Two "food" songs follow each other, *That Sentimental Sandwich* (created by Hollander and Loesser, who should have known better), and *At A Little Hot Dog Stand* (to which Sam Coslow and Larry Spier must plead guilty). During the latter song's denouement, (shared in duet-form by Marion

Mann and Bob Crosby), poor Marion has the epic line "Gallantly you handed me the mustard". Nothing could cure the indigestion resulting from a lyric like that.

A week later, the full band session produced more substantial music, consisting of two Bob Haggart instrumental arrangements, of *When The Red, Red Robin...* and *Them There Eyes... Robin..* gets off to a bright start via a well-thought-out ensemble introduction. The brass dominate the first 16 bars, then hand over to the saxophones who sound rather under-nourished. Butterfield takes a stimulating chorus, sounding on this occasion quite like Yank Lawson, Bob Zurke picks-up Butterfield's concluding phrase and begins building his solo on it, all the while demonstrating his technical mobility and his ambidextrity. In comparison, *Them There Eyes* is something of a pot-boiler, even though it is graced by a decorative chorus from Eddie Miller's tenor sax, and brief solos from Zurke, Fazola and Butterfield. There is also compensation in the sound and spirit of the arranger's own bass-playing, excellent in the four-in-a-bar patterns and in the habanera rhythms that follow. Haggart's balance gain was Lamare's loss, the guitar can hardly be heard, and Bauduc also seems more distant than usual.

The Bob Cats' contingent remained behind in the studio to record two numbers with Marion Mann, *Hang Your Heart on a Hickory Limb* and *Sing a Song of Sunbeams.* Both arrangements were written, allowing brief gaps for solos. Marion seems more relaxed and expressive than she usually does with the big band, and Haggart's bass again sounds superb. During the early years of their existence, the Bob Cats had backed several singers, but not, strangely enough, Bob Crosby himself. The omission seems odd because Bob's singing of bouncy, medium-paced songs was usually more effective than his ballad work. His skills in this direction are made obvious on the full band's bright, up-tempo version of *The Lady's In Love With You,* Bob's vocal is well phrased, rhythmically lively, and neat without sounding too slick.

During the spring of 1939, a big talking point in the musical press concerned rumors of Bob Zurke's impending departure from the Bob Crosby Band. A few days after the recording of *The Lady's In Love With You* Zurke decided to strike out on his own to start a big band (having been guaranteed financial backing by a New York based agency).

The story of his impending departure was on the front page of the May 1939 issue of *Down Beat,* under the headline "Hell, They've Driven Me To It". The "they" were said to be friends and fans of the pianist who had pestered him into forming his own big band, but a cynic might have suggested that "they" were the growing army of people to whom Zurke owed money. Fellow musicians might grouch about the 5 or 10 dollars they had foolishly loaned to Zurke, but they were unlikely to contemplate strong recovery action. However, Zurke had allowed his forgetfulness about debt repayments to extend to his dealings with several Chicago bookmakers, and one of them had apparently promised Zurke another broken leg if the gambling debts weren't swiftly settled.

During this same period, another member of the Crosby entourage also got into trouble about slow settlement of gambling losses, but the threat to his wellbeing disappeared as soon as a relative stepped in and settled the debt. That sort of solution was out of the question for Zurke, the only possibility he envisaged of raising big money was to form his own band. Bookmakers' demands weren't the sole reason for his financial dilemma, for some while he had also neglected to give his wife any money to support her and their two children.

In a press statement, Zurke said "I was offered a swell deal by Ed Fishman (representing the William Morris office), so I gave Gil Rodin my notice, and I'll leave Crosby, May 15th. Fud Livingston is in New York getting men and making arrangements. Everything's all set. We are going to record for Bluebird". The talented pianist went out of the Crosby Band in a blaze of publicity, none of which had anything to do with his musical skills, attention was focused on his personal affairs - amorous and financial.

Zurk's domestic scene exploded when his wife, Hilda, took a policeman to a Chicago apartment to arrest her husband on a disorderly conduct charge. The cop found Zurke in a compromising situation with blonde, Olga Laske, who was promptly given a black eye by Mrs. Zurke. Zurke spent the night in jail prior to appearing before Judge Sullivan. In his plea, Zurke said that Miss Laske was his publicity agent and they had met to discuss business, the pianist admitted getting "very drunk" during the meeting, and after dozing off he was extremely suprised to awake in the girl's apartment. He ended his defence by saying, "My wife hounds me and I drink to drown my troubles". It is now impossible to ascertain whether Judge Sullivan was related to his namesake, Joe Sullivan, what is certain is that the magistrate had a soft spot for jazz pianists, he said he believed Zurke's story, and released him.

A few days after the initial court case, Zurke had to face more charges, this time relating to his wife's demand for maintenance. After a settlement was reached in the court room, Zurke stormed off and, in an Oblomov-like move, retired to bed and remained there for several days. All this took place whilst the Crosby Band was fulfilling its recording commitments. The usually calm Gil Rodin was very angry with Zurke for just dropping out of the band, and as a reprisal attempted to total up all the money that the pianist owed his band colleagues, he stopped when he got to 400 dollars, and lodged an official complaint with the Chicago Musicians' Union.

For the April 19th 1939 session, Floyd Bean took Zurke's place at the piano. Iowa-born Bean, a veteran of the Chicago jazz scene, did a highly professional job during his brief stay with the Crosby band. The first of their recordings that he took part in was a superb arrangement by Matty Matlock of the old favourite *Rose of Washington Square*. The piece ignites from the first notes of the stirring intro, and glows throughout the opening ensemble, just below the scored sections the thick sound of Fazola's low register clarinet bubbles away like hot tar. The tempo suits Bob Crosby, and he takes a relaxed, swinging vocal. Eddie Miller comes forward and creates an inspired-sounding chorus, backed by some exciting high-register bass work from Bob Haggart, in the background the writing is admirably well-spaced. The trombones give out with a strong parade-like motif, which is answered by vibrant trumpets, as a climax Bauduc's drums usher in a variation of the penultimate chorus. The session also produced a charming duet from Bob Crosby and Marion Mann on *Penthouse Serenade* in which there are two short tantalising examples of Floyd Bean's work.

During the Crosby band's stay at the Blackhawk, singer Marion Mann had married a local tennis professional, Jack Macy. In order to settle down she handed her notice in to Gil Rodin, but before she left she took part in recordings with the Bob Cats that produced the four ambitious numbers known as the *Shakesperian Suite*. The four items were devised from Shakespeare's sonnets by composer Arthur Young. The arrangements were well-conceived with being over busy, and Marion Mann rises to the occasion by singing at her best. All of the backings sound appropriate except for Nappy Lamare's shout of "Oh, Play That Thing" (from King Oliver's *Dippermouth Blues*) which provides a non-bardic moment on *Blow Blow Thou Winter Wind.*

Before the Crosby Band left the Blackhawk on May 19th 1939, Gil Rodin received confirmation that a giant breakthrough for the band was imminent, they had been asked to take over the weekly coast-to-coast radio show *Camel Caravan* on which Benny Goodman's band had been featured for the previous two years. The show's sponsors had narrowed the field down to two prospects, Gene Krupa's new outfit, or the Bob Crosby band, and they finally plumped for the latter.

Rodin's satisfaction at gaining the contract was tempered somewhat by his feeling that the band needed a more rugged jazz soloist within the trumpet section. Zarchy was playing excellent first trumpet, and night after night Butterfield stressed his versatility (which had been extended to include skilful plunger-mute playing), but the new man, Bill Graham, despite being a competent improviser apparently lacked the flair that Rodin felt was necessary for establishing musical individualism on a regular radio show.

At the nearby Panther Room in Chicago's Hotel Sherman, the veteran cornet player Muggsy Spanier was making a successful comeback following a near-fatal illness. Spanier had formed up an 8 piece band he called the Ragtimers, and they were getting good receptions at the Panther Room. Rodin went over to see Muggsy and offered him the job with Crosby's band. A few months earlier Muggsy would have jumped at such an offer. After his serious illness he had been written-off by several club owners, and even his former long-time boss, bandleader Ted Lewis, was apparently sceptical that Muggsy could ever resume touring. However, by May 1939 Muggsy Spanier's Ragtimers had started to click, there was the prospect of a New

York residency and of a Bluebird recording contract. Spanier thanked Rodin for the offer, but declined it. Rodin always reluctant to accept an outright "no", told Spanier to get in touch if ever he changed his mind.

Spanier's refusal didn't cause Rodin to abandon his search for a new jazz trumpeter, and a local correspondent in Chicago reported, "Gil Rodin is looking high and low for a hot trumpet man before they start the Camel Broadcasts". One of the candidates was an ex-Ben Pollack musician, Clarence "Shorty" Sherock, another was an ex-Dick Stabile sideman from Texas, Kit Reid. Eventually, after deliberating for a fortnight, Sherock decided to leave Jimmy Dorsey and joined Bob Crosby (replacing Bill Graham). Another change in the brass section took place in June 1939, when trombonist Ray Conniff left Bunny Berigan's Band and swopped places with Jimmy Emert. Conniff's signing was an indication of Rodin's ever wakeful talent spotting, "Gil heard me play a trombone solo (*In a Mist*) with Bunny Berigan on *The Swing Shift* and sent me a telegram with a job offer" says Conniff.

Whilst the band were appearing in Memphis, a new young vocaliste was signed by Gil Rodin, to take Marion Mann's place, the youngster was only 17 but already had a highly individual singing style, her name was Kay Starr. There was also a change in the reed section during the early summer of 1939 when Bill Stegmeyer, a former colleague of Billy Butterfield, joined the band. The move boosted the section to five musicians, and allowed Fazola to devote all of his time to the clarinet instead of playing innocuous alto-saxophone with the section on the more commercial arrangements. Stegmeyer was also an arranger, but this side of his skills was hardly used by the Crosby band, he seems to have done only one chart for them, on *Blue Orchids*. Stegmeyer became known to his colleagues as "The U Boat Commander", (without his knowledge), so he was totally non-plussed when asked drunkenly one day "Where did you park your submarine?".

During the last part of the Blackhawk booking, a new pianist, Norman 'Pete' Viera, began rehearsing with the Crosby band. Thirty two years old Viera had worked in-and-around Chicago for almost a decade, with various leaders ranging from Mezz Mezzrow to Louis Panico. Just as Viera began his stay with the Crosby band, Gil Rodin received a cable from the band's former pianist, Joe Sullivan, who had heard all about the Zurke rumpus. Sullivan who had recently been filming with Bing Crosby, and leading his own small band at the Hawaiian Paradise Club in Los Angeles, indicated that he had completely recovered from the tuberculosis that had laid him low for all of 1937. He was ready to resume touring and offered his services to Rodin. Gil wired back a definite offer, and Sullivan soon began the long rail journey eastwards.

In his usual considerate way, Rodin decided not to fire Viera, but kept him on with the band to alleviate any strain that Sullivan might encounter whilst resuming a full working schedule. Viera, who was, according to Bob Haggart and Eddie Miller, a very capable pianist, agreed to play for part of each evening, leaving the speciality numbers to Joe Sullivan. But this arrangement had hardly taken effect when Viera was taken ill with arthritis, and had to be temporarily hospitalised. Floyd Bean again helped out, then Joe Sullivan settled back into his old job. Gil Rodin was especially pleased to see Joe Sullivan return (the two men were old Chicago pals), soon after Sullivan had rejoined, Gil enthusiastically asked Ted Toll, the *Melody Maker's* American News reporter, "Did you ever hear such piano playing in your life?".

Fazola takes a snack. ▷

Eddie Miller takes off, 1938.

Bob Haggart and Ray Bauduc, 1939.

Fun fair, 1939. Left to right Joe Kearns, Bill Stegmeyer, Shorty Sherock and Irving Fazola.

Bob Crosby, Joseph Lamare (Nappy's father) and Nappy Lamare.

Promotional visit to music store, left to right Warren Smith, Ward Sillaway, Yank Lawson, Gil Rodin, Bob Crosby, and Eddie Miller.

The Andrews Sisters and four of the Bob Cats enjoy a get together, 1939.

Chapter 8

Riding the Camel Caravan

The Bob Crosby band began their CBS *Camel Caravan* radio series on the 27th June 1939, the show was aired each Tuesday night to a vast coast-to-coast audience (Benny Goodman's band played the same product's Saturday programme). Bob Crosby's shows were called *The Dixieland Music Shop* and also featured songwriter-singer and bon vivant Johnny Mercer. An early report said "The air of informality produced by Mercer, Crosby and the rest of the boys contrast sharply with the conservative atmosphere that existed on the Goodman show".

Gil Rodin had managed to resolve most of his personnel worries by the time the series began, but at a late stage of the planning there were new thoughts on a girl vocaliste for the show. It was decided that Kay Starr wasn't experienced enough for the task, and Dorothy Claire, the band's other singer, was considered more of a visual artiste than a radio singer, as a result Helen Ward was brought in to work as a freelance on the radio shows. Kay Starr left the band a mere two weeks after she had joined, and not long afterwards, Dorothy Claire, realising that her chances of national fame with the Crosby band were low, because she wasn't being used on radio and recordings, departed to later work successfully with several top bands.

Just before the Camel radio series began, Bob Crosby's wife June gave birth to a daughter, Cathleen Denyse, whose arrival brought a congratulatory telegram from Bing Crosby which said, "You've nixed the Crosby four boy jinx, but watch out you don't pull an Eddie Cantor and turn up with four girls". That year, 1939, the Crosby band was full of proud fathers celebrating the birth of newly born infants. The Lamares had another son, the Millers a daughter, the Stegmeyers a son, and Billy Butterfield and Warren Smith became expectant fathers.

Because of the need to rehearse and perform the weekly *"Camel Caravan"* show, the Crosby band remained based in New York throughout the summer of 1939. From there they were able to make well-rewarded forays to many eastern cities, either for one-night stands or for short three or four day residencies. For most of these journeys the band hired their own Pullman rail coaches, this meant more comfort - and more gambling, - the space and steadiness offered by a table on a train was more conducive to organised card games than was the top of an instrument case on a shaky band-bus. Not that gambling didn't take place on road tours, but it was less serious, as Eddie Miller says "The usual minimum on the road was two dollars, but on a railroad journey it could get much higher". Shorty Sherock and Bill Stegmeyer were amongst the keenest card-players (Lawson, Miller and Spivak had been the keen ones in earlier days). Billy Butterfield has clear memories of Sherock trying to convert the band to another form of gambling. As the train rides were so smooth, Sherock decided to invest in a small roulette wheel. He took it aboard the Pullman car, and then elected himself as permanent banker. Something went hopelessly wrong with the scheme, for within a week or two, Sherock had lost his shirt many times over in paying out all the winners.

Looking back, Billy Butterfield feels that it was during that summer of 1939 that the sidemen in the band really started to earn big money. Business for the Crosby band boomed, and during a four day booking at the William Penn Hotel in Pittsburgh they achieved the biggest daily gross taken by any band during a five year period.

The band made several return journeys to New England that summer, including a July engagement at the Totem Pole in Boston. During the early part of that date Bob Crosby was noticeably absent from the stage, and the crowd of fans who clustered around the bandstand kept turning toward the entrance door to see if the maestro had arrived. At about 10p.m. their curiosity was amply rewarded, for they enjoyed the rare sight of Bob and Bing Crosby together in public. The two brothers had spent the day watching some of Bing's horses race at the nearby Suffolk Downs track. A wag said that they couldn't get to the gig earlier as they had to wait for Bing's nags to finish the course.

Members of the band were always pleased to see Bing Crosby, his presence added something to any evening. He always had a ready 'gag', but despite the family association, the members of Bob's band never felt that they knew Bing. They had recorded with him, and shared various engagements, liked his jokes and his fooling around but never achieved any degree of closeness. Yank Lawson says "It took us years to get to the point where there was the normal give-and-take of conversation with Bing, but even when we did I always got the impression that he was a guarded man, trying to make certain that nobody took advantage of him. He did several guys in the band various favours, but only of his own accord, if he been asked I'm sure that his reaction would have been different".

The emphasis on the Crosby band's recordings swung round once again to vocals, and as the outfit no longer had a regular female singer, the a-and-r man at Decca, Bob Stephens, suggested that the band use a friend of his, Teddy Grace, on their sessions. The results were far better than any of the band had originally expected, for Teddy Grace turned out to be more jazzy than any of the other girls that the band had previously featured. Eddie Miller still enthuses about her work, "She had a nice, bluesy feeling", and Bob Crosby was quick to add "She swung too".

Teddy Grace, who had worked and recorded with Mal Hallett's band before she linked up with the Crosby group was not as versatile as Marion Mann, nor was she very powerful, but she could phrase herself into the heart of a song, and deliver her lines in a lilting husky voice. Unfortunately, she never worked with the band on engagements outside of the recording studio. Her debut with the band, *You and Your Love* was quite impressive, but better performances were in store, and she soon aquitted herself splendidly on *Over The Rainbow,* timing her phrasing very effectively considering the odd jog-trot tempo of the arrangement. Ray Conniff, the band's new trombonist, takes a short attractive solo, and Fazola's brief appearance emphasises his class.

Bob Crosby takes on a couple of lack-lustre songs, and Helen Ward, guesting with the band, sings *Day In Day Out* to tie in with her appearances on the Camel radio show. On most of the vocals from this period the band's soloists are given a distinctly subsidiary role in the arrangements, but the pattern is broken on a Teddy Grace item, *What Used To Was Used To Was* (sic.) The minor-keyed tune is accorded a thoughtful score (low note trombones, plunger trumpet and tom-tom accompaniment). Ray Bauduc, temporarily indisposed, was replaced on drums by Don Carter, predictably this gives the rhythm section a different feel, but close scrutiny is difficult because through this whole spate of 1939 vocal recordings the rhythm section were distantly balanced.

Two instrumentals shine out from amongst the murky material. One of them was *Boogie Woogie Maxixe*. The Maxixe was a Brazilian dance tune popular in the early years of the century. Matty Matlock's imagination created a swinging up-to-date arrangement of the theme. In between attractive reed-section interludes Joe Sullivan on piano emerges as the principal soloist, revealing both the power of his playing, and the emphatic qualities of his left hand. Matty was always pleased with his treatment of the number, but was greatly suprised to find out some years later that the tune had been copyrighted by Bob Crosby and Gil Rodin, together with writer Sammy Gallop.

Joe Sullivan was also featured on Bob Haggart's arrangement of *The World Is Waiting For The Sunrise,* which is taken at a very fast clip. The pianist never sounds quite at ease during his 32 bar outing, and his tenseness is emphasised by the relaxed quality of Fazola's subsequent solo; the clarinet player again shows how effectively he could tinge his work with perfectly placed "blue notes". Eddie Miller follows on, but after an inventive start he falls back on a succession of familiar phrases, happily they are all ones that belong to him so there is no question of the impetus dropping. The trombone section roars out the melody whilst the rest of the band issue a counter-riff, then a modulation leads into some thickly scored ensembles, which are vigorously performed. Haggart has never felt much pride in this particular arrangement, but it certainly stands the test of time, particularly in demonstrating that the band could still impart a lot of energy to its music even when their working schedule was busier than it had ever been.

The strenuous itinerary began to affect the health of at least one member of the band, and general weariness resulted in several off-stage displays of irritability between the usually affable sidemen. The man with the health worries was Joe Sullivan, who began to feel concerned that he might not be able to keep up with the demanding schedule. During this period, the band did a stint at the Steel Pier in Atlantic City which involved four shows a day, and this almost brought Joe to a state of collapse. He had been encouraged to put on weight to aid his recovery from tuberculosis, but the additional poundage made work more tiring than hitherto. However, Joe soldiered on.

In Atlantic City, Zeke Zarchy and Irving Fazola had what Zarchy has since called "a misunderstanding". The incident was nothing like as serious a fracas as the musical press of the time tried to indicate, but thereafter Zarchy felt he needed a change of scene. After a convivial meeting with Gil Rodin it was agreed that Zeke would leave when a suitable replacement was found. As a result, trumpeter Max Herman joined the Crosby band in October, and Zarchy left. Herman had a few other commitments during his early days with the band, and Johnny Napton briefly took his place, but Max soon returned and became a long-serving member of the band.

The band's recently signed jazz trumpeter, Shorty Sherock, let it be known that he felt unsettled with the Crosby band. At that period of his life Sherock's musical interests were centred on new musical developments, he was happy to be featured on material like *Air Mail Stomp,* but when the emphasis was on Dixieland he seemed less enthusiastic. Sherock and Rodin shared a long talk, and Rodin, mindful of the headaches he'd encountered in signing Sherock, offered peace terms, as a result, the trumpeter agreed to stay on, at least until Christmas.

Joe Sullivan also had a meeting with Rodin to say that he too was considering leaving the band. Rodin was particularly anxious to keep Joe, and offered to use a second-pianist to relieve any physical strain; the matter was held in abeyance. Years later, Mary Anne Nash, who was married to Joe at the time told Richard Hadlock of a reason other than physical problems, "Joe and Bob Crosby didn't really get along. I think it was that each was the baby in his own family".

Pianist Jess Stacy's recent departure from Benny Goodman's band had been widely publicised. Several booking agents had tried to persuade Jess to start his own band, but he refused and left New York to visit his family in Missouri. Whilst there he was contacted by Gil Rodin and asked if he would like to join Bob Crosby's band, Jess asked for time to think things over, apparently both Tommy Dorsey and Jan Savitt had made similar offers.

Joe Sullivan soon got to hear of the Rodin-Stacy discussion and immediately asked Rodin for an explanation, pointing out that he had complied with Gil's request and remained with the band. Things became tangled when Stacy called to say he agreed to join the band, but now Gil

Rodin stalled on a hard-and-fast confirmation. By now, both Sullivan and Stacy were vexed by what Stacy described at the time as "the runaround", and Jess began to seriously think about looking elsewhere. This forced Gil Rodin to act, he explained to Joe Sullivan that he would like to make a firm offer to Stacy, accordingly Joe handed in his notice on September 10th 1939.

Jess Stacy officially joined the Crosby band on October 3rd 1939, but during the previous weeks had played on several gigs with them. Members of the band were relieved that the situation had finally been resolved, they certainly didn't relish the idea of employing a relief pianist to alternate with Sullivan, because a switching to-and-fro would have made it difficult for the rhythm section to settle down. And there were those who, whilst admiring Sullivan's solo skills, felt that his playing was a little too heavy handed for the band's ensembles.

To Joe Sullivan's credit he contributed handsomely to several of the Bob Cats' recordings from this period, playing excellent choruses on *Till We Meet Again, Peruna* and *The Love Nest*, that are positive, full of flowing ideas and totally devoid of lassitude. After leaving Crosby, Joe Sullivan remained in New York and formed his own small band (containing black and white musicians), which was managed by Bob Crosby's brother, Larry. In an interview given shortly after leaving Bob Crosby's band, Sullivan said that it was "mainly health problems" that had caused his departure, but added that he had been much happier with the band during his 1936 stay, simply because he felt that the style of the band, and its general musical policy, had changed. His general tone was not unfriendly, but he concluded "I hope Jess will manage to fit himself into the band properly, they're a swell gang of fellows, but most of them have been together for so long, and they have such strong New Orleans connections it's difficult to feel you're really one of them".

Fortunately, Jess Stacy's initiation into the Crosby Band was easy, both musically and socially. He says himself, "I never found any problems in fitting in. It was a pleasure working in the band. I found it to be good and relaxed". Joe Sullivan's comments about a New Orleans clique has always been denied by the Louisianians who worked in Bob Crosby's band, and Eddie Miller still feels disappointed that Sullivan, "a real pal of mine", ever saw fit to raise the subject. Other Crosby sidemen say that the New Orleans men tended to be autonomous, without perhaps realising it. One remarked "They might not have been the best of pals at all times, but just try saying one word against any of them, or against anything that ever came out of New Orleans, and they would instantly gang up on you". What has to be remembered is that Joe Sullivan also mentioned that many of the band had been together since the Ben Pollack days.

Ben Pollack's shadow actually loomed across the band at the very time that Joe Sullivan was leaving, he announced that he was filing a lawsuit against Bob Crosby's band for "alleged use, without permission, of ten or more of Pollack's arrangements, including *Pagan Love Song*. Pollack's attorney was said to be planning to subpoena ex-Pollack sidemen, Benny Goodman, Harry Goodman, Glenn Miller, Jack Teagarden, Charlie Spivak, Deane Kincaide, Yank Lawson and Joe Harris to prove his point. Pollack hinted that he was also planning to sue Benny Goodman over the use of an arrangement of *Bugle Call Rag,* he also threatened action against various radio companies who hired the Crosby and Goodman bands. Having taken stock of the legal problems involved, Pollack changed his mind and cancelled the action. The affair was soon forgotten, but not before Pollack had gained a lot of useful publicity for his new band's opening in San Diego.

Gil Rodin had never taken Pollack's threats too seriously, he was far too busy dealing with ever increasing administrative problems, and occasionally had to drop out of the band to finalise a business deal. He did this several times during the fall of 1939, and various substitutes came in temporarily on tenor saxophone, including Nick Ciaizza and Nappy Lamare's brother, Jimmy. In October 1939, a permanent change in the saxophone section occurred when altoist Joe Kearns left to lead his own band in Philadelphia, and was replaced by George Koenig, who had previously worked with Benny Goodman and Teddy Powell.

With changes in its brass, reed and rhythm sections, the Crosby band resumed recording on October 23rd 1939. Three of the four titles cut were vocals, two by Teddy Grace and one by Bob Crosby. The one instrumental *For Dancers Only* was untypical Crosby material, its popularity rested on an earlier version by Jimmie Lunceford's band, Decca's Jack Kapp thought it would be a good idea to revive it. The strategy was all too reminiscent of the *Christopher Columbus* blind alley that the band had driven into some years before. Never-the-less, the band make a commendable job of the recording, Butterfield takes a resolutely skilful solo, and Fazola, Miller and Haggart do not shirk their featured spots, but by comparison the band's recording of *Angry* sounds a more attractive proposition. Here the band reverts to its earlier free-wheeling style, with clarinet roaming freely above the main ensemble. Teddy Grace again sings impressively. The overall performance backed up the viewpoint (often expressed in the correspondence columns of music magazines at this time) that the band was at its best when playing its own style. But it must be borne in mind the Crosby band's style was continually undergoing minute changes.

No professional band likes to feel that it is simply going through the motions of recreation, and Crosby's group was no exception. The "roaming" clarinet role was latterly used sparingly within the big band, and the bursts of collective improvisations that rocked the full ensemble gave way to more formal arrangements. On most of the 1939-40 recordings the rhythm section was playing a more sophisticated role (and this particularly applied to Bauduc's drumming), the scoring for the trombones rarely used "tailgate" tactics, instead they were more often used as a two-part "choir". Voicings in general were smoother sounding, and modern chord extensions were gradually being introduced into both Haggart's and Matlock's arrangements.

The commercial influence of the radio show sponsors was a small factor in creating some of the changes, the oft-repeated criticisms about the band's slack approach to ballads also had effect, and so too did the reaction of listeners. Some of the numbers that had "wowed" the dancers three years earlier were now too familiar to evoke a passionate response. Rodin spoke of keeping an open mind about styles and new material, he said in 1940, "It's the commercial sides that make the sugar, and the real jazz that keeps us going". The jazzers within the band, having observed the dramatic increase in their incomes, had no wish to jeopardize the general progress, and they could console themselves with the knowledge that the overall jazz content of each live appearance by the Crosby group hadn't diminished because the Bob Cats were being more heavily featured. It made sense to shift the sound of the big band so that it contrasted more with the "Dixieland" of the Bob Cats.

But the full unit could revert to a jazzier groove with spirit and finesse when they chose to, and *Angry* was just such an example. Jess Stacy plays subtle fill-ins behind Teddy Grace's vocal, Eddie Miller blows an inspired solo and Fazola's playing on the bridge of the final chorus encompasses greatness. The same session produced a fine version of a feature that Jess Stacy had previously recorded as a piano solo for the Commodore label, entitled *Complainin'*. Haggart cleverly scored the piece for the full band without disturbing the enchanting mood of the original. It gives Stacy a fine chance to demonstrate his considerable individuality and his graceful, but highly rhythmic touch.

At the time, Bob Crosby said that Stacy's arrival was "one of the most refreshing things that had ever happened to the band". The new pianist's playing had certainly given a lighter feel to the rhythm section, and this new, springy approach is apparent on the Eddie Miller-Nappy Lamare vocal duet, *Between 18th and 19th on Chestnut Street*. It's a light hearted romp during which both men show good rapport in their unfolding of the eventful lyrics. On the same session, Bob was featured on *Pinch Me* then Teddy Grace, not helped by an undistinguished score, sings *I Wanna Wrap You Up*. The final tune of the date *The Little Red Fox* has a stimulating Matty Matlock arrangement, which compensates for the banal lyric that Teddy Grace was saddled with.

No one left the studio burning with pride after making *The Little Red Fox*, (which had previously been featured by Kay Kyser), but by that strange process known as public taste, the disc became the biggest selling Bob Crosby band record of that period, achieving sales of 140,000 in the year 1939-40. It was, by a twist of fate, the last number that Teddy Grace ever recorded with the band. The band's former singer Marion Mann rejoined the band, so there was no need to use freelance singers. Just before Marion Mann's return, Kathleen Lane temporarily worked with the Crosby band for various bookings including the Strand Theater in New York.

During their stint at the Strand, the Crosby group found they were working close to where Bob Zurke's new band were performing (at the Paramount), he too featured a band-within-a-band called the Tom Cats. Reports were published that suggested the Crosby sidemen were still seething with anger toward Zurke, but Eddie Miller, years later, discounted the stories, "I can't remember anyone in our band getting angry after Zurke had gone, because we just knew, for certain, that it wouldn't work out for him. He just wasn't the band leading type."

The Camel radio programmes had really established the Crosby band, they also brought considerable personal joy to Matty Matlock, because on certain numbers Gil Rodin conducted the band, and Matty resumed a place within the saxophone section. He had been getting distinctly restless about spending all his time arranging. Whilst the band were playing at the Strand, Matlock took the chance to visit Sidney Bechet, who was working nearby, and present him with a soprano saxophone that he felt he would never need again. The band's other principal arranger, Bob Haggart, ended the year in smiles, he had won an ASCAP award for composing *What's New* and this official recognition of his talents was supported by the public, during late 1939, the tune was in the "Top Ten" favourite tune listing for seven weeks running.

Chapter 9
We're in the Money

The fortunes of the Bob Crosby band took another big step forward on the 6th January 1940 when they replaced Benny Goodman's Orchestra on Camel's Saturday night radio show. On these weekly shows, which were originally broadcast on NBC from 10 until 10.30pm, Mildred Bailey worked with the band as guest singer. On the 8th January, the band also began another residency at the New Yorker Hotel, on which they were rejoined by vocaliste Marion Mann.

Things were running smoothly in the vocal department, but attitudes were less happy within the brass section, after having another long talk with Gil Rodin, Shorty Sherock decided to leave the band. He said openly that he wasn't interested in what he termed "two beat Dixieland". He felt happy enough socially, but not musically. Shorty had no enemies in the band, on tour his main interests were in playing cards, or discussing his hobby of cine-photography, when the band was in New York his fellow musicians rarely saw him once the gig had ended, Shorty usually raced off to hear his idol, Roy Eldridge, play. One night, he dashed over to hear Eldridge in between Crosby's stage shows, and in doing so gulped down too much liquor too quickly, as a result he was violently sick. He later said, somewhat unendearingly, that this physical reaction summed-up how he felt about the music he played with the Crosby Band. There were no tears when he left in late January 1940 to join Gene Krupa's band.

Sherock's final recording date with the Crosby band was an unspectacular one, consisting as it did of four vocal numbers, two from Marion Mann and two from Bob Crosby. The pick of the bunch is a Mercer-Carmichael song, *Ooh! What You Said* on which Marion Mann achieves an attractive lilting performance, the arrangement features some incisive plunger playing by Butterfield; the whole trumpet section use their plunger mutes to support Fazola's exquisite half chorus.

Fazola was an extemely consistent musician throughout his entire career, but he rarely played better than he did during 1940. His work on the February 6th Bob Cats session is simply magnificent, producing two solos, on *Spain* and *Jazz Me Blues,* that will be talked about as long as great jazz clarinet performances are discussed.

The basic plot of the Bob Cats' version of *Spain* was devised by Bob Haggart, it is a feature for Fazola's remarkable talent. After playing a stately introduction the clarinettist emotes a chorus of the melody, shaping each phrase artistically and delivering it with a warm, glorious tone. Bauduc's woodblocks sound a little incongruous behind Jess Stacy's piano solo, but the drummer's tango rhythm in support of Eddie Miller's sensitive tenor solo is an inspired touch. Butterfield's leading of the ensemble is a model of mellow power, and Fazola's coda supplies the perfect ending.

Fazola is no less brilliant on *Jazz Me Blues*. The opening ensemble sounds lithe on Tom Delaney's old standard, preparing the way for Fazola's two superlative choruses. The band's re-entry riff was later to become a stock-part of almost every subsequent version of the tune, it heralded a firm ride-out chorus, which swings sturdily through to the final note of the extended ending. Jess Stacy's piano solo, with its contrasting left handed patterns and right handed trills, is the highspot of *Do You Ever Think Of Me*, (from the same date), but Fazola is again in superb form on this number; Nappy Lamare injects all of his considerable charm into the vocal. The session ends with Marion Mann singing *All By Myself*, on which Warren Smith shares the solos with Miller and Fazola.

Billy Butterfield wasn't featured extensively on that Bob Cats' session, but he was given the limelight a week later when the big band accompanied Bob Crosby's vocal on *Shake Down The Stars*. The success of Harry James' approach to ballad playing had not gone un-noticed by rival trumpeters, Butterfield's lush introduction and voluptuous half chorus seems to have been inspired by the Texan trumpeter's work. Marion Mann sings capably on the tasteful *With the Wind & The Rain In Your Hair*, and there are some fine moments from Fazola again, who interprets the melody with an exultant flair.

The band's recording of *Reminiscing Time* is an oddity, it is an instrumental with all the hallmarks of an indifferent vocal backing arrangement. It sounds as though the band were making a half-hearted attempt to capture the sound that Glenn Miller was then making universally popular. The consolation of this dull piece is that it allows us to hear how Eddie Miller was developing a new dimension to his already considerable ballad artistry. His solo here is a model of light-toned expressiveness, pioneering an instrumental concept that is similar to the style that Stan Getz achieved years later. More of Eddie Miller would have redeemed the overall performance, the final chorus of which is a prize example of how a good brass team can sound laboured when the material isn't right.

The Crosby band's contract at the Terrace Room of the Hotel New Yorker was extended until the end of March 1940. By the time the booking had ended there had been two changes in the trumpet section. Shorty Sherock's first replacement was an ex-Paul Whiteman trumpeter, Eddie Wade, who was soon replaced by Bob Peck, an old friend of Billy Butterfield's, who had previously worked with Glenn Miller, Bobby Byrne and Austin Wylie. Peck, in summarising his stay with the Crosby band said, "There weren't too many cliques to contend with. Perhaps I wasn't with the band long enough to pick up on the subtle aspects of relationships, but I felt comfortable with most everyone. Interestingly, the better players and musicians were not in the corporation, Haggart and Miller being the exceptions. Haggart was the most talented and musical one in the corporation. Eddie Miller was an affable person, and next to Haggart the most talented - very musical and consistent".

Gil Rodin, Bob thought of as "the business man, not a musician. Rather quiet, kept to himself. Ran the business end of things and made, or influenced most decisions re. bookings, P.R. etc". Peck found Bob Crosby, "A nice guy to work for. The front man so to speak. Musical decisions were handled by Haggart, Matlock, etc (Matlock was a good musician. He was only writing when I was with the band). As in most bands, the leader didn't fraternise too much with the sidemen, especially in the corporation set-up as this was. Although most everyone got along with one another, there was always the have versus the have-nots syndrome". Bob went on to cite one particular difference that he noticed between the corp and non-corp men, "The band had a radio commercial at that time (Camel Cigarettes). During rehearsals and at show time, the corporation boys, no matter what their preferences were, carried their own particular brands in Camel packs".

Bob Peck's summary emphasised several factors that played a part in the every day life of Bob Crosby's band. The corp and non-corp issue caused no hatred but engendered a degree of envy - not all of it one-sided. For long periods the corp men went without a goodly proportion of their earnings to finance the running of the band; one observer remembers seeing the non-corp men tucking into a four course menu whilst the corp men had to make do by economising over the same meal. Yank Lawson who saw service as both a corp and a non-corp members says he was infinitely happier as the latter, and Bob Haggart points out that he (and Matty Matlock) never received all the money that was due to them as the corporation arrangers, but Haggart also stresses that, in general, the band remained a happy unit, "There were no long sad faces, because if people didn't like it they got out. If a guy joined the band he knew he wouldn't suddenly get fired, and he wouldn't be continually picked on by the bandleader, because that wasn't part of Bob Crosby's job. There were miserable times in other bands usually because the bandleader was a sadistic prick, in fact, looking back to that era it seems you had to be some sort of a prick to become a bandleader at all. Gil Rodin had the authority to go for people, but he rarely did, he liked everyone to be happy and content. If he sensed a second trombone-player, or second alto-player was unhappy with things, he'd do his best to make that man feel he was an essential part of the organisation. If people felt unsettled Gil made them a promise that things would soon get considerably better, we nick-named him 'The Promiser', but most of the time his psychology kept everyone pulling in the same direction".

Bob Peck's dispassionate assessment of Gil Rodin as "a business man not a musician" is all too readily endorsed by the Crosby band members, particularly those who shared places with him in the reed section. As a saxophonist, Gil was not up to the class of the men he employed, and no matter how hard he worked at his music, nothing ever seemed to improve. Matty Matlock, who had affection for Gil, once said "You wouldn't believe the hours that man wasted in practising, it never would come right, but he was keen, after a long wrestle with the saxophone he'd battle with the clarinet for an hour, and then he'd take.on the flute. I tried to make sure that I wasn't within hearing range". Eddie Miller also remembers how seriously Gil tried to improve, "He'd discuss every aspect of the saxophone, and he kept up with every new development, but it never made a scrap of difference, no matter how long he spent wood-shedding. He wasn't a great saxophone player, that's for sure, but he was a good manager, and he was a great diplomat".

Gil Rodin was never accorded any saxophone solos, and this in itself became something of an 'in joke'. By 1940, *Down Beat* magazine had already started its policy of publishing transcribed solos by famous jazzmen, that year, the band arranged that the magazine print a "special" solo by Gil Rodin, the first 12 bars of which consisted of a single long note. Fun aside, Gil's lack of technical fluency caused the band's arrangers problems, and this is why the clarinet trios (from which Gil was usually excluded) are amongst the best executed reed work that the band recorded.

Besides the band's Camel radio shows, they were also broadcasting on CBS and MBS from the Hotel New Yorker, the sidemen got extra money for playing on sponsored radio shows, but not for sustaining broadcasts that were relayed from their place of work. All of this "air" time was helping to maintain the Crosby band's popularity, and in 1940 they again took third place in the "Swing Bands" section of the *Down Beat* poll, behind Benny Goodman who was first, and Glenn Miller. However, the Crosby band were still a long way from the income bracket of both the Goodman and Miller groups, whose quote for a week's stage work at the time was 12,500 dollars, whereas the figure for Crosby's band was 8,500 dollars. As the average weekly wage in the USA was less than 40 dollars, the band business seemed a lucrative one to outsiders.

It certainly was profitable for a successful bandleader, and this fact tempted many sidemen to strike out on their own and form big bands, but, as many of them discovered, the initial outlay for arrangements, transport, uniforms and publicity was often never re-couped, and the money that they had been advanced by band-agents was quickly swallowed up by administrative costs. Several famous players, including Bunny Berigan and Jack Teagarden found themselves bankrupt after being smitten by what was jocularly referred to at the time as batonitis".

Bob Crosby, still mindful of Zurke's recent departure, let his views on the subject of "new" bandleaders come bursting out whilst being interviewed by *Down Beat.* "It sounds terrific to a sideman to hear an agent tell him about a bright future with his own band. But watch out. They advance you a few grand for a piece of the band and from then on it's a struggle. Even if you do click with the band the agent takes a good portion of the profits. As for the Crosby band we aren't worried. We stick together. We vote amongst ourselves on everything that comes up. We have fine esprit d'corps and we don't worry about one of us pulling out suddenly to become a leader". This last comment was an obvious reference to Bob Zurke, but Zurke's attempts to lead a big band were soon to hit a trail of woe, within a year he was forced to disband. Absolutely broke he started to make a living again, playing solo piano, usually in club bars. He died in 1944 at the age of 32.

In the spring of 1940, the Crosby band's long-standing dispute with Tommy Rockwell and Cork O'Keefe was finally resolved when the Music Corporation of America paid Rockwell (whose business was now called the General Amusement Corporation), the sum of 4,000 dollars, in return he agreed to waive any claims he had against the Crosby Corporation. The band had been using the booking services of MCA for some while, but only on the basis that each side had the right to cease dealing with the other providing they gave 24 hours' notice of intent. With the purchase of the release from Rockwell, MCA were able to initiate a mutual six months' notice clause in contracts drawn up with the Crosby Corporation. This suited the agency much better, and gave them the confidence to make long term plans for the band.

The Crosby Corporation did not object to MCA solidifying its connections with them, but it was determined to make it clear to the musical profession that they still felt that they were in the right concerning their dispute with Rockwell-O'Keefe. This attitude was emphasised in a statement from Gil Rodin, who said, "If MCA paid 4,000 dollars for an unconditional release, I assure you that they paid for it out of their own pockets. We refuse to pay Tom Rockwell anything. We won't owe him anything. He owes us!". Rodin's vehemence shows how deeply the band felt about this issue, and in discussing the matter with surviving members of the contretemps one gets the impression that their feelings on the matter have not changed.

It was not surprising that Rockwell held out for a share of the action, a published breakdown revealed that the band had paid 36,000 dollars in agency commission during 1939. That figure was in a listing of the band's 1939 accounts, which were published in *Down Beat*:-

	(in dollars)
Band payroll	157,000
Advertising and publicity	6,315
General expenses	4,602
Telephone and wires	904
Union taxes and standbys	17,059
(standbys - meant payments to local musicians who under union ruling had to standby when a travelling band did a broadcast in their town).	

Theatre talent	9,685
(payment to others who worked with	
the band on percentage theatre dates)	
Miscellaneous taxes	518
Legal fees, auditing	936
Entertainment	778
Hospitalization	566
Hotel, miscellaneous	208
Arranging payroll	5,000
MCA commissions	36,000

No individual breakdown of the band's payroll of 157,000 dollars was given, but in the estimated earnings for 1940, the forecasts were:- Bob Crosby 25,000 dollars, Gil Rodin 20,000, the rest of the corporation men at around 15,000 each, the star sidemen (Butterfield, Fazola and Stacy) at 10,000 each, and the other musicians at 8,000 dollars apiece. Ted Jahns (who was then road manager) was on 3,000 a year, and Jack Cella the band boy, 1,250.

One of Bob Crosby's brothers, Everett, was now on the permanent payroll as Bob's personal manager, and it was estimated he was paid 5,000 a year for his services. A breakdown of money accrued from the band's engagements in 1939, showed that theatre dates were their most lucrative source of income:

	(in dollars)
Location jobs, hotels, etc	44,459
One night stands	79,385
Theatres	83,827
Radio commercials	37,249
Records and Royalties	24,661

The record royalty total showed that neither "The Orchestra" or "The Bob Cats" had hit the jackpot as far as sales figures. Despite the appeal that the Bob Cats had for many jazz fans throughout the world, their record sales (on initial release) were dwarfed by the most successful of the full band's vocal issues. The sales of *The Little Red Fox* have been mentioned, both *Over The Rainbow* and *With The Wind and the Rain in your Hair* achieved over 100,000 sales during their first year on the market, far exceeding the 60,000 copies that *I'm Free* (the best selling instrumental) sold during the same period.

In hindsight, one can understand why Decca, whose job it was to sell records, kept prodding the band to record vocal numbers. They continued to do so in 1940, and the results were often pleasant. The full band give Marion Mann some effective, swinging support to a cheery song of the era, *Run Rabbit Run,* and on *Tit Willow* they really demonstrate their collective attack. Bauduc's press-rolls sound beautifully controlled, and both Miller and Fazola are ultra creative in their solos. Fazola and Butterfield are both featured in a short series of well conceived breaks, and the overall swing carries through to the last notes of one of the band's rare fade-out endings. Perhaps the most novel of all the vocal backings the band provided during this period was the treatment they gave to Bob Crosby's medium tempoed vocal version of his brother Bing's hit *Where The Blue Of The Night Meets The Gold Of The Day*. On the surface it seems an odd choice of material, since Bob was still regularly proclaiming independence from fraternal influence, but the band's arrangement is deliberately tailored to be different, both in tempo and in mood, from Bing's earlier version.

Jess Stacy sets the ball rolling with a superb interpretation of the melody, gently stressing his own highly personal way of trilling upper-register octaves. The piano solo is followed by some ingenious scoring which blends the timbre of Haggart's bowed bass and Eddie Miller's bass-clarinet playing, this sound effectively shares the score with the full brass section and mid-register reed work. Fazola enters the limelight to unexpectedly re-introduce the melody, then the brass dominate with some emphatic phrasing - by this time Miller has reverted to tenor sax. The markedly different planning of this arrangement allocates Bob Crosby the final chorus, and he amply maintains the interest generated during the previous instrumental section. Miller reverts to bass-clarinet for the conclusion which is sealed by an arpeggio from Stacy on piano.

The Bob Cats session of late February 1940, produced four vocals from Marion Mann. The main disappointment of this batch is the subsidiary role that Butterfield plays - he seems to have been placed in a musical "penalty box" and is only allowed out on his own to play brief obliggatos. Eddie Miller and Fazola (brilliant on *Mama's Gone Goodbye*) take the brunt of the solos, but Warren Smith takes a relaxed well-rounded duet with Bauduc to provide a nicely unified introduction for *A Vous Tout De Devey, A Vous*. The piano is almost inaudible behind Fazola's tasteful solo, and this gives added prominence to Nappy Lamare's guitar. The final number of the session, *You Oughta Hang Your Heart in Shame* contains one of the most spirited ensembles the Bob Cats ever recorded.

A month later, there was a breakthrough in programming the Bob Cats recordings, at last Bob Crosby was featured with them. The results are a mixed bag since two of the items are hand-on-heart college songs, but on *It's All Over Now*, Bob reveals considerable elan in his swingy approach. In general, this was a satisfactory period for Bob's vocals, and on the full band's *This Is The Beginning Of The End* he is close to his best.

Very occasionally two takes of a recording by the Crosby musicians were issued, this meant that two differing recorded efforts (usually made one after the other) were pressed up and sold to record buyers. Sometimes, in a written arrangement, the difference between one version and another can be minute, but in the case of the band's *Short'nin' Bread* only one take has a vocal, which is by Eddie Miller. The other take is purely instrumental, and features jubilant solos from Miller's tenor sax and Fazola's clarinet. During the early stages of both versions Haggart's toothy whistling is heard in tandem with Ray Bauduc's drumming, in what sounds like a half-hearted attempt to recreate the *Winnetka* success formula, but Bauduc's drum breaks in the closing section are amongst the most facile he ever recorded. The band's attempt to give a new look to Bob Carleton's old melody *Ja Da* doesn't come off, the juxtaposing of a 12 bar blues with the composer's original 16 bar theme doesn't succeed, despite the excellence of Stacy's piano solo.

The band completed this long bout of New York recordings with a session that produced two triumphs, the first of which was Bob Haggart's sublime arrangement of *Embraceable You*, on which Billy Butterfield is satisfyingly entrusted with the opening chorus. Stacy, Fazola and Miller have small solo roles in an arrangement that had to be cut (much to Haggart's lasting disappointment) in order to meet the time available on a 78 rpm record. The other magnificent item from the four tune session is Matty Matlock's arrangement of *Sympathy*. Fazola plays a dainty introduction after which the muted brass establish the melody which is punctuated first by piano figures, then by a solid counter-melody from the reed section. Fazola re-enters to give an unforgettable interpretation of the tune, remaining mostly in the low register, imbueing every nuance of an excellent melody with his remarkable musical talent. Sadly, this was the last session that the great clarinettist ever recorded with the Crosby band, it was to be five months before the group entered a recording studio again, and during the interim upheavals brought about several personnel changes.

Chapter 10

Hollywood beckons

On April 12th 1940, the Bob Crosby band began another season at the Blackhawk in Chicago. This time the booking was for six weeks, there was no question of optional extensions because the band were already contracted to play a whole string of summer engagements. As far as general popularity, the band were riding the crest of a wave activated by the widely-heard radio shows, but the more popular the band became the more it was criticised by the professional writers.

Throughout its early career, the Crosby band's music had regularly been accorded enthusiastic reviews. Its style, though packaged as "Dixieland" was a refreshing blend of old and new jazz concepts which greatly pleased those who liked to harp on the qualities of yesteryear's jazz, it also satisfied younger listeners, who were moved by the band's spirit and musicianship. By 1940, not only were there other big bands playing scores that were similar to those originated by Crosby's men, but there was also a growing number of small bands who were devoting themselves to reviving an authentic brand of early jazz. A lot of the people who had followed Crosby's band and Bob Cats, because no other permanent groups were attempting to keep certain jazz values alive, were now listening avidly to the revivalist bands.

No one in the Crosby set-up was hyper-sensitive to criticism and all of the musicians were experienced enough to know that a lot of the people who clustered around the bandstand, howling approval, were not likely to develop into life-long fans. The players realised that the upsurge in the number of small bands was likely to attract away some of the jazz fans, but they felt that this did not invalidate their own style of music. They were however, irked by the continual, faintly disparaging, references to their style as "two beat music".

The individual in the Crosby band who received more than his share of criticism was Ray Bauduc. Some critics regarded Ray's volatile, all-action New Orleans style of drumming as passé, even though it was an ingredient that continually affirmed the fact that Crosby's band was not just another swing group. Writers like Barry Ulanov were specific, "Rhythm: Here is where the big faults in the band stand out. Number one is drummer Ray Bauduc. To me, he often seems deficient in his timing, dragging and sometimes rushing the section and therefore the band. The irksome rim-work and the block-work he fills in with don't break up the monotony of the two-beat style they emphasize it. A helluva fine fellow, it seems too bad to this reviewer Bauduc can't drop blocks and rimming and concentrate on solid tempi". Ulanov went on to castigate Haggart, and to suggest that Stacy was out of place in the section, the only one to escape specific criticism was Nappy Lamare, whose "screwy chords fill in his infrequent guitar solos refreshingly, and are quite up to the lax standards of the rest of the rhythm".

Criticisms from other directions were more general, one letter in the February 1940 issue of *Metronome* said, "The Bob Crosby band used to play such great dixieland on its radio shows. Since the change to Saturday nights they are playing mostly sissy stuff". The band's old friend, George T. Simon, put his finger on the dilemma the Crosby band was facing in choosing a programme of popular appeal, he wrote in *Metronome*, "As a pretty band they're strictly second rate, especially weak dynamically and rhythmically, but the public is beginning to love them, and more public than followers listen in on Saturday nights".

The big band's discernible drift towards a more commercial approach was readily admitted by its members, but they were more than suprised to learn that several critics found the "new" rhythm section (containing Jess Stacy) was worse than previous editions. The general consensus of opinion with the Crosby sidemen is that the rhythm section went through a short period of extreme unreliability during the uprise of showmanship that linked in with the success of *Big Noise From Winnetka*. One renowned Crosbyite said "There was more mugging in the rhythm section than there was swinging", another one of the band's stalwarts felt that Ray Bauduc's tendency to speed up was due to "spotlightitis" - the excitement of being featured. But as things were proceeding smoothly soon after Stacy's arrival, the band thought the criticism was unfair. The usually benign Matty Matlock got so angry over the issue he literally pulled one critic up to the bandstand during a performance and demanded to know "What is wrong with that rhythm section?".

The band had no sooner settled into the Blackhawk residency than Rodin became aware that a major upheaval was about to take place. He had recently confirmed to the band members that there were a number of long Californian bookings in the engagement listings. As a lot of the band had made their homes in the New York area the prospect of spending long spells on the other coast was not inviting, as a result several musicians decided to hand in their notice.

Bill Stegmeyer chose to leave, and he was replaced by Arthur "Doc" Rando, a reedman who most of the band's New Orleans contingent had known for years. George Koenig also left and his place in the reed section was taken by Hank D'Amico. Trombonist Warren Smith joined the exodus and handed over his place to Floyd O'Brien. Billy Butterfield decided to leave so that he could work around Chicago (where he, his wife and infant son had made their home), the new man who came in to take most of the jazz solos in the brass section was cornetist Muggsy Spanier. Whilst all of the outgoing men were working out their notices the most dramatic severance of all took place as a result of a brawl between Irving Fazola and trombonist Ray Conniff.

113

The Fazola-Conniff tussle enjoys a special place in the anecdotage of the Crosby sidemen, and I have been privileged to hear several eye-witness accounts. Most of the onlookers agree that there had never been a bond of friendship between the two men, but all goodwill disappeared when Fazola called Conniff "a jerk" on the bandstand at the Blackhawk. Conniff rejoindered by saying "If I'm a jerk then you're a jerk". Unwittingly several members of the band made the atmosphere more tense by laughing out loud at the wildly different pronunciations given to the insult (Fazola was from New Orleans, Conniff from New England). Both protagonists agreed that they would settle their differences physically as soon as the band's set had ended.

Ray Conniff, kindly supplied me with the background to the dispute, "For some reason or other, 'Faz' never liked me too much. I found out later that a drop off the water-key of my trombone occasionally landed on his head as he sat in front of me (unbeknownst to me). The nite of the 'fracas', everyone was very 'loaded'. We came to a spot in an arrangement (I think it was 'Yancey Special') where the saxes had a trill with Faz on top on clarinet. Faz was so full of gin his fingers barely moved up and down, and the trill was so slow the whole brass section broke up laughing. Faz singled me out, and got mad and said "O.K. Conniff upstairs in the loft after this set", being too loaded myself to be afraid I said 'You're on'. There were no blows landed, we both swung and missed, Faz got me in a bear hug and fell on top of me, he knocked my wind out and that was the end of the fight".

Published reports had Ray Bauduc stepping in and landing a right on Fazola's mouth, but no one present recalls that incident. Billy Butterfield summed up the whole incident as being "A donny brook. Many arms flying, few blows struck". Never-the-less the aftermath was serious, Fazola immediately handed in his notice, and nothing could persuade him to withdraw it. But, even if the brawl had never occurred, it is probable that Fazola would have soon left the band anyway. Earlier in the year, he was non-committal when Gil Rodin, sensing that the clarinettist was unsettled, asked if everything was alright.

Rodin, responsive to the moods of various sidemen, came to the conclusion that Fazola, (who had never stayed for more than two years with any band), was planning to move out of the band, so during the spring of 1940 he signed Hank D'Amico, who was a clarinet specialist, to wait in the wings by accepting a non-soloist role in the saxophone section. Rodin was also secure in the knowledge that in any emergency, Matty Matlock, who was ever eager to play, could resume his place as the band's featured clarinettist.

The music magazines tried to suggest that Billy Butterfield left the band because he resented the fact that Spanier's joining would deprive him of many of his featured solo spots, but Butterfield says that he made up his mind to leave before ever Muggsy agreed to join the band. However, the new man's arrival seems to have hastened Butterfield's decision. A particular factor was that Muggsy Spanier was not a good reader, this virtually eliminated the prospect of the three trumpeters swopping the lead parts, and meant that Billy would have increasingly been used as the section leader (a task he could fulfil with ease), whereas his ambition was to express his individuality via solos.

During the period that had elapsed since Spanier had previously declined Gil Rodin's offer to join the band he had enjoyed a good deal of publicity, his "Ragtimers" had excited critics and jazz-fans during a series of New York bookings, and they had also recorded a batch of inspired performances that became known as the "Great 16". But, despite the accolades, offers of well-paid work for Spanier's Ragtimers were not forthcoming, and Muggsy was forced to disband and resume his career as a sidemen. He was delighted to learn that Gil Rodin's offer still held good.

Gil Rodin, the strategist, saw Muggsy Spanier's presence would go a long way towards placating the band's die-hard jazz fans who felt they were being neglected. After Muggsy's arrival a section of the Bobcats programme was allocated to recreating numbers that Muggsy's Ragtimers had recorded.

The band's vocal department also underwent another change. After a bout of illness, during which time she was replaced by Kathleen Lane, Marion Mann returned to the band briefly then decided to quit for good. Her place was taken by a strikingly attractive 16 year old who had adopted the professional name, Doris Day. Doris's real name was Kappelhoff, throughout her childhood she had ambitions to become a professional dancer, but a broken leg had ended those dreams, instead she diverted her energies into singing, and studied under a highly successful teacher, Grace Raine, in her home town of Cincinnati.

Grace Raine's husband, Ferde, a song plugger, heard on the profession's grape vine that Gil Rodin was looking for a singer to take Marion Mann's place. Accordingly Doris Day made the trip to Chicago, accompanied by her mother. After attending a "Camel" radio rehearsal at NBC's Merchandise Mart studio, Doris went to the Blackhawk and successfully auditioned for the vacancy. She agreed to sing with the band for 75 dollars a week, it was the first big move in what turned out to be an illustrious career. She certainly created a good impression with the Crosby musicians, Haggart remembers, "She was so full of life, very tall, with lots of freckles".

The Crosby band played a series of one-night stands after the Blackhawk residency had ended, and on one of these dates the *Down Beat* correspondent in Indianapolis reported that the band "never sounded better". On June 28th 1940, the band began a series of engagements at the Strand Theatre in New York, where Leonard Feather commented on the new vocaliste, "Doris Day is very tall and beautiful, with the usual voice".

Just how much of an asset Doris Day would have been to the Crosby band will never be known, because events that took place during the New York bookings changed her future. The Crosby band were still doing their radio series, and the sponsor's advisers felt that experience was of prime importance on the show. Accordingly, it was suggested to Rodin that Bonnie

King would be much more satisfactory than Doris Day, there were no options. So Gil Rodin reluctantly explained to Doris Day that Bonnie King would be doing the radio shows, and as some of them would be relayed from venues away from New York, Bonnie was also to be featured on one-night stands. Rodin softened the blow by saying that bandleader Les Brown was going to call in to hear Doris Day, with a view to offering her a place with his band. Les Brown duly arrived and within minutes had offered Doris Day 75 dollars a week to join his band - by the time she left Brown's band in 1946 Doris was on 500 dollars a week.

A published report later suggested that Doris Day left the Crosby band to escape the unwelcome attentions of one of the members of the group, but this was denied by Doris, who at the time was engaged to Jimmy Dorsey's trombonist, Al Jorden. She told author A.E. Hotchner (who worked with her on "Doris Day - Her Own Story"), "Actually I never had a hard time with any of the men in the band, I was their kid sister". At the same time she also said, "Bob Crosby himself contributed little or nothing to my singing education because he was really only a front man for the band". Unfortunately, due to a gap in the band's recording activities, Doris Day was not featured on disc with them. Bob Crosby candidly says that he doesn't think that any of the band's girl vocalistes ever liked him very much. He thinks that they imagined he was creaming off all the best songs for himself.

Whilst the Crosby band were at the Strand Theatre, Rodin outlined their future musical strategy in *Metronome,* "We're going to have a more versatile outfit. It's true that we all feel the two-beat type of jazz more, but there's no getting away from it that many of the kids who come to hear us want us to play some four-beat-so we're going to give it to them from now on". Rodin pointed out that the band's most frequently played record during that period was *For Dancers Only,* "waxed after much prodding from Decca Records prexy, Jack Kapp". He went on to say, "We didn't like the idea then, and even after listening to the recording, we're still not convinced that it's the kind of jazz we play best. But if the kids want some of that, they'll get it". Rodin also said that to broaden the scope of the band it was using the work of two new arrangers, Jimmy Mundy (who had written for Earl Hines and Benny Goodman) and Paul Wetstein, who as Paul Weston later gained an international reputation as a composer and arranger. Rodin concluded by saying, "I'm in the market for a good vocal rhythm trio".

After the New York bookings ended the band moved westwards on a journey that eventually took them to a summer season in California. Whilst the band were on this odyssey they played at the Eastwood Gardens in Detroit, where Rodin found a vocal group to work with the band. He chose a 3 men and 1 girl line-up thus competing with many other big bands of the period who featured similar singing groups, (*The Pied Pipers* with Tommy Dorsey, *The Modernaires* with Glenn Miller, etc). The group that Rodin signed was originally known as "The Downbeaters", but after joining the Crosby set-up they were re-named "The Bob-o- Links", one of its members, Johnny Desmond, later became a nationally known music personality.

For the journey west, the band welcomed back its former road-manager, Joe 'Red' kearney, who had been recuperating from a serious illness in his home town of Spokane, Washington. Joe briefly resumed his duties working alongside a Texan, Ted Jahns, who had recently celebrated his first year with the band, but Kearney didn't stay long and left to become a Jesuit priest. Kearney was following in his brother's footsteps, who had worked as a missionary in China. Later when Father Kearney had taken his vows, he was asked if he too would go to the Orient, he replied "No, I think I'll get a trailer and follow the Bob Crosby Band around, there's much more work to do there than in China". A young man from Chicago, Bill Black came in to fill the vacancy caused by Kearney's departure, Black later became a successful band agent. An Ohioan, Larry Barnett, who became a powerful figure in MCA, was also for a time a bandboy with the Crosby crew.

In the summer of 1940, the trumpet section underwent one of its periodic changes, Bob Peck left and his place was taken by ex-Freddie Martin trumpeter Al King, who joined the Crosby band whilst they were appearing in Salt Lake City. At the same venue, Ruth Keddington, who later married Johnny Desmond, joined the Bob-o-Links.

The band's season on Catalina Island (which began on August 17th 1940), provided many happy memories for the participating musicians. The ballroom where the band worked was owned by the Wrigley Spearmint Company, and so too were many of the island's leisure facilities, thus the golfers, tennis-players, swimmers and fishermen amongst the band were able to easily follow their sporting pursuits. The band's ball team was revived, now greatly strengthened by three fine players, Muggsy Spanier, Hank D'Amico and Doc Rando.

En route to the Coast, a local music correspondent in Ohio had specifically mentioned the high morale and good humour of the "new" band, and this happy spirit continued to flourish on Catalina. The band's new arranger, Paul Weston, went with them to the island, and recalls the period with affection, "The band was good, Catalina was beautiful. We played golf every day, and the men in the band were some of the finest people I've ever met, and we became life-long friends. I was paid by the arrangement. Bob Haggart and Matty Matlock did most of the instrumentals, and I wrote some ballads for Bob and the Bob-o-Links - I can't remember one title!".

In September 1940, near the end of their Californian season, the Crosby musicians went into the recording studios in Los Angeles to cut a series of 14 vocal numbers, spread across three sessions. From the first track of the batch it is apparent that the recent personnel changes had affected the overall sound of the band. The reeds have a lighter sound, by then Matlock was playing alto-saxophone within the reed section, and Hank D'Amico was the featured clarinettist. D'Amico was a highly competent improviser with an individual flair, but he was no Fazola. his tone was much thinner for one thing, and also lacked Faz's considerable musical presence, but the band were pleased that D'Amico always retained his own style.

Bonnie King proved that she was a good professional vocalist. She sang with confidence and technique, but lacked the individuality that instantly establishes a great singer's identity with an audience. A lack of originality also marred the work of the Bob-o-Links, their shared feature with Ray Bauduc, *Drummer Boy,* sounds too ordinary, but the number does feature the inimitable sounds of Muggsy Spanier's cornet for a brief 8 bar solo. Jess Stacy also has a short outing on the same tune, but it is one of his lesser musical offerings consisting as it does of a series of arpeggios somewhat haphazardly performed. The next number recorded, *Cow Cow Blues,* finds Stacy in a much more constructive mood. The arrangement consists of a series of piano phrases being answered in double-time by the rest of the ensemble. The effect soon wears thin, but Stacy is relaxed and eloquent throughout, and Spanier enlivens a late part of the plot with a resounding solo.

Muggsy also shines through the dust stirred up by the Nappy Lamare, Bob-o-Links shared vocal on *Dry Bones,* his bright 16 bars of muted playing saves the side. Hank D'Amico shows that he could add elegant touches to a ballad in his playing of *I've Got a One Track Mind,* which features a competent Crosby vocal; both men are hampered by the paucity of the material. Eddie Miller plays bass-clarinet in the reed section on several band numbers from this period, but remained on tenor sax throughout the four Bob Cats' sides recorded in September 1940.

Bob Crosby takes a bouncy vocal on *Take Me Back Again,* which is also graced by a Muggsy Spanier solo. Trombonist Floyd O'Brien gets one of his rare solos with the group on *I'll Come Back To You,* his devotion to the work of the great tailgate trombonists is apparent, but the actual delivery of his lines, as opposed to work he had recorded in the 1930s, seems to lack energy. This doyen of many fine Chicago sessions seems subdued, and this approach led one Crosby sideman to suggest, jocularly, that at this period of his life, Floyd was too tired to even add a vibrato to his notes.

Hank D'Amico's clarinet sounds impressive both in the ensemble and throughout his immaculately played solos, but overall, this version of the Bob Cats lacks the homogenity of its predecessors.   Two of the numbers recorded, *Don't Call Me Boy* and *You're Bound To Look Like a Monkey,* are vehicles for the jollier side of Nappy Lamare's vocal style, here the bonhomie is stacked even higher than usual by the inclusion of shouted responses from the Bob Cats. D'Amico and Miller solo skilfully on both, but during the final chorus of each tune it becomes apparent that Muggsy is content to intone his stock phrases.

Muggsy's musical imagination may have been restricted, but he had his own, positive style, and he endowed all of his phrases, muted or open, with panache and feeling. The band followers liked Muggsy's playing, and his colleagues on the bandstand found him pleasant to work with, though some of them were wrily amused to observe that Muggsy couldn't resist dropping coins into a jukebox to share the sound of his own Ragtimers' recordings.

After their season at Catalina had ended, the band played for a week at the Paramount Theatre in Hollywood in late September 1940. During this period they took part in the filming of the movie *Let's Make Music*. The film, a low-budget RKO affair, was the story of a staid music teacher learning about jazz and "jive talk", it is not considered to be an epic, however it gave cinema-goers the chance to see and hear *Big Noise From Winnetka*, and to catch a glimpse of the Crosby musicians. Bob Crosby's role called on him to leap out of bed wearing some loose-fitting pyjamas, he did so with more vigour than he intended and the result produced an "out" take in more ways than one; that piece of film hit the cutting room floor.

The band's contribution to the film was impressive enough to gain them appearances in several other movies. One distinction of *Let's Make Music* was that the screen play was by the posthumously famous author, Nathaniel West. It was released in the States in December 1940. In October 1940, after their filming duties had ended, the Crosby band moved north to play dates in San Francisco where they did good business at the Palace Hotel, and at the Mark Hopkins Hotel, from where they broadcast regularly. These radio shows produced a large number of postcards all requesting that Muggsy Spanier be featured more. The band were amazed at this response, but they were less impressed when it transpired that they had all been sent by Muggsy's brother.

Kay Weber

Dorothy Claire

The Wilde twins, Lyn and Lee

Doris Day

120

Bob Crosby, Raymond Scott, Louis Armstrong and Connie Boswell rehearsing for CBS's Saturday Night Swing Club, California, November 1937.

Judy Garland, Bob Crosby and Van Heflin in a scene from the movie, Presenting Lily Mars.

Fazola, with members of Ben Pollack's Band in New Orleans, 1936, Harry James on extreme right.
(photo courtesy of New Orleans Jazz Club Collection of The Louisiana State Museum)

Irving Fazola (third from left, top row) in the New Orleans ROMA Band, c. 1926.
(photo courtesy of New Orleans Jazz Club Collection of The Louisiana State Museum)

Irving Fazola's Band at Tony's Cafe, Canal Boulevard, New Orleans, c. 1947. Left to right Joe Rotis,
Howard Reed, Irving Fazola. Charlie Duke and Ogden Lafaye.
(photo courtesy of New Orleans Jazz Club Collection of The Louisiana State Museum)

Gil RODIN   **Irving FAZOLA**   **George KOENIG**   **Bill STEGMEYER**   **Eddie MILLER**

The Bob Crosby Orchestra's saxophone section, 1940.
(photo courtesy of Selmer Instruments)

Nappy Lamare, Bob Haggart, Muggsy Spanier and Ray Conniff, 1940.

Chapter 11

Californian pleasures

The results of the 1941 *Down Beat* poll were a disappointment to most of the Crosby band's devoted fans. The band dropped four places to finish 7th in the "Swing" section placings . Consolingly, the Bob Cats retained their general appeal, gaining 3rd place in the small band division; four of the band's individual musicians, Eddie Miller, Ray Bauduc, Bob Haggart and Jess Stacy were outright winners in their instrumental sections.

Whilst it is easy to dismiss music magazine polls as frivolous attempts to make league tables out of performers' artistry, there is no doubt that high placings affect business, because they stimulate that mysterious quality called "box office appeal". During the "Swing Era" people flocked to see a "winning band". Both Gil Rodin and the MCA agency were sorry that they couldn't splash the news of a poll success for the Crosby band across the show business pages of every big city newspaper. *Down Beat* in summarising the big band scene during 1940, certainly didn't alleviate Rodin's dismay with the item "Many observers believe Bob Crosby's band was the most disappointing of the batch. After five years, the band suddenly went commercial and began stressing the leader's vocals along with the undistinctive Bob-o-Links Quartet and Bonnie King".

The magazine's suggestion that the Crosby band had suddenly begun emphasising vocals did not refer to the recorded output, which was at about the same ratio as before, it was directed at the preponderance of vocal numbers heard on the band's peak-time radio shows. But then, as now, the average listener preferred vocal numbers to instrumentals, and the programme sponsors were well aware of that fact. In the radio popularity ratings conducted by the Crosley Company (who organised a telephoned survey in American major cities) the Crosby band gained a higher placing than that achieved by Benny Goodman's Orchestra in a 1940 sampler.

However, the Bob Crosby band was soon to lose its long-held residency on the Camel Caravan radio show, and the change had nothing to do with the quality of music, or of audience response. In 1940, a disagreement arose between ASCAP (American Society of Composers, Authors and Publishers) B.M.I. (Broadcasting Music Incorporated) over the rights to collect fees for the radio transmission of copyright music. As a result, ASCAP banned the radio useage of music that came under its auspices. This move meant that only material owned by BMI could be broadcast in the U.S.A. for the length of the dispute (January 1st to October 30th 1941).

As very little of the Bob Crosby band's repertoire consisted of BMI tunes the ASCAP ban meant that the group was prevented from broadcasting most of its usual arrangements. The Camel sponsors were forced to dispense with the services of the Crosby band and they were replaced by Xavier Cugat's Orchestra, whose repertoire of Latin-American numbers was comprised mostly of BMI material. On off-shoot of the dispute was an upsurge in the popularity of Latin-American music, for a brief while it seemed as if North America had gone rhumba crazy.

In December 1940, after the Crosby band had finished its six week residency at the Mark Hopkins Hotel in San Francisco, Ray Conniff, the band's up-and-coming trombonist left to join Artie Shaw's band, who were then working in Calfornia, he was also able to start his illustrious studio career by playing for the Burns and Allen radio show. Conniff (who was replaced by Elmer Smithers) had already developed a reputation for arranging before he joined the Crosby band, but that side of his talents were hardly used during his stay. A Crosby sideman, recalling the reason said "Ray certainly had technique as an arranger, nice ideas and good voicings, but his charts made us sound just like any other big swing band, and that was just what we didn't want". Conniff did some writing for the Crosby band, "Mostly ballads" he recalls, one of them *Maybe* he particularly remembers as being a vehicle for what he calls a "great solo" from Muggsy Spanier.

Soon after Conniff's departure, Muggsy Spanier also decided to leave the Crosby band. In January 1941, whilst the group were in Los Angeles, Muggsy informed Gil Rodin that he would soon be leaving to form his own big band. Consequently, on the 24th January 1941, Spanier moved east to organise a large New York-based ensemble. The band, which was backed by a consortium of Chicago businessmen, recruited by Bill Spanier (he of the postcards), was firmly modelled on the big band style originated by the Crosby ensemble. Its principle arranger was the Crosby "pioneer" Deane Kincaide, and, a little later on, its premier soloist was none other than Irving Fazola.

Spanier's closest pal in the Crosby group was his old Chicago colleague, Jess Stacy, (as early as 1930, Spanier had praised the pianist's talent to the French writer, Hugues Panassié). The cornetist enjoyed himself throughout his stay, and said a few years later, "One of the greatest thrills was playing with the Crosby band". This was some compliment as Muggsy had worked with a number of groups, including Ben Pollack's band, his replacement in the Crosby group was trumpeter Bob Goodrich, who had also been a Pollack sideman.

During the last part of Spanier's stay with the Crosby band he appeared with them in a Republic movie called *Sis Hopkins* which featured the young actress, Judy Canova. Cy Feuer, a former trumpet player, then head of Republic's music department, was a great fan of the Crosby band, and actively encouraged them to play jam sessions on the set, to the delight of the rest of the cast. Muggsy Spanier's final recordings with the band, in December 1940, were a mixed bunch. The *Mark Hop*, an instrumental composed by Bob Haggart and dedicated to the Mark Hopkins Hotel, is a superior model of many tunes seemingly spawned by the success of *Tuxedo Junction*. The compact scoring of the opening chorus is neatly answered by Stacy's piano figures. D'Amico takes a thin-toned but well-devised half chorus then hands over to Stacy, whose solo labours along for a while, but finishes with an inspired display of ambidexterity, as his right hand emphasises an even tremolo whilst his left hand builds a dramatic, ascending phrase. Muggsy plays a warm-toned solo over the band's gentle riffs, replaying phrases he had recorded before, but making them sound spontaneous and apt. Trombone glissandos herald the final theme, the trumpets counter effectively, and the saxophones play well-drilled phrases that handsomely fill the gaps.

Burning the Candle at Both Ends is charming original from Jess Stacy, who leads off with a chorus of the melody. The ensemble introduces a tuneful second theme, then the piano re-emerges for a further solo, which is backed by some discreet writing for the saxophone section (in which Gil Rodin plays baritone sax). Muggsy chips in with a breezy 8 bar solo, then the ensemble reprises the catchy opening theme. The balance is superb throughout, each section blending cohesively with its counterparts; the sound of the drums remains crisp without being too obtrusive. All round this is one of the band's best instrumental recordings, underlining the merits of the 1940 band.

Alas, the remake of *Big Noise From Winnetka* does not measure up to the original. The 1940 band version, which has Bob Crosby singing lyrics written by himself and Gil Rodin, is considerably slower than the earlier version. Haggart's whistling and Bauduc's drumming are featured at the beginning and at the end, in between there is an undistinguished vocal collaboration between Bob Crosby and the Bob-o-Links, plus a weary-sounding clarinet trio interlude.

On *Something I Dreamed*, Bob Crosby proves that his vocal performances could vary drastically within the course of a single session. After his limp efforts on *Winnetka* he rose to the heights and recorded one of his best ever vocals. He makes the melody sound truly effective, and his satisfying efforts are given neat support by the Bob-o-Links. The arrangement introduces D'Amico's mellow low-register clarinet work, which sets the mood nicely for the warm vocal. On *Blue Echoes* Bonnie King is featured with the Bob-o-Links, the arrangement, which is spiced with Latin-American rhythms, gives the trombone duo a rare burst of prominence.

After playing a February 1941 stint at the Paramount Theatre in Los Angeles, the Crosby band moved across to begin an 8 week residency in Chicago, this time in the Panther Room of the Hotel Sherman. For the first part of this booking the band played without Bob Crosby, who remained in Hollywood to put the final touches to his performance in the *Sis Hopkins* film. he rejoined the band in time for the March 28th recording session, which produced *Well, Well,* an invigorating romp which contains a supple vocal from Bob, a pleasant dixieland interlude (led by newcomer Bob Goodrich), and some flamboyant drum breaks from Ray Bauduc.

The one instrumental amongst the five numbers recorded on the session was *Flamingo,* a contemporary song that stayed the course and became an evergreen. Its lasting quality cannot be ascribed to the Crosby band's version, which apart from Eddie Miller's interpretation of the melody, and his superbly constructed cadenzas, has little to recommend it. The quasi-dramatic beginning sounds inappropriate, and D'Amico's 16 bar solo emphasises the spikey, unattractive aspect of his upper-register tone.

On the following day, the Bob Cats backed four Bob Crosby vocals. *Those Things I Can't Forget* is scored, none too effectively, with a tenor-sax lead, things loosen up after Bob's vocal, but the ad-lib finale sounds reticent. Jess Stacy is the main soloist on *I'll Keep Thinking of You* (with vocal asides from Nappy Lamare), and on *A Precious Memory,* both of which have ensembles that sound neat rather than inspired (the latter has a brief interlude in which the ensemble intriguingly offers a few quotes from Louis Armstrong's *Cornet Chop Suey*). The liveliest item amongst the four sides is *I've Nothing To Live For Now,* which has a good relaxed vocal from Bob, and sparkling choruses from D'Amico and Miller. The most jarring aspect of this date was the choice of material. The four songs recorded (all by different composers) sound like entries for a contest to find the most unsophisticated combination of melody and lyrics ever devised.

The band were happy to be back in Chicago, particularly Jess Stacy, who had many old friends to see. He also met a new friend whilst working with the Crosby band in Chicago, her name was Patricia, years later they re-met and were married in 1950. During the early 1940s Jess's wife was the noted vocaliste, Lee Wiley, but that union soon ended in divorce. Jess's sensitivity extended beyond his piano playing, and during one Crosby session he thought he was the target for some vicious glances emanating from Hank D'Amico. With worry written all over his face Jess apologised to a non-plussed D'Amico, who later explained that the hard looks were directed at drummer Ray Bauduc.

Following their stay in Chicago, the Crosby band moved off to play a long series of one-night stands, which in a series of stepping-stone hops took them into New York City for the first time in 15 months. En route the band had a worrying experience whilst playing a theatre date. One of their trombonists was missing when the band took its place behind the closed curtains. Various telephone calls were made, but the missing man couldn't be traced anywhere, the full band played the show one short, then handed over to the Bob Cats for their featured spot. As a fresh set of Bob Cats drums were unveiled on stage, in front of the audience, the missing trombonist was found. He was happily sleeping off a hangover seated behind Bauduc's spare kit.

Usually a self-imposed discipline avoided mishaps like that one, and even when the individual members did long road journeys on to the next gig they maintained punctuality. The Crosby band suffered very few road mishaps despite their busy touring schedule. Bob himself had a scrape during the band's early tour in Georgia, and Zurke once nonchalantly turned an auto on its back at high speed without doing much damage to himself. Driving in heavy rain near Philadelphia in the early summer of 1941, Jess Stacy narrowly averted a nasty accident when he temporarily lost control of the car. Fortunately, Jess avoided any serious injury, but admitted at the time, "It shook the hell out of me", however he was able to travel on to link-up with the band on the last stages of their trek to New York.

During the Crosby band residency at New York's Strand Theatre, Gil Rodin decided to implement an idea that he had been toying with for some months. He made contact with the band's former star trumpeter, Yank Lawson, and asked him to rejoin. Because of a Musicians' Union ruling Yank couldn't suddenly quit the theatre orchestra with whom he was then working, he had to complete a long period of notice, but he assured Rodin, that if terms were agreed upon, he would be willing to rejoin his old colleagues. The news had an up-lifting effect on all of the founder-members, particularly Ray Bauduc, who had sorely missed Yank's emphatic leading of the Bob Cats' ensembles.

Whilst Lawson was fulfilling the last part of his run-of-the-show contract, the Crosby band did two recording sessions in New York. The first title cut, *Do You Care?* is one of Bob Crosby's superior vocals, he pitches his low notes with ease, and sounds romatically expressive throughout. The Bob-o-Links flutter around him then after a brief Eddie Miller solo, Bob is granted a reprise and the song ends with a 16 bar vocal. On the next title, the band's new vocaliste, Liz Tilton, recorded her first song with the band, *Will You Still Be Mine?*, a pleasant enough ballad. Liz Tilton (whose sister Martha sang with Benny Goodman), had a voice which didn't transmit a vast depth of feeling, but both her pitching and her range were satisfactory, and the light texture of her singing had a certain charm.

The first of the two instrumentals from the May 1941 session, *You're a Darlin' Devil,* is a Paul Weston arrangement of his own composition. Unison saxophones play the inoffensive theme, then a modulation introduces some elegant rhapsodising from Eddie Miller, the emphasis remains on the reeds as some "Glenn Millerish" scoring ends the piece. The next title *Big Tom* is much more interesting. It opens with Bauduc producing a tympani-like effect from his tom-toms, the timbre of which is echoed by low register trombones, then, (not quite so effectively) by low-register trumpets. Bob Goodrich plays a genteel 16 bar plunger-muted solo, followed by some atmospheric D'Amico clarinet playing (similar in mood to Artie Shaw's earlier performance on *Traffic Jam*). The trombones pump emphatically at a simple, hauntingly repetitious figure, prior to the trumpets' strident motif. The arrangement ends in rondo with the tom-toms and trombones repeating their opening ploy.

The June 30the 1941 session began with a vocal feature for Eddie Miller, Big Bill Broonzy's composition *It Was Only a Dream*. Eddie usually sounded effective when singing the blues, but he never seems to settle into this four chorus vocal. The next item recorded, *Elmer's Tune*, is a long way, musically, from Bill Broonzy's Chicago South Side, it was a popular song of the period, catchy without a trace of significance. The Crosby band's version juxtaposes a commercial reading of the melody with some unrestricted piano work from Jess Stacy. The pianist's 24 bar solo is a pearl within a Tin Pan Alley oyster, the pieces other attraction is a brief, but pleasant-toned trumpet solo from Bob Goodrich.

This was to be Goodrich's last recording with the band, it was also Hank D'Amico's farewell date. D'Amico's clarinet is featured on the third cut of the day, *The Angels Came Thru'*, he makes it a telling final appearance by performing the opening melody with a superb amount of expression. Recordings were not always kind to D'Amico's tone, but this sounds to be a warm, attractive performance.

In July 1941, the Bob Crosby band began a three week vacation, its first lengthy break for several years. Almost all of the New Orleans members made a pilgrimage back to their home city, most of the remainder of the band relaxed at sea-side resorts with their families. Rodin, as usual, was the last one in the organisation to sign off, before he could take things easy he had to make sure that all the details concerning Yank Lawson's return to the band had been finalised. He also had to finalise the acquisition of a trumpeter new to the band, Lyman Vunk, who was planning to leave Charlie Barnet. Vunk replaced Al King, whilst Lawson took Bob Goodrich's place. Another newcomer was trombonist, Moe Zudecoff who was added to the band to augment the trombone section into a three piece unit.

When his administrative tasks had been completed, Gil Rodin issued a press statement: "We'll have the greatest band, musically, in the business. When we open at Catalina Island in August, the Crosby Band will be at its peak. The Bob-o-Links are finishing up with us this month. Lyman Vunk will leave Charlie Barnet and join us August 1st in Oklahoma City. Yank Lawson, and Moe Zudecoff will be with the band when we get together again shortly after our vacation is ended".

In general, the music critics were delighted with the personnel changes, which *Down Beat* magazine said had "re-dixied" the band. George Frazier, the often hard-hitting New England critic, welcomed them enthusiastically· "Yank Lawson, or what his playing represents, is what the band has needed desperately for some time. The Crosby brand of jazz requires, above all else, an authoritative driving trumpet, and ever since Muggsy Spanier left there's been no one to fill the bill. The chief change though will have taken in the band's attitude toward the kind of music it should produce. Gil Rodin has witnessed the enthusiastic reaction to the head arrangements that have been tried out lately, and is finally convinced that the band's strongest point is its unsullied jazz".

George T. Simon of *Metronome* pointed out that Rodin's strategy during 1940 and 1941 showed he wasn't infallible, "Gil proved that when he suddenly decided to change the band's style and went out and hired a vocal quartet called the Bob-o-Links, and put in orders for a lot of dull, schmaltzy arrangements. And, as a further de-emphasis upon the band's dixieland style, he also got some killer-diller arrangements. Commercially, the move wasn't bad. In fact, the band went ahead and made some movies and a lot of money. But after a year of this, the monotony began to tell on Messrs. Miller, Bauduc, Matlock, Haggart and others, and the band began to sound worse and worse. Come to think of it, it sounded down-right terrible. If one man ever remade the Bob Crosby band that man was Yank Lawson".

Hank D'Amico's departure, (he left to lead his own band in upstate New York), meant that Matty Matlock again resumed the role of clarinet soloist, and he was delighted to do so. After Rodin had dispensed with the services of the Bob-o-Links, one of its members, Tony Paris, stayed on for a while to assist with the band's administration, and to take the occasional vocal.

During the Crosby band's season on Catalina Island they played from 9pm until midnight at the Casino Ballroom on weekdays, on Sunday evenings they only played for one hour, from 6pm until 7, providing dinner music at St. Catherine's Hotel. This schedule gave the members of the band ample time to follow various sporting pursuits. The ball team was again revived, and soon trounced a team of Fuller's Brush Men 24-4, however they failed against their adversaries of the previous year, the Catalina Police team. Eddie Miller still smarts over that defeat, "They were supposed to be the local police team, but they were all the police force's own physical training instructors, and I'm not kidding. They sure didn't want to lose to us musicians, and as I was running for a base, with time to spare, one of these great big guys charged into me and sent me flying. I went yards up into the air, and landed completely winded, but with no bones broken, and nobody said a word".

Yank Lawson issued a challenge to all-comers at tennis and this led to a memorable victory over Bob Crosby. All of the golfers made sure they were on the course early. Matty Matlock was a keen golfer, but he was a much better musician. On one of his early visits to the Catalina course he managed to drive a ball straight on to another player's head, rendering him unconscious. When the cry went up for a doctor, it was discovered that Matty had knocked out the only m.d. on the island.

Besides tennis and golf, several of the band also went on fishing expeditions. Yank Lawson was one of them, "The ballroom that we played in was owned by Wrigley's, they also owned the boats that were hired out to the holiday makers. We were allowed concessions, we could hire a boat out for a dollar a day, so we went fishing, you could catch King Mackerel, Yellow Tails, all sorts of fish. Come evening time, we changed and went to work, and we'd all line up outside on the ballroom balcony and play *Avalon* (which was composed on Catalina Island). The dancers would then know that things were about to get under way".

"It was very peaceful on Catalina, they didn't allow automobiles. Once a week we'd catch the water'bus into Los Angeles, which was about 26 miles away, so that we could do our regular radio show and recordings. The water sometimes got bumpy on that run, and not every one in the band was a good sailor. There were often green faces by the time we reached L.A.".

The Crosby band did two Los Angeles recording sessions for Decca during September 1941. Eight of the nine titles were commercially slanted vocals, but on the one instrumental, *Take It Easy* (composed and arranged by Bob Haggart), Yank takes a 32 bar plunger-muted solo that exemplifies the very merits that the critics had been stressing. It exudes virility, but does not generate into a show of brute force. The ideas are all rhythmic and skilfully shaped, and they are presented in Yank's unique sound. The opening theme, played by the trombones, has some delightful piano interjections from Stacy, and following Lawson's estimable solo, the band builds up a telling series of call-and-answer patterns that are climaxed by the phrases of the high register clarinet trio.

One thing that becomes immediately apparent from these sessions is just how much difference the presence of a third trombone had made to the band. Zudecoff's arrival at last ensured that the trombones had a satisfying section sound, which is heard, giving a sturdy edge to the lively two-beat treatment afforded *A Gay Ranchero*. The trombone choir also performs the opening melody on *I'm Trusting In Love* in fine style. Moe Zudecoff (who later became famous as bandleader, Buddy Morrow), wasn't restricted to a section role, he also plays melody solos on *Something New, A Sinner Kissed an Angel,* and *Two in Love*. He makes the most of these half-chorus spots, playing them in a style reminiscent of Tommy Dorsey (without quite achieving Dorsey's velvet tone).

The Catalina season ended in September 1941, but the band remained in California, combining its radio studio work with a residency at the Trianon Ballroom, in Southgate, Los Angeles. The band also made broadcasts from the Trianon, and it was noticeable to listeners that successes from the band's earlier period, like *Honky Tonk Train Blues* and *South Rampart Street Parade,* were being reintroduced. The band's regular Friday evening radio show was the prestigious "Three Ring Time" sponsored by Ballantine's Ales. During late 1941, singer Liz Tilton left and was replaced by petite Gloria De Haven.

The Crosby band were particularly delighted to be chosen to provide music for the Paramount movie *Holiday Inn,* which featured Bing Crosby and Fred Astaire. Their assignment was to record part of the soundtrack, and in order to do this they were booked for a sixty day schedule. Paramount not only had to pay the Crosby band for this period, they also had to book an equal number of local musicians to 'stand by', as per a local union rule which insisted "only musicians who had been members of the Hollywood Branch of the union for a year or more could take part in film recordings". The band felt an affinity with the film's musical director, Robert Emmett 'Bob' Dolan, and enjoyed working with him, But, whilst the production of *Holiday Inn* was being finalised, the history of the world was dramatically changed by the Japanese attack on Pearl Harbour.

Chapter 12
Wartime woes

Because of the possibility of a suprise attack by the Japanese on California, the West Coast entertainment industry went topsy-turvy during the early days after America's entry into World War II. Ballrooms were temporarily closed, and those that remained open were subject to sudden blackouts throughout the evening. After the Californian authorities took stock of the situation they eased the restrictions and allowed most entertainments centres to resume their activities. Having suffered a temporary deprivation, the public flocked to the dance halls when they were re-opened and for several months there was an attendance boom.

The Bob Crosby band were not only kept busy in the Californian ballrooms during the early part of the war, they also spent a good deal of time working in various film studios, making appearances in *Reveille with Beverly, Presenting Lily Mars* and other movies. When the band had finished their work on the *Holiday Inn* film soundtrack, thev began another residency at the Trianon Ballroom (starting there on the 19th February 1942). For arranger Paul Weston, working on the *Holiday Inn* movie proved to be one of the most important assignments in his career, "I did all the writing for Fred Astaire's dance numbers, and some of the Bing Crosby and Fred Astaire duets and this got me started at Paramount studios".

Because of these growing commitments, Paul Weston's work as an arranger for Bob Crosby's band was gradually coming to an end, this brought more prominence to the work of another arranger, Norman "Buddy" Baker, hired by Gil Rodin as a freelance whilst the band were playing their initial residency at the Trianon. "At the Hollywood Palladium, Gil Rodin heard some of the arrangements that I had written for the Casa Loma Band, he approached me and asked me to write for the Crosby band. Gil said he wanted both Paul Weston and myself to try and change the "all-dixieland" approach, to develop a style that was something that was as recognizable as Benny Goodman's Band, but without copying any aspect of Goodman's style. So we set out to find a unique sound for the Crosby band, one that all the musicians would feel at home with. But to tell the truth I don't think we ever found anything original in the way of a sound or a new style for the band, and Bob Haggart and Matty Matlock continued to write excellent Dixieland styled things for the band. I was paid per arrangement, and never travelled with the band. I found scoring for the Crosby band quite unusual at the time, because there were three alto saxophonists (Art Mendelsohn, Doc Rando and Matty Matlock), one tenor sax (Eddie Miller) and Gil Rodin on baritone sax."

Gil Rodin was pleased that the band was again getting highly favourable reviews, but he was uncertain as to whether it was a good idea to return wholeheartedly to a dixieland policy, hence his request to Buddy Baker. This same edging of bets caused Gil to commission several arrangements from Phil Moore. Moore, who had been a staff arranger at MGM in Hollywood for several years, had recently moved over to begin a successful stay at the Paramount studios.

The work of both new arrangers, Baker and Moore, was featured on the Crosby band's first recording session of 1942. The first tune cut, *Vultee Special* was a musical tribute to the aircraft manufacturers, Vultee, it was a straightforward 8-in-the-bar blues, which is introduced by a repetitive trombone figure. Yank Lawson solos briefly then Jess Stacy plays two choruses of boogie-woogie neither of which carry much punch. Buddy Morrow plays two muted choruses, then Stacy is allocated another solo, which he happily performs in his natural style. The opus, co-composed by Bob Crosby and Gil Rodin, is not the prototype of anything new.

The next number, *Russian Sailor's Dance* was labelled as being arranged by Crosby and Rodin, whereas it was actually orchestrated by Buddy Baker. Trombonist Morrow displays considerable technique in the opening cadenzas, then the saxophones pick up the main theme in tempo, their phrasing is superb and sounds as well co-ordinated as any sax team the band ever had; Nappy Lamare's guitar is also well presented. After Jess Stacy's subtle 24 bar piano solo, the clean-cut saxes repeat the opening theme with an admirable mixture of precision and enthusiasm.

A Zoot Suit feature some effective singing by Nappy Lamare, who wails a plea for one of the sartorial extravaganzas of the early war period; Miller and Matlock play brief fluent solos. On the next cut it was Eddie's turn to sing. His offering is a long, anecdotal saga about *Barrelhouse Bessie*. Yank Lawson's open tone gives a muscular lift to a mechanical tune, then Eddie begins expounding the lyrics of a convuluted tale. He sticks to his task manfully, but the length of the ditty only allows time for him to play a few bars of sumptuous tenor saxophone.

Phil Moore's *Brass Boogie* was issued on two sides of a 78 rpm recording, a procedure usually reserved for auspicious creations, unfortunately the piece is all too ordinary, in effect, a twelve bar blues plus trimmings. The saxophones are absent from this title. A deliberately dissonant beginning gives way to four loosely connected, tritish ensemble choruses. Jess Stacy is featured at length, but sounds stiff-backed and cautious in each of his three long innings. Bob Haggart is heard soloing on bass, and later has the opportunity to revive his whistling party trick; Yank Lawson and Buddy Morrow (both muted) have walking-on parts each lasting 12 bars. In the final chorus the trumpets are given the chance to demonstrate their "shake" effects, an opportunity they don't make the most of. A brief coda from Stacy leads the brass ensemble on to a rich-sounding finishing chord. Nothing memorable happens in either part one or part two.

As if to keep all options open, Gil Rodin arranged that the next recording session, a week later, was devoted entirely to recordings of established dixieland favourites, such as *Sugar Foot Stomp, Eccentric,* and *Milenberg Joys,* all were up-tempo pieces. *Sugar Foot Stomp* and *King Porter Stomp* (both scored by Bob Haggart), closely follow the arrangements originated by King Oliver's Creole Jazz Band and Fletcher Henderson's Orchestra respectively. Yank Lawson performs the expected three chorus trumpet solo in blazing style, but still manages to stamp his own personality on the recreation. Matlock sounds faintly unhappy about his part in the piece, and the final ensemble remains a little too non-feverish. The standout feature of this title, and indeed, for the whole session, is the superb lift that Bauduc's drumming gives to the proceedings.

Matty Matlock's arrangement of *Jimtown Blues* (a tune originally published in 1925) is the best item from the date. Here the arranger's clarinet playing sounds warm and vital, relaxed but involved. Eddie Miller creates yet another vibrant solo and the drums (aided by Haggart's energetic bass-playing) bring the super-charged arrangement to a stirring finish. *Eccentric* begins with a time-honoured introductory format, but gradually welcome new effects and ideas surface within the arrangement. A nice melody duet between Matlock and Miller transpires, and later the same two musicians vie for top soloist's role in their abundantly friendly way. The final chorus is truly ingenious.

Rumbustious trombones give a rousing start to *Milenberg Joys.* The first ensemble chorus is full of harmonic depth and subtlety, then comes a vigorous interlude played by the Bob Cats contingent, who temporarily separate themselves for the main group. Matlock solos convincingly, then Miller excels his own high standards by playing one of his most hard-hitting choruses. In the final chorus, Haggart echoes the three-ring circus effect of his earlier arrangements. The least satisfactory arrangement of the bunch is Matlock's *Original Dixieland One Step,* on which the writing takes on a stilted quality, making it difficult for the band to drop into a swinging groove, but there is consolation in the earthy sounds of Floyd O'Brien's trombone solo.

On a test of performance, the "Dixieland" recording session was far superior to the "Swing" date, both in spirit and invention. Broad minded fans who liked swing and dixieland saw nothing reactionary in preferring the Crosby band to stress its unique qualities rather than belatedly chase after the swing express long after it had moved on.

Gil Rodin's vacillation between swing and dixieland was partly caused by a worsening in relations between the band and its recording company, Decca. A big selling record, in either style, would have ended the seemingly inevitable disagreements that both sides had over the sort of material that the band should record. *Metronome* magazine mentioned this rift in March 1942, "The Crosby band has repeatedly expressed dissatisfaction with recording tunes it has been assigned during the past months".

The Crosby band drew huge crowds to the Trianon ballroom during their second residency, but beneath the happy party spirit that the audiences generated there were undertones of apprehension. Nearly every family in the USA had been affected by service recruitment, and restrictions were making travelling for pleasure increasingly difficult. After the Trianon stay ended the band did a series of dates in N.W. California then returned to Los Angeles.

During this period, the vocal department saw yet another change, Gloria De Haven left to fulfil a lucrative film contract. Muriel Lane temporarily filled the vacancy with the band, but in April 1942, Gil Rodin made a more permanent change and brought in two girl singers - the identical Wilde twins, Lyn and Lee. The two youngsters, who had previously worked with Ray Noble and Charlie Barnet, were still only 18 years old. Lee spoke of her days with the Crosby band: "Sis and I were so young, shy and fearful. All the guys were great to us (more like father figures). I remember while we were at the Rendezvous Ballroom in Balboa Beach, I got a painful case of impetigo and 'Doc' Rando cured it for me. Yank Lawson, who has twins of his own, was another one who was particularly kind to us. I also remember that when we sang, Bob Crosby would introduce us as 'the two frightened gazelles'."

Lee Wilde's story of Rando's remedial skills is only one of many such tributes, on several occasions "Doc" gave medical aid to members of the Crosby band and their families. Bob Haggart's infant son's distended umbilical cord was successfully treated, as was Billy Butterfield's eye, which was injured by a tiny metal fragment that flew off a Chicago Loop train. Arthur Rando had been a dentist in New Orleans before he became a professional musician, after he left the Crosby band he qualified as a doctor and became an eminent cardiac specialist.

In May 1942, just prior to playing a residency at the Casa Manana Ballroom in Culver City, the Crosby band completed their *Holiday Inn* duties by backing Bing Crosby, Fred Astaire and Margaret Lenhart in various recordings. Buddy Morrow's trombone is featured, and Yank Lawson contributes a scorching solo to Bing's *I've Got Plenty To Be Thankful For,* but mostly the band's task is to provide a melodious background. The two loosest arrangements are the Bob Cat backings for Bing's *When My Dreamboat Comes In* and *Walking The Floor.*

Early in June 1942, Bob Crosby temporarily took over brother Bing's role as master of ceremonies on the Kraft Cheese radio programme *The Kraft Music Hall.* Bing went off on vacation, taking time out to play some exhibition golf games. The Bob Cats, and not the full band, accompanied Bob on the show, and apparently went to their task with alacrity.

This new edition of the Bob Cats, (with the Lawson/Matlock/Miller/O'Brien front line), generated a broad, healthy sound on the recordings they made in

Los Angeles during this period, particularly noticeable on the stirring version of *It's a Long Way to Tipperary.* Yank Lawson's trumpet sets things going with a reveille call, but seemingly this fails to rouse Jess Stacy, for there is no sign of the pianist on either take of this number. Matlock is in inventive form on all four items from the session, the regular playing schedule had redeveloped the pleasant sound of his low register. Miller is his usual effervescent self and Floyd O'Brien is given more limelight than usual, taking robust solos on *Sweethearts on Parade* and *Tin Roof Blues,* a week later, O'Brien was also featured on two of the Bob Cats' accompaniments for Bob Crosby. All three of Bob's offerings are country-and -western numbers, two of them written by the famous cowboy-actor, Gene Autry. The fourth title of the session was a happy-go-lucky version of *Way Down Yonder in New Orleans,* which begins with Eddie Miller and Nappy Lamare chatting about the virtues of Creole cooking, and various other Louisiana delights, Nappy then takes the medium-tempo vocal. Matlock, Miller and Stacy all contribute gorgeous solos, and the final ensemble bustles with invention and musical team spirit.

The same cannot be said about everything on the big band session that took place later that month, even though all four items were instrumentals. Two of them are Phil Moore orchestrations, *Black Zephyr* and *Black Surreal.* The band perform these pieces well enough, and there is no question of slacking by the soloists, but the transmission of feeling that graces all memorable recordings is missing. *Black Zephyr* is a well constructed melody, taken at medium tempo. It is introduced by Matlock's clarinet, the supporting brass play background phrases 'in hat' utilising harmonies that are more chromatic than those usually employed in Crosby band arrangements. Eddie Miller plays a long, exploratory solo that is full of interesting ideas, and Yank Lawson shares out energy and enterprise in his muted solo; Buddy Morrow on trombone sounds svelte and well in command. The companion piece, *Black Surreal* is distinctly Ellingtonish, with Matlock being cast in a Barney Bigard-like role, given the task of playing swooping runs over a figured bass line. Lawson fashions a Cootie Williams-like growl here and there, and the blending of muted trumpets and clarinet revives an old Ducal tone colour. The rhythm section deliberately stresses four-beats-in-a-bar behind Eddie Miller's well defined solo then Lawson's sturdy, plungered sound re-enters to wrap things up.

Equally adventurous harmonically, but with a much more interesting format is *Chain Gang,* an extended composition by Bob Haggart, which richly deserved being granted a 12 inch 78 rpm issue. It is virtually a miniature tone poem, one that opens with a melange of varying timbre, supplemented by the simulated sounds of anvil tapping. Lawson's plunger playing is again highly evocative, as is Matlock's clarinet solo, played over an ostinato rhythm. Both O'Brien and Miller create absorbing patterns on a simple chord sequence, then Lawson re-emerges, more ferocious than usual, and yells out another convincing plunger solo. The reed scoring in the final section is highly reminiscent of Duke Ellington's 1940 innovations, but overall the piece gives more than a glimpse of Haggart's vast store of originality.

The original coupling for *Chain Gang* was a Jess Stacy piano feature, given the witty title *Ecstacy,* by record producer Milt Gabler. On this, his own composition, Stacy is superb throughout, conjuring up wistfulness, elegance and warmth with seeming ease. The band's role is a subsidiary one, but the clarinet team's trilling is delightfully performed.

In March 1942, the band concluded its recording activities for five months by cutting five vocals, four from Bob Crosby (supported by a vocal quartet) and one - a novelty offering of *Dear Old Donegal* in 6/8 time - by Muriel Lane. Bob imparts a gentle lilt to the up-tempo *Don't Sit Under The Apple Tree,* which has nuggets of improvisation from Lawson and Miller. On *Last Call For Love,* Lawson plays a delightful obligatto to Crosby's vocal, using a solotone mute with considerable finesse and delicacy. The balance on these five sides, and the scoring, allows us to clearly hear Gil Rodin playing a robust, not unattractive section role on baritone sax. Rodin was no threat to Harry Carney, but despite the five packs a day intake, his lungs certainly filled the big saxophone.

The Bob Crosby band had been offered a return booking to play again on Catalina during the summer of 1942, but by then Californian Defence Regulations decreed that the island was officially a "war zone", and this meant that the Wrigley Company had to abandon its holiday entertainment plans. A new season soon materialised for the Crosby band which took them to the Rendezvous Ballroom at Balboa Beach, about 60 miles south of Los Angeles. Throughout their stay there (July 3rd to September 5th), the band did "turnaway" business.

Several personnel changes occurred within the Crosby Band during the summer of 1942. Trombonist Elmer Smithers left to join the musical staff at Paramount Studios, and his place was taken by ex-Ben Pollack player, Bruce Squires. Then a little later on, when Buddy Morrow departed to work in the east coast studios he was replaced by Pete Carpenter, who had previously worked at Balboa with Gil Evans' Band. Carpenter, now a highly successful composer of film and television scores, recalls the events, "Buddy Morrow left, and Paul Weston who was arranging for the band asked if I would like to work for the summer at Balboa. I really was thrilled to work with the Crosby Band, and was in awe of players I had heard for some time. I enjoyed the summer and subsequently played a few one-nighters with the band then left to do studio work for ABC and CBS".

Art Mendelsohn left the saxophone section before the Balboa season started and his place on alto was taken by Ted Klein, who as Ted McKay had been working as a copyist for the Crosby band. By the late spring of 1942 the band had five full-time singers, Bob Crosby, David Street, Tommy Skeffington and Wilde twins. Both Street and Skeffington did solo numbers but they also teamed up with the two girls to resurrect a "Bob-o-Links" type quartet. Two new arrangers, Billy May and Axel Stordahl occasionally contributed scores for the big band.

The Wilde twins got the break that changed their lives whilst the Bob Crosby band were taking part in the filming of *Presenting Lily Mars*. The band, augmented by a string section, appeared in a night club sequence, during which Bob Crosby was given a brief chance to act alongside the film's stars, Judy Garland and Van Heflin. Originally there were no plans to include the Wilde twins in the film, but things turned out differently, as Lee explains, "We were not supposed to be in the picture, but we were visiting on the set. Joe Pasternak, the producer, saw us and asked Bob Crosby to let us sing for him. As a result, we were in that picture, and subsequently put under contract to M.G.M.". The twins were later to feature in many other movies, they were also seen with the Crosby band in *Reveille with Beverly*.

The Crosby band were easily able to make the trip from Balboa Beach to Decca's Los Angeles studios, and during July 1942 they made the journey several times in order to help the record company's plans to stockpile material in the face of an impending strike by the Musicians' Union. The Union eventually forbade its members to record from 31st July 1942 onwards, as a move to obtain fees for recordings played on juke boxes and radio stations. The ban affected Decca and Capitol's output until mid-September 1943, the dispute with other recording companies was not resolved until November 1944.

The martial times were reflected in almost all of the numbers the Crosby band recorded during July 1942, they included *The Marine's Hymn*, *Anchors Aweigh* and *Army Air Corps*. Bob Haggart conceived some spirited arrangements for these various anthems, often allowing Matlock's clarinet to roam over the scored arrangement, as in days of yore. The band's version of *Over There* (complete with verse) brings back strong memories of *South Rampart Street Parade*, particularly in the presentation of the low register clarinet solo; Yank Lawson plays a particularly spectacular solo on this one. Eddie Miller contributes brief forthright solos to several numbers, but is heard at length on *Where Do We Go From Here?*, and the ultra-lively *Pack Up Your Troubles In Your Old Kit Bag, and Smile, Smile, Smile*. The one Bob Crosby vocal from the three sessions is the light hearted *When You Think of Lovin'*, on which the Wilde twins are also given the chance to shine.

On *Army Air Corps*, the last title that the full band recorded, both Lawson and Matlock deliberately stress the melody in their solos. During two atmospheric interludes, band members shout "Clear, Clear, Contact, Contact", bringing a reminder that in those days twin engined bombers were the rule. For some of the musicians the service shouts turned out to be a rehearsal for events in real life. The Bob Cats recordings on the 30th July proved to be their last, it was not a glorious finale to years of magnificent achievement, but simply a series of polite backings for singer Mary Lee. The only lasting joy that emerges from this unlikely liaison comes from Eddie Miller's consistently swinging tenor-sax solos.

The false optimism engendered during the heady summer of 1942 evaporated with the news that from October 4th 1942 there were to be severe restrictions affecting the use of passenger trains. These new rules concerning travel priorities were certain to disrupt several long journeys that were to form the basis of the Crosby band's scheduled winter tour. New, more stringent regulations on the private use of gasoline were also introduced.

Faced with the ever-increasing problems of travel, and of finding replacements for musicians called up in the draft, Glenn Miller, one of the most successful big band leaders of the era decided to call it a day. He disbanded and entered the services, he was soon a commissioned officer in the Army Air Force, detailed to organise a big service band.

To the astonishment of their colleagues, Gil Rodin and Ray Bauduc announced that they were going to enlist in the Artillery. Eddie Miller recalls the shock, "We were all taken completely by suprise. We thought that they would wait to be called like the rest of us, but I guess that because they had no children, they thought they might as well volunteer as be drafted". Rodin and Bauduc left together and on the 28th September 1942 joined the Coast Artillery Band stationed at Vallejo, California. Musically, Bauduc was the greater loss, he had long been one of the band's star performers, but Rodin, having been President and Business Manager of the Corporation, was virtually irreplaceable as an administrator.

Chapter 13

The final tour

In the last week of September 1942, the Crosby band, with several new-comers within its ranks, left California for a 10 week tour of theatres. Their itinerary included Omaha, Minneapolis, Milwaukee, Chicago, Detroit, Cleveland, Buffalo, Newark, Philadelphia and concluded with a week's booking (11th-17th December) at the RKO Theatre in Boston, Massachusetts. Eddie Miller recalls. "We knew the end of the band was near, so we decided to make as much money as we could in the time left to us. This meant playing a whole string of theatre dates, but even then the transport problems gave us a continual headache. I can remember seeing all of the band's gear being piled high on a rail station and thinking 'How are we ever going to make the next date?' But we did somehow".

The band set out to earn big grosses on that tour, and they succeeded. Working on percentages of the door take they grossed an average of 20,000 dollars on each week of the tour, topping 36,000 dollars for their week's stint at the Michigan Theatre in Detroit. Plans for the tour had been finalised by Gil Rodin before he left to join the services. Rodin's place on baritone saxophone was taken by Bob Mario (then known as Mario Bobadilla), Ray Bauduc was replaced by an ex-Glenn Miller sideman, drummer Cody Sandifer (from Arlington, Texas). Other personnel changes had taken place before the theatre tour began. Trumpeter Max Herman left at the end of the Balboa engagement to join the U.S. Coast Guard Band, he was replaced by Johnny Best. Trombonist Bruce Squires enlisted in the Ferry Command Band, and his place was taken by Harry Uhlman, who in turn was replaced by Blaise Turi, who joined the band in Omaha, Nebraska, after the tour had begun. "I flew from Los Angeles to Omaha after working out my two weeks notice with Abe Lyman's Orchestra, and almost immediately went on stage with the Crosby band, wearing a jacket 3 sizes too big for me. Bob and the guys were very nice to me. I was the baby in the band, 18 years old".

When Gil Rodin joined the services, the rest of the band decided that it would be best if Eddie Miller kept a watchful eye on the band's organisation and travel arrangements. All went fairly smoothly, except for one occasion when part of the band's equipment went astray and some of the band had to borrow instruments from a pit orchestra who were working at the theatre with them. As usual, each man in the band maintained a totally professional outlook on behaviour and timekeeping, though there was one small blemish which is still remembered with humour. Somehow Yank Lawson and Johnny

Best misjudged the time it would take them to get to the theatre from where they were relaxing, the result was that Lyman Vunk had to play most of the show as the sole member of the trumpet section. Johnny Best, a newcomer to the band, apologised profusely to Miller, who gave him a cool look, and said "Look, you're over 21 aren't you?". This cryptic admonition remained a running-gag in what turned out to be a life-long friendship between the two musicians.

Word of the band's intention to make this a farewell tour reached *Down Beat*, who published an item in its November 1st 1942 issue hinting that the end was near "because of draft losses and transportation problems". This story was emphatically denied by MCA, the band's agents, who were hoping against hope that a magical solution could be found to the difficulties caused by World War II. Their optimism was unfounded, things soon got decidely worse, and before long, one bandleader, Jack Teagarden, lost 17 musicians to the services during a space of four months.

Originally, the Bob Crosby band had planned that there sould be a neat cessation of their activities following the December booking in Boston, but as no-one in the band was certain of the date on which they would be called up, MCA persuaded the corporation to consider working together for as long as possible. But, by late 1942, Bob Crosby, acting on the previous decision to disband, had accepted a contract to become a film actor, and he was also in line for the job of compering a regular West Coast radio show. There was no Gil Rodin on hand to engineer an easy solution to the problem, so the matter was put to the vote and it was decided that if Bob Crosby was otherwise engaged, then Eddie Miller would be appointed as the band's leader.

A trade magazine made the situation seem more acrimonious than it was, by reporting, "When Gil Rodin bowed out there was a psychological clash between Bob Crosby and the bandsmen as to who was the most important - the 'name' front man or the band. Bob with the new MGM contract in his pocket evidently turned up his ace-in-the-hole, and said 'Here you are boys. You can go to the coast with me as leader, and I mean leader, or I go to the coast alone and you go on your way'." The report was an over-dramatic exaggeration, no such ultimatum was presented by Bob Crosby, and writer George T. Simon, who was at the band's December 1942 Boston date, stressed, "Despite erroneous reports there was no semblance of hard feelings, whatsoever. Not only were all the men high in their praises of Crosby, but Bob himself couldn't rave enough for his men". Simon added ruefully that the engagement "ends an era in jazz history, perhaps just for a spell, perhaps forever".

When the Boston engagement ended, most of the musicians made their way back home to their families in California, some via New Orleans. Yank Lawson and Bob Haggart, who still had homes in the New York area, remained in the east to await a call from their local draft boards. Jess Stacy also stayed in the east in order to rejoin Benny Goodman's band.

To all intents and purposes it seemed as though the Bob Crosby band had played its final date, but when the musicians who had returned to California took stock of the draft sitution, they realized that it might be months before any of them were called, so, early in 1943, Bob Crosby took a big band out for a brief series of dates in Southern California. The engagements were billed as the Crosby band's "farewell appearances", within the personnel were Eddie Miller, Matty Matlock, Nappy Lamare, and Doc Rando. During the tour, Eddie Miller confirmed to a local *Down Beat* correspondent that there was no question of a permanent reunion of the band, Bob Crosby's impending commitments in the film studios made this impossible.

When the tour with Crosby ended, Eddie Miller was approached by the GAC agency and asked to form up his own big band, which he did, using several ex-Crosby musicians, including Matlock, Rando, Lamare and Floyd O'Brien. The band got off to a fine start by immediately gaining a contract to work on a Universal movie featuring Donald O'Connor and Jean Ryan, entitled *Mister Big,* in the billing for the film the group was listed as "Eddie Miller's Bob Cats".

Offers of West Coast work came flooding in for the new band, and Eddie Miller's friendly personality and superb musicianship soon won over the Californian ballroom crowds. An early appearance at the Hollywood Palladium in the spring of 1943 received an enthusiastic review in *Down Beat,* which began, "The Bob Crosby Band - without Crosby", and went on to say "the flavour of the old band remains, but there's a new spark here that promises to flare into something mighty good. Miller's book is studded with standards associated with the days when the Crosby Band was in its never-too-happy heyday as a co-op unit".

Eddie's great pal, Matty Matlock, did most of the new arrangements for the 15 piece band (5 saxes, 3 trumpets, 3 trombones and four rhythm). Nappy Lamare was featured on vocals, and Eddie sang a few numbers himself, but most of the vocalising was done by a girl singer who was new to California, Mickey Roy, originally from Kansas City. Eddie Miller occasionally broke the band down into a small Bob Cats like unit, with a front line consisting of himself, Matlock on clarinet, O'Brien on trombone and Hal Barnett on trumpet. Nick Fatool, on drums sparked the four piece rhythm section, which had Lamare on guitar. The *Down Beat* review was typical of the favourable reactions that greeted the formation of Miller's band, the unusual, almost unique, aspect of the magazine critique was that it specifically mentioned that all had not been heavenly bliss in the old band.

Meanwhile, Bob Crosby's commitments at the film studios proved to be nothing like as time-consuming as he had originally envisaged, and he found himself with ample time to guest on various radio shows. For these broadcast dates Bob fronted a pick-up band consisting of freelance studio musicians, and although the unit was announced on the air as Bob Crosby's Orchestra, Bob pointed out in print that the acceptance of these dates did not mean that he was contemplating a return to full-time bandleading. Despite Bob's attempts to make the position clear, many of the old band's fans found the situation extremely confusing, particularly since what had been the Bob Crosby Fan Club Magazine was now devoted to Eddie Miller's Band. It led to a situation where people were confused as to whether the Bob Crosby band was the Bob Crosby band, or was the Eddie Miller band the real Bob Crosby band.

The position seemed even more complicated when Bob Crosby returned to the east coast in March 1943 to front a 15 piece band organised for him by arranger, Van Alexander. This was part of an MGM promotional drive, and when it ended Bob returned to Hollywood where he began hosting a weekly NBC radio show sponsored by Old Gold cigarettes, on this he was backed by an 18 piece studio band. A press announcement said that the band would not be playing Dixieland, but would instead concentrate on "a sweet groove".

The merits of Eddie Miller's band were emphasised when their contract for weekly appearances at the Hollywood Palladium was extended to make their initial stay cover a record-breaking 18 weeks. Trombonist-vocalist, Joe Harris, (a member of the original Bob Crosby band), joined Eddie's group and commented on the freedom he enjoyed with it, "I could play the way I wanted to" he said. The faint element of rivalry between Miller and Crosby soon evaporated, and a trade press item in September 1943 reported "Bob Crosby and Eddie Miller aren't mad any more".

An English emigré, Bill Harty, who had formerly played drums with Ray Noble, briefly became Bob Crosby's manager, and soon organised what was virtually a full reunion of the West Coast based ex-Bob Crosby musicians for a series of dates (for the MCA agency) in California. Eddie Miller, Matlock, Lamare, Rando and O'Brien all agreed to work again under the Crosby banner, but Miller pointed out that this did not mean he was giving up his own band (who were still being handled by the GAC agency).

On ballroom dates Eddie Miller's band were given ecstatic receptions by servicemen who were temporarily stationed in California prior to being posted overseas. At one such engagement, at the Pan-Pacific Ballroom in San Diego, a 6,500 crowd (comprised mainly of sailors and marines) whistled, stamped and cheered for minutes at a time to show their appreciation of the music. It was an emotional time, both for the audience, and for the musicians on stage, none of whom knew how long it would be before they too were in a service uniform.

The fact that most of the Bob Crosby alumni were family men with children meant that their names were low down on the draft priority lists during the first years of World War II, this allowed both Bob Crosby and Eddie Miller to continue working throughout 1943. Bob organised pick-up bands for live appearances, he also appeared on several radio shows, and continued with his film career, which involved him being featured in several movies, amongst them the picture he always gleefully castigates, *The Singing Sheriff.* Eddie, when he wasn't occupied with the administration of his own band, played many studio dates in Hollywood, including regular appearances in Billy Mills Radio Orchestra, but gradually time ran out for Bob and for Eddie.

Eddie Miller's invitation from Uncle Sam eventually reached him in March 1944, accordingly he reported for duty at Fort McArthur. A few weeks later it was Bob Crosby's turn to be called up, and he reported to the US Marine Base at Camp Pendleton, California. Crosby was given the rank of Second Lieutenant and soon posted to the Pacific War Zone. Thus the great era of the original Bob Crosby band finally ended.

Bob Crosby, and most of his original musicians, were destined to enjoy many varied successes when World War II ended, but the calls of that conflict meant that the musical organisation that had given listeners so much pleasure since 1935 ceased to exist. Over the years, since the mid-1940s, there have been countless re-unions of ex-Bob Crosby sidemen, often organised by Bob himself, all have served to remind the music world of the original ensemble's non-pareil reputation.

It was, as writer Dave Dexter said recently, "A truly distinctive and 100% original organisation". One of the band's original members, Deane Kincaide, wrote in 1982, "It was the most unique sound that ever hit the airwaves, the discs or the ear drums. I'm disgustingly proud to say I was in that group". Arranger Paul Weston commenting on the merits of the group said "The Crosby band was unique in that it was a real family - the men who made up the nucleus were remarkable people as well as musicians".

As if to suggest that performing the Crosby brand of music has the qualities of a magic elixir, most of the original group are still at the top of their profession. Bob Crosby, Eddie Miller and Nappy Lamare thrive from their homes in California, and Yank Lawson and Bob Haggart still make world-wide tours from their east coast bases - their joint leadership of the World's Greatest Jazz Band (a pedigree off-spring of the original Bob Cats), was one of the musical success stories of the 1970s. Ray Bauduc lives in Texas, Jess Stacy in California, and Billy Butterfield is constantly travelling from his home in Florida to star at jazz festivals all over the world.

I have been fortunate enough to have had help from all of these men. When I began this study I wondered if my research might reveal that the almost legendary camaraderie of the old Bob Crosby band was all a facade; I conjectured that the report that mentioned the band's "never too happy hey-day" might prove to be the tip of an iceberg of solidly cold relationships. Happily, I found that the Crosby band existed in an atmosphere that was a cross between a family and a highly successful sports team. There were no lasting feuds, no exclusive cliques, and considering the often exhausting touring schedules, very few serious rows.

This does not mean that the Crosby musicians wanted to spend all their waking hours together, they did not remain blissfully unaware of each other's foibles and weaknesses, but they did, as a group, always try to look on the bright side of life, and placed team spirit high on a list of important qualities.

They were bound together by a genuine love of jazz, by a shared sense of humour, and by a pride in their musical achievements. The uneasiest period socially seems to have occurred immediately after World War II, when each player wanted to prove that he was able to excel at music away from the Bob Crosby band, and Bob himself wanted to show the world that he didn't have to be surrounded by members of his original band to have a successful group. Memories of minor aggravations were still fresh but these faded quickly, and both the leader and his former sidemen came to realize that they were part of a unique success story. They were all well aware that they churned out some unmemorable commercial offerings, but to balance any regrets they can think about the honest way they played their own brand of jazz without too much compromise.

The groups shared love of jazz played a big part in smoothing over many differences. Money has always been one of the main causes of discontent amongst musicians, and there are some within the Crosby group who feel that their financial affiars could have been better handled, but as none of the original shareholders ended up poor, the discontentment never gets beyond ruefulness. Occasionally eyes narrow when the subject of composer royalties is mentioned, no-one begrudges Bob Haggart and Ray Bauduc the money they made from their own efforts, but somewhere a feeling lurks that there should have been more sharing on other items, and that opportunism in copyrighting has benefitted some more than others, but even this is not a deep rankle.

None of the Crosby entourage can remember any rows about politics that left permanent bitterness, and, even though there were Catholics, Jews, Methodists and Baptists in the band, there were no serious disagreements about religion. North v. South rivalry hardly ever got beyond the bantering use of "Damn Yankee", and the only lasting grudges seem to concern old comments about various inept golf shots made over 40 years ago.

At the various reunions, the Crosby musicians are genuinely pleased to see one another and to catch up with the news of each other's families, and of various mutual friends. Each of them is likely to post his ex-colleagues a newspaper clipping that will provide information or amusement, and sometimes unsolicited gifts are despatched, thus Nappy Lamare has more old cameras than nearly anyone else on the West Coast. More recently, the ex-Crosbyites have begun to take a greater interest in reissued albums of their work, keeping one another posted about re-releases or newly-issued broadcasts from the 1930s and 1940s. Almost all of the participants got pleasure from hearing the recently released albums of transcriptions they did in 1941-42, and those from 1938, which they recorded pseudonymously as Bert Castle and his Orchestra.

The Bob Crosby veterans have observed many changes in jazz styles since they first became professional musicians, but being individualists they have retained their own way of improvising jazz, putting self expression first. Bob Crosby feels that his colleagues elevated their style of music without taking away any of its vital jazz qualities, "I think we took it out of the Honky Tonks into the top spots, and your traditionalist, your purist, probably felt we had done a disservice to Dixieland for that reason". That may be so, but open-minded jazz listeners realise that the Bob Crosby group made three big contributions to jazz. Firstly, they assembled a big band that was able to transmit the surging excitement and flair of a superb jazz group, secondly, by forming the Bob Cats they created a small unit that reintroduced cohesive, joyful sounding ensembles, and inspired rhythmic improvisations in the manner of earlier great jazz bands. Thirdly, the aggregation kept the flame of jazz alive at a time when interest in it was very low. From faint flickerings a conflagration of interest in the music and its history developed, and happily that fire still burns bright today.

Matty Matlock and Eddie Miller help Tony Paris load up after a location job, 1941.

Steel Pier, Atlantic City

Strand Theatre, New York

Bob Crosby's Orchestra, 1941.
Top row, left to right Jess Stacy, Ray Bauduc, Elmer Smithers, Yank Lawson, Bob Crosby, Liz Tilton, Bob Haggart, Lyman Vunk, Buddy Morrow and Tony Paris.

Bottom row, left to right Nappy Lamare, Eddie Miller, Art Mendelsohn, Max Herman, Doc Rando, Floyd O'Brien, Matty Matlock and Gil Rodin.

The Bob Crosby saxophone section, 1941.
Left to right Gil Rodin, Art Mendelsohn, Doc Rando, Matty Matlock and Eddie Miller.

Manuscript conference, left to right Matty Matlock, Bob Haggart, Gil Rodin, Jess Stacy and Bob Crosby.

Gil Rodin gives the word, 1940.

Cody Sandifer, Jess Stacy and Isabel Richardson (Bob Crosby Fan Club organiser) 1942.

Eddie tries it the hard way.

◁ *Eddie Miller joins up, 1944.*

Dig For Victory, 1943. Nick Fatool, Doc Rando, Eddie Miller, Nappy Lamare and vocaliste Mickey Roy.

Bing polishes Second Lieutenant Crosby's new bars, 1944.
(photo courtesy of US Defense Dept.)

Eddie Miller and his sax section, 1943.
Left to right Eddie Miller, Rosy McHargue, Vic Garver, Doc Rando and Matty Matlock.

Matty Matlock, Mickey Roy, Eddie Miller, Helen Forrest and Nappy Lamare, 1943.

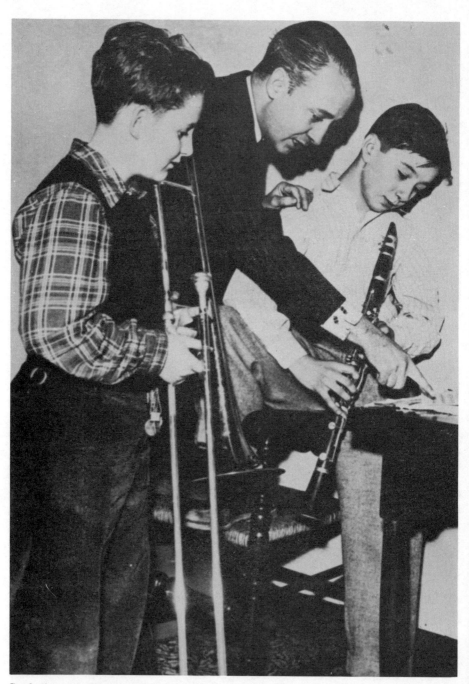

Good advice from Matty Matlock.

Bob Crosby and Yank Lawson during the 1950s.

Eddie Miller (photo: Teresa Chilton)

Chapter 14

Eddie Miller

There can be no doubt that the most popular member of Bob Crosby's Band was Eddie Miller, revered both for his musicianship and for his friendly personality. Eddie's appeal spread all across the board, from fellow musicians and devoted jazz record collectors through to dreamy-eyed fans who hung around the bandstands where Bob Crosby's Band played. As time passed, Eddie's popularity grew, and long after Crosby's original group had disbanded he was still being cited as a favourite musician. His artistic consistency has been truly amazing, over fifty years after he made his record debut he still plays exemplary jazz, and he still wins friends wherever he plays, home or abroad.

Those who have known the diminutive Miller since his early days in New Orleans maintain that he has always been "a great musician and a great guy". One veteran, bandleader Norman Brownlee, who saw Eddie grow up and lived to see him become a world-famous jazz musician, said "Eddie has always been well-liked everywhere he goes". Brownlee's personal nickname for Miller was "The Little Prince". To be well thought of by musicians from his home city means a great deal to Eddie, his life and experiences there are never far from his conversation.

Edward Raymond Müller was born in New Orleans, Louisiana on the 23rd June 1911. His actual birth place was in the Irish Channel section of the city, but when he was two months old, his parents moved to Magnolia Street, and that was where Eddie and his sister were raised. Their mother was of French extraction, their father was German, Eddie's grand-father and great grand-father had travelled together to the USA from Germany, after a brief stay the elder man returned there, but his son stayed and made his home in America. Eddie kept the original spelling of the family name until the 1960s when he officially changed it to Miller.

Eddie's father was a keen amateur accordionist - and a devout tee-totaller - he had no objections to Eddie showing an interest in music, but he was continually trying to dissuade him from ever considering it as a profession. "He had no time for musicians, he thought they were all bums, who spent their time drinking and chasing girls" says Eddie, who realised that it was going to be a long hard job persuading his father to buy him a clarinet. When Eddie heard that the local "Newsboys' Band" were willing to loan instruments to boys who followed that trade he took a weekend job selling copies of the *New Orleans Item*. Thus Eddie was able to borrow his first instrument, he was soon spending all his waking hours either practising the clarinet, or thinking about musical theory. For Eddie, and for many of his school friends, the great musicians of New Orleans were heroes, as god-like as famous sportsmen, to emulate them seemed the supreme ambition.

One of Eddie's older pals, Wilfred 'Bill' Bourgeois, was able to afford clarinet lessons from the noted Italian-born teacher, Santo Giuffre. The Müller family budget didn't allow for private musical tuition, so Bourgeois dashed home as soon as his lesson had ended so that he could immediately share what he had learnt with his eager friend. By this relay, Eddie learnt the secrets of good tone and smooth articulation, he gleaned his knowledge of jazz improvising by hanging around the various dance halls and music bars that flourished in New Orleans.

There were no mixed jam sessions (with black and white musicians) during Eddie's teen years, but all of the youngsters that were interested in jazz avidly followed the personnel changes that occurred in both white and black jazz bands. When Louis Armstrong left King Oliver, it was a major talking point. Eddie remembers being called over by Harold Peterson, an ex-drummer who owned a music and record store, to hear the newly arrived recordings by Louis Armstrong's Hot Five.

Throughout his career, Eddie has always stressed the importance of music in the New Orleans way of life. In one of his first published interviews (in 1937) he said that his influences were Leon Roppolo, Johnny Dodds (and Coleman Hawkins), and also cited "the general playing of New Orleans Parade Bands, and the coloured bands that would gather at the corner where I lived and have battles of music". One of Eddie's earliest memories is of seeing clarinettist George Lewis lubricating his instrument with oil from a giant can.

Eddie made rapid progress, both in reading music and in improvising. Whilst still at the Warren Easton School he earnt money playing clarinet in "Miller's Musical Masters", a group co-led by three Millers, none of them related : Eddie, Benny on banjo, and Lloyd on drums. The quartet's other member was Irving Caro on trumpet.

By 1926, Eddie's skills, both on clarinet and on alto-saxophone, had gained him a good reputation amongst the young musicians of New Orleans, that year (Eddie was still only 15), he went to Gulfport, Mississippi with the "Jack O'Lantern's Band" for a week's booking. During time off he travelled to nearby Biloxi to listen to two brass players he had heard a great deal about, Wingy Mannone on trumpet and Jack Teagarden on trombone. They were playing with a band that was resident at a pier hall, but when Eddie got to the place he felt too shy to go in, instead he sat on the sea-wall enraptured by the marvellous music that floated to him across the water.

On another music seeking trip, this time to hear the legendary Fate Marable's Band playing aboard a steamboat, Eddie met Edna Damerall, the girl who was soon to be his wife. Eddie was a mere 16 years old (in 1928) when the couple married, a year later he was the proud father of Eddie Jr the first of his two children.

Whilst Eddie was working at the Little Club on Bourbon Street with Abbie Brunies' Band he met up with his principal musical hero, the ex-New Orleans Rhythm Kings clarinettist Leon Roppolo, "I always loved Roppolo's playing, he had a tone all over the instrument, he influenced me more than anyone on clarinet". Roppolo who had spent time in a sanitarium because of a mental condition was temporarily at home with his family, he called into the club where Eddie was working, principally to see a girl who worked there. Seeing the great man near the bandstand, Eddie played a solo that was full of his fastest and most spectacular phrases. Roppolo appeared unmoved, but smilingly passed on some advice that encouraged Eddie to shape his own distinctive style, he simply said "Hey kid, it's not how many notes you play, it's how you play 'em". Eddie took heed and a new degree of feeling entered his playing. Older musicians began to take heed of the brilliant youngster who was admitted to the Musicians Union at the tender age of 16, on June 15th 1928. In 1929, he was asked to join one of the city's most renowned bands, "The New Orleans Owls", whose line up at the "25 Club" consisted of Eddie, Bill Padron on trumpet, Armand Hug on piano, John La Porte (drums), Angelo Palmisano (guitar) and the leader, Frank Netto on trombone and bass. Unfortunately this illustrious group was soon to disband.

The Depression hit New Orleans as hard as any other American city, and musical excellence did not guarantee a regular wage packet. In 1929, Eddie, with a wife and child to support, was only making 17 dollars 50 cents for a full working week. The union minimum was 35 dollars, but the management of the speakeasy where Eddie worked got around the rules by perpetually owing musicians the balance of their wages, needless to say, the debt was never settled.

A cousin of Eddie's, who was doing well from a bootlegging sideline, offered to act as Eddie's sponsor in getting him up to New York. "Get your ass up there, where the action is, I'll give you the money for the journey" he said. Eddie had heard from several experienced musicians that times were also tough in the north, but he came to the conclusion that long-term prospects would be better in New York than in poverty stricken New Orleans.

In 1930, Eddie, and another fine musician, reedman Sidney Arodin, and two other passengers set out for the long journey to New York in an old Model T Ford. The trek took them four days and four nights. During a snow-storm that they encountered near Baltimore the car occupants realised to their horror that the only thing holding the doors on was a rope with which they had lashed the suitcases on to the running board. The bedraggled quartet hit New York and parked their vehicle in a lot that belonged to the Roxy Theatre, when they went to collect it they discovered that the parking fee was more than the car was worth, they settled the debt by leaving the jalopy behind.

Eddie found a temporary home in the Lansdale Apartments, near the Roseland and Arcadia Ballrooms, which made it a popular dwelling place with many other musicians. Eddie soon found that the old world courtesies that flourished in New Orleans were not encouraged in New York. On one of his first strolls around the city he said "I beg your pardon" to someone he had accidentally bumped into, he was given a stare that radiated both amazement and deep suspicion.

After four days of exploring the city, Eddie met up with Ray 'Slim' Evans, a tenor sax player from Cincinnati, who told him that there was a vacancy for an alto-sax player in a band led by Julie Wintz. Eddie got the job and found himself working with two other musicians from New Orleans, pianist Horace Diaz and bassist Frank Ermeier. Besides making his record debut with Wintz's band in April 1930, Eddie also did two CBS broadcasts a week with them, that were relayed from a studio that was in an old brownstone building on 59th Street. The pay per man was a mere three dollars each, per broadcast, but as Eddie says "This was the toughest part of the Depression, and people who had been comparitively rich were selling apples on the street, just to make enough to live on".

Wintz, who was a conducting leader, picked up quite a lot of work around New York, including a three week residency at the Roseland Ballroom, where Eddie was able to listen closely to Coleman Hawkins, who was then starring in Fletcher Henderson's Band. Miller was not only struck by the colossal tone and abundant ideas of the great tenor saxist, he also vividly remembers that Hawkins was so troubled with his feet that he had cut the sides out of his expensive shoes to make life more comfortable. Eddie spent the early hours of many mornings listening to the fine jazz that was being performed in New York, one his favourite ports of call was Small's Paradise, the home of Charlie Johnson's Band.

When not working with Julie Wintz, Eddie did a variety of gigs some in bands organised by the Dorsey Brothers. On one of these , he could hardly believe his eyes when he saw that both Bix Beiderbecke and Bunny Berigan were sitting in the trumpet section. Through the Dorseys, Eddie got introduced to the clique of musicians who frequented Plunkett's, the notorious speakeasy on West 53rd Street. Eddie saw the two brothers have some ferocious rows over seemingly inconsequential issues, but he was always impressed by their muscianship, and Jimmy Dorsey went out of his way to help with any musical problems. On one gig when Eddie and Jimmy were working in a Sam Lanin Band, Jimmy asked, "Why are you playing that wreck of a clarinet? Try this one, Selmer made it for me when I was in Europe with Ted Lewis". Eddie borrowed the custom-built instrument, which was part-Boehm fingering and part -Albert, and fell in love with it, whereupon Jimmy sold it to him for the bargain price of fifty dollars. The instrument gave Eddie many years of service.

Julie Wintz's supply of work seemed to temporarily dry up, and Eddie spent an enjoyable month working in a group led by singer Red McKenzie. Then, in September 1930, he had a casual meeting with trumpeter Charlie

Teagarden (brother of Jack), who told him that Gil Rodin, the alto-saxist with Ben Pollack's Band had decided to leave the band, and Pollack was looking for a replacement. Eddie passed the audition then learnt to his dismay that Rodin had changed his mind about leaving, however a vacancy was about to occur in the reed section, tenor saxist Babe Russin was definitely leaving. "Do you play tenor sax?" asked Pollack. "Sure he does" said Ray Bauduc, before Eddie had a chance to say that he didn't. Nappy Lamare, (another newcomer to the band), emphasised Bauduc's New Orleans camaraderie by borrowing a tenor sax from his brother Jimmy so that Eddie could get used to the larger horn.

Ben Pollack liked what he heard and arranged for Eddie to buy a brand new Conn tenor saxophone. The question of salary hadn't been settled, and Eddie was uncertain how much to ask for, his previous employee, Red McKenzie, advised Eddie to stick out for 85 dollars a week. Pollack's opening offer was 75 a week, but heeding McKenzie's advice Eddie asked, "Can you do a little better, please?", and bandleader responded with 85 a week, much to Miller's relief.

At the start of Eddie's first booking Pollack called all of his band musicians together and told them that the manager of the club in which they were booked did not allow musicians to drink before midnight. This deprivation meant no hardship to Eddie, but to some of the heavy drinkers in the band it was a prospect of agony. Jack Teagarden certainly failed to hold out until midnight struck, and at an early stage of the evening was quite plainly drunk, so much so that he couldn't hold on to his trombone slide, never mind manipulate it. Every few seconds, the slide shot out of the instrument and sailed over saxophonist's Gil Rodin's shoulder. Rodin simply picked it up and replaced it in Jack's trombone.

At the end of the set, Pollack mustered a posse from within the band and asked them to carry Jack out to the parking lot that adjoined the club, Eddie was amongst the bearers. No sooner had they got Jack into the fresh air than he began bellowing "Why is it always me who has to be the get-off man, why can't you guys play like me?". Ray Bauduc carried a cup of black coffee to the scene, which Jack accidentally spilt down the front of Bauduc's dress shirt. Gradually the ace trombonist sobered up. When he returned to the bandstand he was grateful to find that the ever-enterprising Bauduc had devised a system of linking elastic bands to stop the trombone slide from falling out of the instrument.

Not all of Miller's nights with the Pollack Band were as dramatic as that early fiasco, but many were very rewarding in terms of experience. Besides the supremely talented Jack Teagarden, the band also featured Ray Bauduc, Nappy Lamare, Gil Bowers on piano, Jerry Johnson on bass, Matty Matlock on clarinet and alto sax, Gil Rodin, also on alto and clarinet and Tommy Thunen on trumpet. Eddie regularly doubled tenor sax and clarinet. Miller and Matty Matlock soon struck up an easy friendship, and their musical empathy led them to experiment with ways of livening up the dreary commercial stock arrangements that the Pollack Band occasionally performed. The two men, Matlock on clarinet and Miller on tenor sax, devised a system of playing octave unison figures, and this simple effect gave a new timbre to some rather banal orchestrations. This was some while before Glenn Miller utilised an extension of a similar idea.

Eddie Miller soon established himself as one of the Pollack Band's premier soloists, but unlike Matlock, he never showed any inclination to become an arranger. "I just couldn't get interested in writing out an arrangement, years later, in Hollywood, I tried to learn the technique of orchestration via the very talented Lyle 'Spud' Murphy, but I just found it all very boring, and none of it stayed in my head".

The Pollack Band usually enjoyed success wherever it played, but one particular booking could be marked down as a failure. The band were hired to play in a 'battle of the bands' contest against Joe Haymes Band. The venue was a usually popular New England ballroom, and band-wives from both contestants arrived early to take sides in the action. Unfortunately, one of the worst rainstorms in living memory hit the area with the result that no-one at all attended the much heralded musical combat.

Eddie was never the victim of Pollack's occasional ferocity, but he always remembers one display that occured at the Casino De Paree in New York during cabaret time. The band were accompanying an act called Gomez and Wynona, and Pollack and Gomez had never seen eye to eye on any music matters. The bandleader beat in an opening tempo that Gomez plainly thought was wrong, and this caused him to hesitate in the wings. Pollack spotted the indecisive dancer and bawled out, in his most genteel manner, "I'm not stopping this band for you, you dago. Get your ass out here on stage!"

The outline of the Ben Pollack Band saga and its vicissitudes are dealt with elsewhere in this book. Eddie Miller was not an instigator in the walk-out from Pollack, but as a key soloist, his presence in the move to New York was a great morale booster for the new group, and there is not doubt that Eddie's influence played a big part in the moulding of the Crosby Band's style.

Within the Bob Crosby Band, Eddie was certainly a premier soloist, not only in the quality of his work, but also in the quantity, he was more heavily featured than anyone else in the band, both on fast and slow numbers. This led one long-time Crosby member to say that Eddie was something of a "teacher's pet" when it came to the allocation of solo space, but this comment was said without any trace of malice. Eddie also played a key role in the band's stage routines, as a member of the ever-popular fan-dance trio, and as a participant in other light-hearted features. His triple threat was the ability to sing the blues with more sincerity than anyone else in the band. Nowadays Eddie rarely sings, "In those days I didn't care, but now I'm a little self-conscious". The only disappointment concerning Eddie's music-making was that he rarely played clarinet solos with the Crosby Band after 1938.

During the 1930s, Eddie's talents graced many recordings by various pick-up groups, these included dates with Glenn Miller, Louis Prima, Wingy Mannone, Bunny Berigan and Frankie Trumbauer, and the Metronome All Stars. For one brief period in the Crosby Band's history it seemed as though Eddie had grown stale through over-exposure to the same type of chord progressions, and he became slightly repetitive in his solos. But the malaise was only temporary and Eddie soon bounced back, as full as invention as ever.

As a generalisation, dullards have tended to regard Eddie as simply a lighter-toned echo of Bud Freeman, but anyone familiar with the two men's work could hardly mistake the diverse styles. Freeman's more rugged sound, emphatic single-note syncopations and repeated arpeggios contrast dramatically with Miller's floating rhythmic phrases, more regular use of the upper register, and easy, legato constructions. The two musicians developed their own styles independently, all the while enjoying a friendly rivalry.

Eddie's musical heritage came from New Orleans' musicians originally, a fact that he is justifiably proud of, but on one of the Crosby Band's rare trips to Louisiana, he thought the subject of his musical tuition was going to be the cause of trouble. The band were playing a date in Opelousas and Eddie noticed three young Cajuns staring hard at him from close by his music stand, "This went on for number after number. I was turning things over in my mind, why could this be? It could have been a tricky situation, they looked so hostile. At the intermission they surrounded me, and I thought 'this is it', then one said 'Is it true that Howard Vorhees taught you the saxophone?', I gulped out a 'yes' and one of these guys turned to his friends and said 'You see that Vorhees wasn't shitting after all'."

When the United States entered World War II in December 1941 it was obvious that most of the members of Bob Crosby's Band would eventually be drafted into the armed services. It was decided by the band members that if Bob Crosby was called up, or decided to do other things, then Eddie Miller should take over the leadership of the band. Eddie's talent and popularity (outside of the band and within) made him the number one contender, he also had a good sense of business acumen and a sound knowledge of the behind-the-scenes workings of musical administration. He agreed to lead the 'new' band until his period of deferment expired.

The band clicked emphatically with Californian audiences, as was proved by the long run at the Hollywood Palladium, and by the wealth of bookings that they were offered. Most of the group's key members, such as Matty Matlock, Nappy Lamare, Floyd O'Brien and Doc Rando (who assisted Eddie with the administrative side of the band) were ex-Bob Crosby sidemen. The group's girl singer was Mickie Roy, who had previously worked with Sonny Dunham, and the drummer, Nick Fatool, was someone regularly listed by Eddie as a favourite player.

The band featured many of the instrumental numbers that had been part of the Crosby Band's repertoire, including *Sugar Foot Strut, South Rampart Street Parade, Louise, Louise, Muskrat Ramble* and *Wolverine Blues*, but they also played arrangements of current popular songs. At the time, Eddie said "Sure, we're playing a lot of Dixieland. That's the only music we know how to play - I mean play well. But we don't want to be billed as a Dixie band. Too many kids and musicians stick a corny tag on anything they hear that's called Dixie".

Most of the ex-Bob Crosby sidemen are irked by the fact that they were often referred to as "two beat musicians". The issue has always been a sore point with Eddie, and one that is likely to evoke a warm response from this usually equable man. "They used to say two-beats-in-a-bar equals the south, and four-beats-in-a-bar meant the band was from the north, that was all crap. Bands from the south played four beats, and bands from all over also played two-beats-in-a-bar. It got to the point where you'd been playing four-in-a-bar for a whole set and you'd get off the bandstand to hear some guy say 'Gee, I love this two beat music'. It carried on for years. When I worked in the studios we were making a recording with a well known singer, and the question arose as to whether the 'feel' of the arrangement should be two-beat or four-beat. This gal crossed the floor and called out to me in the reed section "Do you think it should be two-beat, Eddie?" Well, I really got a burn on, and I called back "I'd make it five beats in the bar if I were you".

Eddie's 1943 band was based in Los Angeles. War-time travel restrictions made it nearly impossible for the band to undertake any lengthy tours. Even the railroads had a priority system for long distance travel, this meant that a booking no further away than Ocean Park in Southern California could be fraught with transport headaches. During one period, Eddie and the band were flown to play engagements at various Californian service bases, then a service order grounded all transport planes immediately, with the result that the group were stuck in San Francisco without any means of getting home. One highspot in the band's career was their appearance (as Eddie Miller's Bob Cats) in the 1943 film *Mister Big* (also titled *School for Jive*) which featured Donald O'Connor, Gloria Jean and Peggy Ryan.

Earlier in 1943, Eddie toyed with the idea of accepting an offer to join Benny Goodman's Band, who were then working in California, but after attending one rehearsal, simply as a spectator, and observing how mercilessly hard Goodman was on Miff Mole and Lee Castaldo, making them endlessly repeat phrases long after their lips were raw, he declined the invitation. Eddie did however play with Goodman's Band for the soundtrack of the film *The Gang's All Here*.

After a year of band-leading headaches (connected with travel problems and draft losses) Eddie decided, in early 1944, to discontinue the big band on a regular basis. This decision meant he was free to work in the film studio orchestras, but he had no sooner settled into that lucrative groove when his draft notice arrived, summoning him to report to the Army Air Force induction unit at Fort McArthur in April 1944. From there he was posted for 'boot training' at Camp Roberts, (where he enjoyed a brief reunion with Gil Rodin and Ray Bauduc who were already well past their rookie days in the service).

Eddie found that his musical reputation had preceded him to Camp Roberts, the Band Sergeant there immediately assured Eddie that there would be a regular place for him in the station band when he had finished his basic training. The idea sounded fine to Eddie, it meant he would be based fairly close to home, 'I was pleased to get the offer, my wife and children were in California, so I could get to see them regularly. The Sergeant mistakenly believed that I was getting lots of offers from other service bands, and this made him all the more keen to have me in his outfit".

"My stock rose when Bing Crosby came to the camp. Before he arrived a special communique came through from headquarters saying, 'Bing Crosby requests that Private Miller accompanies him as he knows all of his tunes'. Bing really thought he was doing me a big favor, saving me from drill, but I was actually due for a weekend pass at the time of his visit. I had to stay on camp and play the gig, but it turned out to be fun. Next week, on his radio show, Bing spoke of me being in uniform, and said I was 'the saddest sack he'd ever seen'."

But before Eddie had finished his basic training his hands became very swollen and painfully contused. He was taken to the service hospital where arthritis was diagnosed. After several weeks of treatment, it was realised that Eddie's ailment was of a chronic nature, he was recommended for a medical discharge and left the service in August 1944.

Fortunately, Eddie's arthritis did not greatly affect his nimble technique on the tenor saxophone, and he was soon playing regularly again. In 1945 he resumed leading a big band, assembling it for specific bookings; this time the repertoire was less inclined towards "Dixieland". the band had lots of specially written arrangements, many of which showcased Eddie's wonderfully expressive ballad playing, but the band could also swing powerfully, and Eddie's exciting playing on the *Hum Drum* feature he shared with drummer Nick Fatool was a real show-stopper.

However, the problems of leading a big band again outweighed the joys, and Eddie was pleased and somewhat relieved to be offered a regular place on the musical staff of the 20th Century Fox studios; it turned out to be permanent berth, Eddie stayed there for almost nine years.

The pay for working in a Hollywood studio band was excellent, and the schedule allowed time for Eddie to work numerous club dates, and to play regular golf. More time at home meant that Eddie (who has always been keen on electronics) could relax whilst tinkering with the various amplifiers he had built himself.

Eddie doubled tenor saxophone and clarinet in the studio orchestra, and this meant he finally had to lay aside the clarinet he had bought from Jimmy

Dorsey twenty years earlier. "I had to change to Boehm system, because even the third clarinet parts contained fingering that was just too fast for my old clarinet. But I still think that the Albert system suits jazz playing more than the Boehm (which Eddie, like most New Orleanians, pronounces Bayem). I maintain that you get a bigger tone out of an Albert system clarinet".

Listeners to old film sound-tracks will often hear bursts of Eddie Miller's superb tenor-sax playing, usually uncredited. Occasionally, Eddie was seen on the screen, but for the most part he led an anonymous well-paid existence in the studio band. Recordings from this period show that he had lost none of his guile, or his flow of inspired ideas. Occasionally his extra-curricula jobs involved reunions with ex-Bob Crosby Band pals, and often Eddie guested with eminent jazzmen who visited California. A gig with Louis Armstrong provided some outstanding musical memories for Eddie, and a chuckle. "Louis said he would love me to see some of the films he'd shot on his own cine-camera. I was pleased to be asked, but I couldn't help smiling whilst I was watching them, because it seemed as though every shot had Louis coming out of the same doorway and waving straight at the camera. Whilst they were being shown, Louis tugged me and said, 'That was me in Detroit, or that was me in Philadelphia, or that was me in Dallas', but they all looked identical. Still it was great seeing Louis's enthusiasm".

It would need a fat discography to list all the many recordings that Eddie Miller had made since the demise of the first Bob Crosby Band. He was particularly active in the late 1940s when he played on countless sessions for the Capitol label - this was at the time that Johnny Mercer was one of its directors, and Dave Dexter one of its a-and-r men. "Matty, myself and a few others were practically the house band there. We accompanied all sorts of singers. One day I'd be the leader, and the next day someone else whould be the boss, using exactly the same musicians".

The nucleus of musicians involved in these projects included Matty Matlock, Nick Fatool and pianist Stan Wrightsman, all of whom were featured in the film *Pete Kelly's Blues* and in the long-running television serial of the same name. Matlock and Miller shared hundreds of sessions and still remained close friends; Eddie made his only recorded appearance on baritone saxophone for one of Matty's recording dates.

After Eddie had completed his studio contract, he found himself with time to travel, and during the late 1950s and 1960s often worked outside of California. One notable journey in 1964 took him to Japan and Australia, as part of Bob Crosby Bobcats' reunion, he also went to New York in 1966 to play in the Crosby get-together at the Rainbow Grill. During the 1960s, Eddie played many seasons in Las Vegas in various bands, including one in 1965 that was the last gig Red Nichols ever played.

In 1967, Eddie toured Britain, guesting with Alex Welsh's Band. This proved to be the first of many trips to Europe, in the late 1970s one six week jaunt took him through a dozen countries. Eddie, who worked with the embryo version of the World's Greatest Jazz Band at a Dick Gibson party in Aspen, Colorado, later guested with the band and toured Europe with them.

Eddie's longest spell away from California was spent in his home city of New Orleans, where he worked as a member of the band led by clarinettist Pete Fountain, from 1967 until 1976. "I had known Pete since he was a teenager, way back in the 1940s. Monk Hazel took me to hear Pete and George Girard on trumpet play, and they were only about 17 then. We always kept in touch, and when Pete came to the coast to work with Lawrence Welk we spent a lot of time together. He went back to New Orleans, and then asked me to join his band. It was a great time. I like Pete, he is a fine player, and a nice guy. He'll stop and speak with the guy who is sweeping the street, there's nothing big time about his attitude at all. My only regret is that I took my bass clarinet down there and left it, it's there to this day".

During the 1980s, Eddie kept up a regular playing schedule, appearing at numerous jazz festivals. In 1982 he was chosen by the American magazine *Jazz Forum* as *Jazzman of the Year* (a remarkable achievement for a man in his seventies), but even more remarkable was the inspired performance that Eddie gave at a celebration concert held in his honour at Rosemont, Illinois in November 1982. A month later, Eddie was stomping his way through a feature at a Bob Crosby re-union session in New Jersey, and his playing at another Crosby date a month later had to be heard to be believed.

These days, Eddie gets a lot of relaxation from his hobby of renovating antique furniture, he also finds he can relax more on the bandstand. "Nobody is pressurising me to make things happen. I just relax and have a ball". The man is in great shape musically and mentally. He gave up drinking a few years ago, after being what he calls "a vodka champion"; at 65 he was told by a medical examiner that he had the liver of a 25 year old, Eddie says "I decided to quit whilst I was winning, you can't be lucky all the time". Eddie, a grandfather several times over, has no intention of giving up playing, "You just don't retire from music. It's been my life, and I always tell myself how lucky I've been in earning my living by playing the music I love".

A 1943 reunion, left to right Ray Bauduc, Bob Crosby, Max Herman and Gil Rodin.

Chapter 15

Gil Rodin

During his days as a teenager in Chicago, Gilbert Rodin dreamt of becoming a great jazz soloist. Together with other young musicians he listened open-mouthed to King Oliver's Band play at the Lincoln Gardens, amazed to hear the skills of Louis Armstrong and the Dodds brothers. He also developed a great admiration for Jimmie Noone's facile, warm-toned clarinet playing and went to hear him as often as possible. Originally, Gil couldn't decide which instrument to specialise on, he made tentative efforts on the trumpet, tried out a flute that belonged to a brother, then settled on saxophone. With a good deal of diligent practice Gil became a competent saxophonist, but his dreams of becoming a great jazzman were never fulfilled, his ability to read music developed rapidly, but he was never able to improvise fluently.

Gil wasn't born in Chicago, his detailed memories of growing up in that city often gave that impression, but he, and his five brothers and one sister, were all born in Russia. Gil, the sixth of seven children, was born on the 9th December 1906. His parents moved to the United States during Gil's infancy and settled in Chicago.

Like the children of many Chicago immigrants, Gil was fascinated by the sounds of jazz, and even though he soon realised that he was never going to be an accomplished jazzman the disappointment never diminished his love of good jazz playing. Years after he first heard King Oliver's Band he described the experience as one of the "greatest thrills". What struck him at the time he said was that the Oliver Band "played arranged hot music and still kept swinging". It was this very quality that was to prove a vital asset for the Bob Crosby Band, a unit that would never have come into being without Gil Rodin's ingenuity and acumen.

Gil's first regular work as a musician was in Chicago with pianist Art Kahn's Band, which featured drummer Vic Berton. The repertoire of the band was fairly progressive, and featured many of the tunes that Rodin listened to at clubs that flourished after his night's work with Kahn had ended. At these early hours' sessions one particular local white musician impressed Rodin, and that was drummer Ben Pollack, who was enjoying considerable success with the New Orleans Rhythm Kings. Rodin instantly recognised him as being one of the other youngsters who regularly went to hear King Oliver's Band.

Feeling like a change of pace, Gil Rodin made his first trip to California, principally to take a vacation, but not discounting the idea that he might work with local bands. On a casual visit to a ballroom in Venice, California, he saw to his suprise that the drummer was none other than Ben Pollack. He struck up a conversation, the upshot of which was that Pollack invited him to share his apartment. The two young men became good friends, and Pollack soon got Rodin into the band at the Venice ballroom. When Pollack returned to Chicago because of a family bereavement, Gil travelled back with him.

Whilst the two musicians were in Chicago, Pollack, who was temporarily kept at home by family ties, asked Rodin to go and hear a young clarinet player who was working at the Midway Gardens on the South Side. Rodin obliged and later reported, "I heard the most astonishing clarinet I had ever heard - coming from a kid!". The talented youngster was none other than Benny Goodman; Rodin offered him a job with Pollack's Band in California, and was delighted when the Goodman family raised no objections. It was an early indication of Rodin's considerable gift for spotting talent, a quality he shared with Ben Pollack.

Pollack himself was certainly no slouch when it came to finding gifted musicians for his band, after he and Gil returned to California, trombonist Glenn Miller joined the entourage. Soon most of the arrangements that the band played were either by Glenn Miller, or by reedman Fud Livingston, of whom Rodin said "his arranging set the style that the Pollack band followed for many years".

A spirit of jovial camaraderie filled the Pollack Band at this time, and there were many happy gatherings at the Haley Hotel in Venice, where the musicians had their rooms. But eventually it was realised that a move to Chicago would benefit the long term interests of the group. They arrived back there in early 1926 to find that work was temporarily scarce. Rodin soon found out which jazz haunts were thriving, and spent pleasant hours listening with, and talking to, young up-and-coming jazz musicians like Frank Teschemacher, Joe Sullivan, Dave Tough and Jimmy McPartland who were drinking in the sounds of the band that Louis and Lil Armstrong had at the Dreamland, the same clique listened regularly to Jimmie Noone's group at the Nest Club on 35th Street.

Eventually, Rodin persuaded Pollack to hire some of these young musicians and make the move to New York. When the band arrived in Manhattan, Gil shared a room with two of his Chicago buddies, Jimmy McPartland and Bud Freeman. One night the three of them visited a musician' get-together at the Louisiana apartments on 47th Street, and heard for the first time the amazing talents of trombonist Jack Teagarden. Next morning, Gil called Ben Pollack and told him about Teagarden's superb artistry, "I told Ben all about him. I'm afraid I probably became a little incoherent in telling him how much Jack impressed me".

Glenn Miller's decision to stay in New York rather than move with the Pollack Band to Atlantic City, meant that Jack Teagarden was immediately able to fill the vacancy. Not long after Teagarden's arrival Benny Goodman and Pollack had a bitter row, Goodman left the band, and in came reedman Matty Matlock. A further upheaval brought Eddie Miller and Nappy Lamare into the band, drummer Ray Bauduc was already a member. Gradually the Pollack Band took on a new look, and a new sound, as fresh emphasis was put on the creation of head arrangements. Unfortunately Jack Teagarden left the band whilst they were working in Chicago in 1933, but that same year saw the arrival of the dynamic trumpeter Yank Lawson.

Rodin, who was ever shrewd in sensing new developments in the music world, felt that a change would follow the repeal of Prohibition. He said, "It was about this time that one could definitely notice the rise in public favour of that thing called Swing". But Pollack seemingly had no desire to stay in New York and exploit developments that Rodin felt sure would soon greatly enhance the band's progress, instead the band leader wanted to concentrate of furthering the career of the band's vocaliste, Doris Robbins. The band moved to Galveston, Texas, then on to California, leaving the New York scene wide open for a new band that was blending good arrangements and imaginative jazz solos in a manner similar to Pollack's style, the up-and-coming unit was led by Pollack's former star, Benny Goodman.

Rodin felt, with some justification, that Pollack was totally ignoring any advice he gave him, worst still, Pollack was destroying the goodwill that Rodin's diplomacy had carefully built up with various club owners and ballroom managers. Gil did not engineer the eventual walk out that occurred in late 1934 when Pollack's musicians left en masse, he was simply on hand to give the younger men advice. He did so with such wisdom and experience the musicians called him 'Pops', though he was still not yet thirty. It was inevitable that they asked him to manage the new band, he not only became manager he also became its chief policy maker and its father-confessor.

In summarising the walk out, which caused him much heart searching, Rodin said "For some time prior to our opening in California, there was much unhappiness and dissatisfaction with the musical policies and it was only a reluctance to split up that kept us together so long. We had and still have a great admiration for Ben Pollack, both personally and as a leader, and hated to see this happen".

Once the "Pollack Orphans" reached New York, Rodin immediately set about finding work for the group. He knew most of the band agents personnally, and was on first name terms with almost every song-plugger in New York. Word soon spread about the new band, and as a result Rodin not only secured radio and recording work for them, he also attended the meeting at the Rockwell-O'Keefe office that brought Bob Crosby into the organisation.

Cork O'Keefe and Gil Rodin, both adroit businessmen, had a good deal of respect for each other. but O'Keefe felt he was never able to get close to Rodin, even when their negotiations were proceeding smoothly. "It was as though Gil wanted to keep you at arm's length. He'd have a laugh and a joke with you, and give you a warm smile, and a friendly handshake, but all the while you felt he was holding back. He never really changed, I knew him for most of his life".

Although Eddie Miller, Matty Matlock, Lamare, Bauduc and Lawson, had been working with Rodin for some while before the Bob Crosby Band was formed, it was Bob Crosby himself, a virtual newcomer to the group, who settled into the easiest relationship with Gil. Even so, Crosby found Rodin to be what he called "a correct person". "He never did find the right girl. He was good looking, but not the romantic type. I think he had casual affairs with anonymous women, he was certainly secretive about anything like that. In fact, he was pretty secretive all around, but a stickler for detail and efficiency. He did have his occasional lapses, once after a tour of New England, we boarded the train to return to New York, as we did Gil turned white, he'd left all the money we'd taken on the tour in his hotel drawer - 30,000 dollars in cash. He raced back, and there it was, untouched. I think I'm right in saying that he only ever loved one woman, and that was one of the Williams Sisters, a singing act".

Noted writer George T. Simon was a long-time friend of Gil Rodin, and greatly admired his dedication to business. "For years, Gil devoted every waking hour to his life with the Crosby Band. He'd sit down, with a cigarette always dangling from his mouth, and plan a campaign like a general. Although he kept in the background, and let Bob actually front the band, the musicians recognised him as the headman. I think Gil would have been happy to have got married, but he promised his mother that he would marry a Jewish girl, and the right one never came along. I think he had a brief romance with the band's singer, Dorothy Claire, but it didn't last. Even then I had to tell him that Dorothy was mad about him, his mind was so much on band business he hadn't realised it".

Simon feels that Rodin was perhaps the musician who got closest of all to Benny Goodman, Goodman once said "Gil Rodin is liked by more people in the business than anyone I know of". Glenn Miller, who shared with Goodman a reputation for failing to develop warm friendships, was also a close friend of Rodin's, it was as if Rodin, a reserved man himself, made friends mostly with people of a similar disposition. He could however be expansive and chummy, particularly late at night when the band had packed up their instruments, then he began his "real work", talking over business deals with guests he had specially invited, or listening to the pleas of an army of song pluggers.

Rodin was not a ruthless disciplinarian, but everyone who worked in Bob Crosby's Band seems to have respected his wishes without too much hesitation. Everyone realised that no matter how many hours of practice that Gil put in, on saxophone, clarinet, flute or oboe, he was never going to be a brilliant musician, but, everyone acknowledged that he was a wily businessman, and clever strategist. He occasionally made mistakes in policy, but none of them were disastrous, and throughout the time he handled the band's interests there was never a period when the group were scuffling for work, each year things improved financially for the musicians. "We always played the best locations" stressed Jess Stacy, and Matty Matlock emphasised "Whatever Gil did was for the good of the band". Writer and recording company executive, Dave Dexter, wrote that Rodin was "a man of great integrity".

In 1940, Gil admitted that he left little to chance, "It's been a lot of work. Bob Crosby has proved himself a damned swell leader. We all like him personally, and he has worked hard to learn more about music". The two men shared a cordial relationship, and Bob regularly listened to Gil's advice, Crosby, more impetuous than Rodin, occasionally let fly when a journalist adopted a beligerent attitude, but Gil would soon smooth things over. He was, as Bob Haggart said, a man who wanted to see everything always running smoothly. The musicians dubbed him "the promiser", because he tended to iron out any difficult situation with a series of promises - a good many of which came true.

The only lasting grudge that some of the corporation men retain towards Gil concerned his allocation of the money that went into the band's coffers. Most expense outlays were authorised personally by Gil, and some musicians did not always agree with his order of priorities. Gil, ever one for planning ahead, tended to want to pour money back into the band fund, or use it to establish goodwill for the future. This policy caused musicians like pianist Gil Bowers and arranger-saxist Deane Kincaide to leave the band, and even now veterans look back and reflect that the share-outs that the corporation men enjoyed were few and far between.

When the World War II break up of the Crosby Band was imminent, Gil Rodin and Ray Bauduc joined the Coast Artillery Big Band, once again Rodin's organisational skills came to the fore as he became the band's "manager" (with the rank of sergeant), he also played saxophone in the group. After the two men left the service, Rodin played baritone saxophone in the band they co-led in 1944 and 1945. As the new band's spokesman he said "We wanted a young band, a fresh band. We didn't like the idea of going over old trails", for a time it seemed as though the policy would triumph.

In October 1945, a *Down Beat* reviewer commented on the work of the two leaders "Rodin, playing in the saxophone section, virtually unknown to the public, but a real power behind the throne. Bauduc, the smiling showman, complements stern-visaged Rodin very satisfactorily" Despite this optimistic report, the death knell was already sounding for the band. Both co-leaders decided to disband, Rodin quit playing and moved back to Los Angeles to concentrate on management. He was weary of touring, and was beginning to suffer from recurring back trouble. He soon began another partnership with Bob Crosby, helping him to organise bands for live appearances, and becoming responsible for the production of the Club 15 radio show.

Gil Rodin's canny outlook served him well again, he decided to learn all he could about television production well before it became an international art. Under the auspices of the G.I. Bill of Rights he was able to study the subject free of cost at the U.C.L.A. After gaining some practical experience in West Coast studios, Gil moved out to Australia from 1962 until 1964, and worked as a producer for Channel 7 television. By then television production occupied all his thoughts, just as organising a band had done formerly, and Australian jazz fans eager to talk about the Crosby Band days were disappointed by Gil's peremptory reflections.

Rodin's speciality in Australia was working on the news-magazine show *To-night*, but after his move back to California in 1964 he concentrated on utilising his specialised knowledge of the music business and became the producer of Eddie Fisher's regular show. He also produced some prestigious specials for Fred Astaire and for Nureyev. His other successes included the 13 part series *Feather on Jazz* (featuring Leonard Feather) and two Swinging spectaculars that were devised by George T. Simon and compered by Ronald Reagan.

Throughout his travels, Rodin always kept in touch with Bob Crosby, often speaking fondly of Bob's family (he was godfather to Crosby's first born, daughter Cathleen), he also never once forgot to send a Christmas card to Isabel Richardson, the ex-organiser of the Bob Crosby Fan Club. When any of his former colleagues played engagements close to where he worked he always dropped in to see them, and was delighted to pay a well-wisher's visit to The World's Greatest Jazz Band when they played in California.

Late in life, he discussed Bob Crosby's work with Charles Thompson, Bing Crosby's official biographer "Bing's success was something I always regretted for Bob's sake. He always had this big shadow there. 'Bing's Brother. Bing's Brother'. He didn't know which way to go and became a meek little fellow instead of really doing something on his own. They tried to compare his singing, they tried to compare his talking. It was a spiteful kind of thing".

Rodin did not thrive on enmity, and felt happiest when he was at peace with former antagonists. He and Ben Pollack, after a long period of non-communication, occasionally met socially during the 1960s, by then, Gil had long repaired the rift with agent Cork O'Keefe, whose period as the Crosby Band's agent had ended in acrimony. The two men often saw each other when O'Keefe visited California. He recalled their last meeting, "I saw him not long before he died. I visited him at his home in Palm Springs, he was very thin, and behind that deep Californian sun-tan they all get out there, he looked ill. He had heart trouble, but he kept saying 'I feel fine'. He didn't have any financial worries because by then he had done really well as a television producer for Universal".

Gil Rodin died alone, suffering a fatal heart attack at his Californian home on the 10th June 1974; he was active right until the day of his death. Eulogies were paid by countless people from all walks of show business, ranging from veteran jazzmen who had shared Prohibition sprees with Gil in Chicago, to famous actors and actresses who had worked with Gil in radio and television. Members of the Bob Crosby Band sent warm tributes.

Bob Crosby felt a genuine sense of loss for someone who he once described as "Just about the finest guy who ever stepped on this earth", but, still maintains that Gil Rodin could not have known how ill he was. "I was amazed to learn that Gil hadn't made a will, he was not only a very methodical guy, but he also had studied various aspects of the law. I still find it incredible that he could have overlooked something as important as that. Maybe he was one of the type who doesn't want to tempt fate by making a will".

In California, Gil's associates at Universal organised the Gil Rodin Scholarship at U.C.L.A. in honour of his memory. In the East, a collection for this was organised by Cork O'Keefe, "I went round to many musicians who had known Gil, but some refused to give anything, including a couple of former Bob Crosby Band members, however I did get a hundred dollars from Benny Goodman, which can be called one of the biggest accomplishments of my life".

Without doubt, Gil Rodin was the vital factor in the organisation of the first Bob Crosby Band, as President of the Corporation he felt that true success had to be long lasting, and some of his methods of achieving that aim left a few musicians aggrieved, but no one who ever worked with Rodin regularly ended up hating him. Gil saw himself as a sort of benevolent father to the Crosby musicians, and at the heyday of the band he said "We are strictly a family group and proud of it". A close relative summed up Gil's total involvement with the Bob Crosby Band "Gil never looked for credit or glory for his efforts with the Bob Crosby group, or for any of his efforts. His fulfillment was in doing his best, those days were happy ones for Gil".

Ray Bauduc

Chapter 16
Ray Bauduc

All of the founder members of Bob Crosby's band were experienced professionals, but the most travelled and seasoned trouper amongst them was drummer Ray Bauduc. He was making his living at music by the time he was 15, at 18 he toured all over the States, at 20 he made his recording debut, and at 21 he worked in Europe as a drummer and speciality dancer. For six years, from 1928 until 1934, Bauduc drummed in Ben Pollack's band whilst the leader conducted out front, and it was during this period that he perfected his own style of drumming, which became an inimitable part of the Bob Crosby band's rhythm section.

Bauduc, who was born at 1101 North White Street, New Orleans, on the 18th June 1906, came from a musical family, his father Jules Snr played trumpet, and Ray's elder brother, Jules Jnr, was an eminent banjo player and guitarist, who died at an early age. Ray first fell in love with the idea of becoming a full-time musician when he helped his brother carry instruments to local gigs. He was given an old set of drums to practice on, and after showing early promise was sent for lessons to George 'Kid' Peterson and to Paul DeDroit. Ray responded well to formal tuition, but he was also very interested in producing the beat, and the effects, of black drummers like Baby Dodds and Zutty Singleton (both of whom he heard playing in riverboat bands), he also loved the flair shown by Emil Stein, the house percussionist at the New Orleans Palace Theatre. During all the early studies, Ray was still a pupil at the Delgado Trade School, where he was learning to become a mechanic, one of his fellow pupils was Emmett Hardy, who later became a renowned cornetist.

Ray never lost his considerable aptitude for mechanical engineering, but it took second place to music in his life. His first regular work as a drummer was at the Thelma Theatre in New Orleans, where he shared musical duties with a pianist for three dollars a week. From there he graduated to the Six Nola Jazzers, and experienced his first stint of touring, which ended with him being stranded in Birmingham, Alabama.

New Orleans trumpeter Johnny Bayersdorffer was re-organising the band he led at the Tokyo Gardens in the Spanish Fort (close to the Crescent City), he heard about Ray and clarinettist Bill Creger being holed up in Birmingham and sent them their fares for the journey back to New Orleans, together with an invitation to join his band. Bauduc joined Bayersdorffer in the late summer of 1924. During the following October, the band left New Orleans to play a season in Chicago, from there they moved on to the Rainbow Casino Gardens in Indianapolis, then in March 1925 they returned to New Orleans to begin another season at the Spanish Fort.

For the 1925 Spanish Fort season, Bayersdorffer added a newcomer to the band, banjoist Hilton 'Nappy' Lamare, who was to be a working companion of Bauduc's for the next thirty five years. An intense and persistent plague of mosquitoes caused the Spanish Fort ballroom to temporarily close in August 1925. This invasion of insects forced the band out of work, but fortunately allowed Bayersdorffer to accept some bookings offered in Los Angeles, so Bauduc and Lamare got their first look at California, riding there with Bayersdorffer in an open Ford Model T. The band played a happy season at the Roseroom Ballroom in Los Angeles, and on a night off, Bauduc entered and won a Charleston dance contest at the Aragon Ballroom.

Whilst in California, Bauduc had the pleasure of meeting Ben Pollack, the two men swopped drum talk, each expressing the hope that they would meet again, neither realising that their professional futures were soon to intertwine. From the West Coast, the Bayersdorffer band moved back to Indianapolis to play a return season at the Rainbow Casino Gardens prior to making the return trip to New Orleans. Back home, Bauduc temporarily linked up with Ellis Stratakos (trombone), Pinky Gerbrick (trumpet), Frank Mutz (piano) and Eddie Powers (alto sax) to play local broadcasts as "The Dixieland Roamers".

Meanwhile, Bayersdorffer decided to merge with violinist Billy Lustig (who had led the Scranton Sirens). Lustig had the work contacts, and Bayersdorffer a ready-made band (which was soon augmented by several newcomers). In 1926, the new enlarged line-up played at the Little Club in New Orleans, then, minus trombonist Santo Pecora, they left to play for a month at the Rendezvous Club in Chicago. Pecora's replacement, a brilliant young musician, joined the band there, his name was Tommy Dorsey.

When the Rendezvous booking ended there were no further prospects for the band in Chicago, so an off-shoot group consisting of Lustig, Dorsey, Bauduc and pianist John "Chummy" MacGregor moved north and became part of a new version of Billy Lustig's Scranton Sirens. After working in Pennsylvania the band moved on to Detroit and there they were joined by Tommy Dorsey's brother, Jimmy, who doubled on alto-saxophone and clarinet; on some engagements the band recreated an earlier billing and became known as "Dorsey's Wild Canaries".

The band moved on to Atlantic City, and there another splinter group consisting of Jimmy Dorsey, Bauduc and MacGregor attached itself to a new band being formed by violinist Joe Venuti, and guitarist Eddie Lang, these five, plus Red Nichols on cornet and "Chi Chi" Carmen on bass, went to New York to open at Tommy Guinan's "Playgrounds" Club. In New York, during November 1926, Bauduc made his record debut as a member of the Original Memphis Five, some earlier efforts with Bayersdorffer were thwarted by technical problems and never released.

Jimmy Dorsey recommended that bandleader Fred Rich use Bauduc on some of his recordings, Rich was pleased with the results and this led to him offering some theatre work to the drummer, who was able to "double" between the theatre and the Playgrounds club. Eventually, when the club gig terminated, Ray concentrated exclusively on working with Fred Rich, whose itinerary included a 1927 tour of England.

Bauduc's extrovert nature was made obvious by the eye-catching way he played the drums, Fred Rich soon discovered that Ray's flamboyance extended to dancing. The New Orleans drummer had devised a routine on the exotic steps he'd seen performed in carnival parades back home, he added some ideas of his own, and the result was a series of contortions that were a mixture of shimmies and snake-hip movements. The dance became a standard part of Fred Rich's stage show and later enjoyed lasting popularity with audiences who went to see Bob Crosby's band.

In November 1928, the British *Melody Maker* announced that Ray Bauduc had left Rich, the item also paid tribute to his terpsichorean skills: "Ray Bauduc, who caused a sensation when over here with Freddie Rich's Band, with his showmanship and splendid dancing, no longer with Rich". By the time that transatlantic news item appeared in print, Bauduc had joined Ben Pollack's Band on the recommendation of Pollack's trombonist, Jack Teagarden.

The American dance-music profession was suprised to learn that Ben Pollack, generally regarded as one of the leading jazz drummers of his era, and still only in his mid-twenties, had signed a young up-and-coming percussionist to take his place behind the drum kit. The background emerged that Pollack had accepted the job of providing a band for the "Hello Daddy" musical show, this meant he would have to conduct for part of each evening, hence the need for a drummer.

Bauduc joined Pollack's Band (which then included Benny Goodman, and Jack Teagarden) at the Park Central Hotel in New York, so that he could get accustomed to working with the band before they left, a month later, to go to Philadelphia, where in Bauduc's words "they began to rehearse and break in the 'Hallo Daddy' show".

After its out-of-town tryouts, the show opened in New York in December 1928, and ran until the following June. As soon as the Pollack Band had settled into the show's routine they were able to double engagements by resuming their residency at the Park Central Hotel. The band also managed to find time to broadcast regularly, and to appear in a short Vitaphone film that featured Estelle Brody.

The competent way that the band handled its chores in the "Hallo Daddy" show led them to be offered a similar spot in Ginger Roger's first big show *Top Speed,* which ran from November 1929 until March 1930. When this show ended Pollack made no move to resume his place at the drum kit and settled for the position out-front, occasionally moving back to play a drum feature.

Bauduc found that he had to adjust his drumming when he joined Pollack's Band, so that he sounded closer to the leader's style, "because the band wouldn't swing otherwise", like Pollack, he began to play on brushes for quieter effects. Pollack was not the easiest of mentors, he had his own drum kit set up in front of the band, and often made his point by forcibly demonstrating what he required, naturally this didn't altogether please Bauduc, but when there was no spare drum kit, Pollack often outlined his requirements by hitting Ray's cymbals, and this was even more annoying.

So despite the admiration that both men had for each other's skills, arguments tended to develop between them during the early days of their working together. Onlookers in the band talked for years afterwards about a flaming row the two men had when Pollack accused Bauduc of speeding the tempo on one of the band's big numbers, *Pagan Love Song*. Touchy situations were not helped by Pollack often muttering that there was only one drummer in the world for him, one Chiefy McIlroy, an obscure Chicago musician. However, in time things settled down between the leader and his drummer, and a bond of mutual respect and friendship grew between them. Bauduc's inspiration came from various New Orleans drummers, and from Pollack, but he also profited from regular visits to hear George Stafford playing in Charlie Johnson's Band at Small's Paradise in New York.

When the Pollack band broke up in late 1934, Bauduc drove east with Yank Lawson, he left Yank in Minneapolis and went across to nearby St. Paul to see his fiancee, Edna. Later, Yank, Ray and their wives shared an apartment in the Whitley Block when the band members reached New York. During the period that Pollack's "Orphans" were rehearsing, Bauduc took various freelance gigs, and also played on recordings with Glenn Miller, Wingy Mannone and Louis Prima.

Bauduc became a vital force in the new Bob Crosby band, he was a constant fund of worthwhile ideas, and put forward many useful suggestions during the band's embryo period. He did the same sort of thing for Wingy Mannone, who acknowledged Bauduc's help in the autobiography *Trumpet On The Wing*.

Bauduc's keeness was such that he could hardly wait to begin playing, his eager spirit hustled anyone who looked like being late on the band-stand, and once the performance got under way, Ray appeared to be, and most often was, in seventh heaven. Leonard Feather, on a visit to the United States in 1936, saw the drummer in action,"As for Ray Bauduc, he is more than a showman. He is a great big boy having a grand time, to the equal delight of himself and the lookers-on. With head lurched forward and swaying, teeth projecting a broad grin, he lets his sticks run riot on the tap-box, traps and everything on his kit, doing things that might be indefensible in a lesser artist".

Ray's agile and intricate dancing also wowed audiences and critics alike, in October 1936, *Metronome* reported "Ray Bauduc went through a routine which would have taxed a python and raised a cackle at a funeral". But plaudits for Bauduc weren't restricted to his flamboyancy, and in 1936 when Louis Armstrong's book *Swing That Music* was published, Ray was cited as 'a foremost performer on the drums'.

Besides being part-composer of several of the Crosby Band's most important recordings, Bauduc's livewire nature also led him to coach anyone in the band who hadn't quite grasped the subtleties of New Orleans Jazz. Bob Haggart remembers Bauduc handing out advice, literally, by banging out rhythmic patterns on the steering wheel of his Plymouth, and several band members recall Bauduc regularly saying "What this number needs is a good rat-a-tat lead". "The New Orleans drop beat" was probably the phrase that entered into Bauduc's musical discussions more than any other, he felt its useage was vital for the correct interpretation of New Orleans jazz, and elaborated "Dixieland is characterized by light accents played on the second and fourth beats, I always try to keep such accents sounding, whether playing a basic two beats or four beats in the bar".

One of Bauduc's great assests was his ability to create many varied effects on his drum kit. Like Zutty Singleton, and many other great New Orleans percussionists, he was not afraid to provide a change of tone-colour by using his woodblocks, playing press rolls, or tapping a long series of rim-shots. In March 1937, a *Down Beat* writer summarised the drummer's work, "Ray Bauduc's ability to change the rhythmic background several times in an arrangement without spoiling the solid groove of the whole band, whilst still giving the soloist the kind of rhythm or beat that inspires him most, is one of the secrets of the Crosby Band's interesting personality".

Bauduc was not averse to punctuating the band's phrasing or a soloist's improvisations with a perfectly timed 'splash' from his Chinese cymbal. The effect became an easily identifiable part of his playing, but for a time its use was threatened when the cymbal developed a crack. Ordinarily, Bauduc could have simply ordered a replacement, but at the time, China and Japan were at war, and none were being exported. Ray got the Avedis Zildjian company to make a close copy, which had rivets inserted into it to capture the required sound, this proved to be the proto-type of the "sizzle" cymbal, which gained popularity with drummers all over the world.

Ray's natural aptitude for understanding mechanical problems allowed him to repair all sorts of devices, and this led to Eddie Miller nick-naming him, 'the Fixer-Up'. Bauduc regularly repaired other drummer's accessories, and helped the Ludwig company design the "Speed King" foot pedal.

Bauduc's battery of sound effects was anathema to some critics, who pounced on the fact that he sometimes tended to speed up in solos, other drummers equally guilty of this offence were left alone, but for a good deal of the Crosby band's existence Ray's playing was criticised regularly in print. The detractors would have been happier if Bauduc had chosen to adopt the conformities shared by most of the swing band drummers of the period. Had he have done so, the Bob Crosby Band would have lost one of its instantly recognizable aural trade-marks.

During the Crosby Band's heyday, Bauduc was something of a dandy, always well aware of the latest fashions in men's clothes. Arranger Glen Osser, who wrote for the early Crosby Band, has good reason to remember, with affection, this side of Bauduc's interests. "At that time, 1936, the syle of men's pants was big pleats and pegged bottoms (16 inches). Ray Bauduc was the "fashion plate" of the band. I had read in *Esquire* magazine that wide bottoms were going to be the coming style, so I had a suit made up with wide bottoms. When I showed up at the rehearsal with my new suit, Ray wanted to know who told me to get the wide trousers. When I told him about having read it in *Esquire* I broke him up. The band kidded me about the suit for a long time, and they called me 'Esquire'."

Bauduc's jocularity existed alongside his dedication to New Orleans jazz, and his desire for individualism. In 1939, a time when he was the victim of much critical sniping, he said "I play a different style of drums than most guys do; yet I'd never say they're wrong, and Gene Krupa and Ray McKinley and them guys don't tell me I'm wrong either. Music's like a guy's religion. It's something he feels inside of him and nothing that any of us says or does is going to make him feel different. As long as a musician is sincere in what he's doing, he's doing right. The only time we got a real right to criticize is when a guy knows that he's playing the wrong kind of music. They probably come apologizing to you saying it's all wrong musically, but they gotta make money someway. Boy, let's let them have it!".

Bauduc's heart was always in jazz, and although he turned in some admirably competent performances on the Crosby Band's commercial recordings, his efforts there do not compare with his superb drumming on the jazz numbers. It was common knowledge that he disliked accompanying ballads, and stories about him tuning and tampering with his drums whilst vocalists were trying to emote are true. Bauduc was highly responsive to the music that was being created around him, and he liked nothing more than accompanying a free-flowing jazz soloist. Eddie Miller, who of all the Crosby Band's New Orleans contingent was probably least close to Bauduc, says, "Ray always played good for me. At various times, Warren Smith and Hank D'Amico called me aside and said 'How come Bauduc plays good for you and not for me?'. I don't think it had anything to do with New Orleans, it was because I used to turn around and smile at Ray as I was about to begin my solo, and this would make him feel good, and he'd start to lay it down behind me".

But if Bauduc detested ballads, he loved the blues, and was prone to say so. "Without the blues there wouldn't be any of this 2-beat or 4-beat jazz of today. For the blues is the basis of all real jazz and a musician who doesn't know and love the blues - the real authentic blues of New Orleans - hasn't a chance. Down south, the blues really stands for something. Once you've heard those colored workers along the levee of the Mississippi singing and chanting the blues in their bluest, most sincere form, you can't get away from them. That's why the New Orleans school of musicians play the blues better than says the Chicago style guys of the Kansas City style men or any other style you want to name".

Bauduc joined in most of the band-room fun that the Crosby group enjoyed, without ever making a nuisance of himself. The New Orleans bandleader, Norman Brownlee, who had known the drummer for many years said "Ray Bauduc was outstanding in his carriage, and his appearance. He loves a good time but always knows when to stop". Away from the Crosby Band's gigs, Ray usually spent most of his time with his wife, Edna. The couple had no children and this allowed Mrs. Bauduc to travel more regularly than most of the other band wives. Both Ray and Edna maintained a canny outlook and preferred to shop around before buying anything, carefully selecting those restaurants that served good food cheaply when the band were on tour. Ray drove from one band job to another whenever he could, but if he had to travel in the band bus he usually spent most of that time deep in slumber.

Bauduc could be outspoken, but this never affected his friendship with Gil Rodin, the Crosby's Band president, and during the first year of World War II both men decided to enlist together. They joined the Coast Artillery Unit 211 Big Band, which was based at Vallejo, California. The big event for the band was their annual stage show, "In 1942 we did a Christmas show like *This Is The Army* and next Christmas we did another show, but there was no touring, we played around Vallejo to sell war bonds, and we sold quite a few million dollars worth".

Bauduc left the service on November 23rd 1944, and Gil Rodin was discharged a little later, both men decided to pool their experience and start their own big band, "We did a lot of Armed Forces camps all over the USA, with Army transportation flying us. We had 26 people in the show, and played about four Army camps a week, taking other work on the remaining three days to make the payroll up, we also did Coca-Cola radio shows. We didn't make any recordings, but we had a wonderful book of arrangements, by Tommy Todd, Johnny Plonsky, Eddie Sauter, Billy May, Justin Stone and many others. We went to Jerry Jones' Rendezvous in Salt Lake City for a one month booking, and we stayed there for twelve weeks. We worked on the East Coast, then we were due to start flying to the Army Camps again, but then the project was grounded so we broke up the band and went back to Los Angeles".

Ray soon bounced back into action and in February 1946 started leading his own quintet at the Susie Q Club in Hollywood, featuring Joe Graves on trumpet, who had been in the Artillery Big Band with Bauduc. The line up was a trumpet and tenor sax front-line, with a three man rhythm section. A reporter covering the quintet's opening said, "There's not a dixie beat in the carload". Bauduc, like most of his ex-colleagues from the Crosby days, was by now weary of the seemingly continuous disparagement accorded to dixieland, and he let his feelings known when he formed the new quintet, "I'm sick and tired of being labelled a Dixieland drummer. I've got nothing against Dixie music, or any other kind, but I'm out to prove to a few zombies that I'm not restricted to the so-called two beat style".

The quintet played a six month residency at the Susie Q, during which time its personnel changed several times, the working schedule at the club allowed the group to play a scene in movie called "Stallion Road" which featured Alexis Smith and Ronald Reagan. After the Susie Q booking ended, Bauduc took a small band to play a brief season at the Club Brazil on Catalina Island.

In October 1946, both Bauduc, and trumpeter Joe Graves were set to join Tommy Dorsey's Band, but at the last moment both changed their minds, Joe Graves went to work briefly with Jimmy Dorsey, and Ray decided to accept Nappy Lamare's suggestion that they form up a co-led sextet. This group, which was the fore-runner of the two men's later joint venture, made its debut on October 19th 1946, but it soon disbanded, because Nappy had become involved in running the Club 47 night club, and Ray had accepted an offer to work in a big band that Bob Crosby had formed up in Los Angeles, in preparation for a widespread tour (which was to include dates in Chicago and Philadelphia).

Ray Bauduc rejoined Bob Crosby early in 1947, replacing Ralph Collier. At that time, Crosby was having a hard time keeping the taxman happy, and this meant that the budget for the band tours was severely limited, there was no money for band-boys or road-managers, and Bauduc had to look after his own drum kit on the road, and set it up for each show. Even so, there were happy moments on the tour, and plenty of friendly faces from the past, but by the late summer of 1947 Ray decided to resume leading his own quintet.

Bauduc's new five piece band played mostly around Los Angeles, its trumpeter Joe Graves soon left to join Charlie Barnet and after Danny Kenyon had taken his place the quintet played another season on Catalina Island. Bauduc's quintet didn't make any recordings, but in late 1947 Ray was given the chance of leading an all-star group for a Capitol date. The personnel included his three ex-Crosby colleagues Lamare, Matlock and Miller, the group's four sides were issued as by 'Ray Bauduc and his Bobcats'.

It was ironical that a revival of interest in Dixieland sounded the death knell for Bauduc's 'jump' quintet. Good class work for the group became scarcer and in early 1948 Ray decided to accept an invitation to join Jimmy Dorsey's Big Band - over twenty years after he had worked with Jimmy in the Scranton Sirens. The reunion lasted for two years, then Ray moved back to Los Angeles and freelanced there for a while before spending three years (1951-54) on the road with a small band led by another of his pals from the 1920s, Jack Teagarden.

Bauduc kept in close touch with Nappy Lamare, and when Lamare relinquished his interest in the Club 47, the two men decided to make a wholehearted attempt to co-lead their own small band. In 1956, they launched the group that became known as Ray Bauduc and Nappy Lamare's Riverboat Dandies, during the following year they made their first album.

The group, which specialised in dixieland, did good business on their wide-ranging tours, playing New York, Chicago, Las Vegas, etc. But by 1960, Ray Bauduc felt that he had done his share of touring, he returned to California and led his own six piece Dixieland band around Los Angeles, playing various residencies, including one at Ben Pollack's Club. During the early 1960s, Ray and reedman Albert 'Pud' Brown worked in a band that played a two year residency at the Roaring Twenties Club in La Cienaga, after that Bauduc began a long association with Texan clarinettist Bob McCracken, the two men occasionally worked in a trio with ex-Bob Crosby pianist Jess Stacy.

Finally, in late 1960s, after spending over 20 years based in California, Ray and his wife decided to make their home in Texas. To his disappointment, Ray had rarely been called on to take part in the various re-unions of Bob Crosby alumni, either in California or elsewhere, so it was not as though his move was going to greatly affect his work prospects. Once he had settled down in Texas he resumed regular playing, and got a great deal of pleasure from sitting in with The World's Greatest Jazz Band during one of their visits to Texas.

Bauduc still keeps in close contact with his old pal, Nappy Lamare, and Bob and Helen Haggart always call into the drummer's Bellaire home when they are en route to their winter retreat in Mexico. Ray lives in highly comfortable surroundings, in a well appointed house complete with workshop and lathe. He is now a widower, his wife Edna having died early in 1983. Bauduc enjoyed many successes during his varied career, for the most part he looks back with contentment on his musical achievements, "All my times were happy", but his special memories concern his years with the Bob Crosby Band, "they were a great bunch of guys".

Bob Haggart

Chapter 17
Bob Haggart

Fellow musicians who grew up with Bob Haggart are convinced that he could have become a world-class performer on trumpet or guitar if he had chosen to specialise on either of them. Both instruments played a big part in Bob's musical adolescence, so too did the piano, but by the time Haggart was 17 he had graduated to the string-bass, and it was on that instrument that he made all the prophecies of international fame come true. By way of underlining predictions about his versatility, he also became one of the best big-band arrangers that has ever lived, and a superb composer.

No one is more aware of a musician's limitations that those who share a bandstand with him regularly, but even men who worked with Haggart for years, have always been emphatic and unstinting in their praise of his talents. Bob Crosby said, "I think he could have been another George Gershwin if he'd chanelled all his talents into composing", Gil Rodin called him "One of the greatest talents in America", and Eddie Miller said "The man himself will never realise just what talents he possesses".

Robert Sherwood Haggart was born on Friday the 13th of March 1914, in New York City, he was raised in Douglastown, Long Island (a place affectionately acknowledged in Bob's magnificent composition, *Dogtown Blues*). Bob was given a banjo-uke for his 13th birthday, he soon mastered it and began yearning for the mellower sounds of a guitar, his mother realised this and bought one for him. Bob began taking weekly lessons from the renowned George Van Eps, and made rapid progress. Creativity and fun went hand-in-hand at the Van Eps's musical household, and soon Bob was asked to join in the jam sessions that the Van Eps brothers, Bobby, Freddy, John and George held in their home. Bob even bought a long-neck tenor banjo so that he could share duets with George.

During his early teens, Bob also played the vast E flat sousaphone in the school band, this led to him playing tuba in a band organised at summer camp. Weary of carrying the heavy brass-bass, Bob auditioned for the job of duty bugler at the camp. Blowing the smaller mouthpiece came easy, and Bob soon graduated on to cornet, buying a beat-up second-hand model for 12 dollars.

Hag, the name he was commonly known by, took his cornet with him when he entered the portals of Salisbury School in Connecticut. There amongst the staid world of prefects, gowned masters, and a regular black-tie dinner routine he became an invaluable member of the "Salisbury Serenaders". His long-time friend, Harlow Atwood, Jr., remembers that Bob showed an early aptitude for arranging by 'doctoring' the printed arrangements that could be bought at a local music store, Bob turned these into 'specials' by re-writing whole portions of the orchestrations. Bob and Harlow's deep affection for jazz made them immune from suffering long-term effects of the school's rigid protocols, Atwood remembers the place as 'a snob factory'.

Bob doubled on cornet and guitar with the band, but for Christmas 1929, he persuaded his parents to buy him a trumpet. But this stimulus didn't cause him to abandon the guitar, thereafter he shared his practice time evenly between the two instruments. "I always have a soft spot for the guitar. My very first gigs were as a guitarist, with Fred Petry's Happy Daze Orchestra, so called because Fred had a big picture culled from a *Saturday Evening Post* which showed a drunk, with the caption *Happy Daze*. Fred had no foot pedal and used to kick his bass drum with a sneaker. The front-line was two saxophones, an alto and a 'C' Melody".

Fred's brother Vic, who was also a musician, remembers when Bob began to double, "He turned up at the Knickerbocker Yacht Club in Port Washington, New York carrying both the trumpet and the guitar asking the band-leader which he would like him to play". The wise leader allowed Bob to switch between the two, which he did with great facility. Hag shared a friendship with the Petry brothers, and it was at their home that he heard his first jazz recording. It was the Frankie Trumbauer recording of *Singing The Blues* (featuring Bix Beiderbecke on cornet), brought to the Petry house by Ward Byron, a young local musician who later became a musical director in radio. Byron, and Fred Petry, who later worked with Artie Shaw, Jack Teagarden and Alvino Rey were only two of several local musicians who made the big time. At jam sessions in the Douglastown area, Bob played alongside the Eps brothers, Will Bradley (trombone), and Stew Pletcher on trumpet. Texan Ray McKinley, on drums, was also a regular at these get-togethers.

In discussing this period of his life, Bob recalls the surge of pleasure he got from listening to *Singing The Blues,* he also recalls the tremendous impact of the first jazz recording he ever bought, Louis Armstrong's *I Can't Give You Anything But Love*. "That one turned my life around, I guess if I had never heard jazz like that I might have become a hosiery salesman like my father. Louis's music seemed to have so much more feeling than most of the white jazz I'd been listening to. It swung harder and it led me to go to the Roseland Ballroom, and to the Savoy, to hear the great black bands of that period, Fletcher Henderson, Chick Webb, Claude Hopkins and so on".

Bob's introduction to playing the string bass came at the Great Neck High School, he saw one leaning against the wall of the school's music room and asked if he could be allowed to play it. As no-one else in the school looked like volunteering to take on the rather unglamorous role of school bassist the teacher readily agreed. With permission under his belt, the long, lanky teenager asked to be shown how to play the scale of 'C' on the bass, the music teacher demonstrated the fingering, then left Hag to his own devices. Before the day had ended Haggart's agile musical brain had worked out the fingering positions for all of the major and minor scales, "I've been making sausages ever since" says Haggart, referring to his round-fingered approach to fingering the sound-board.

Word about Hag's skills on string-bass spread like wildfire amongst the bands in the Douglastown area - here was a kid who not only played the right notes, but imparted a swing to them that lifted even the most stodgy ensemble. At 17, Bob bought his own double-bass (which he nicknamed 'The Black Maria') from Charlie Barber who played in Milt Shaw's New Music (a band that also employed Haggart's pal, Ray McKinley).

Hag and his old Salisbury School friend, Harlow Atwood, (who later also became a professional bassist) spent most of their waking hours listening to jazz, either live or on record. Atwood recalls, "In those days, Bob and I were strongly moved by the playing of Pops Foster, Ernest 'Bass' Hill, and Bill Johnson, as well as the work of Steve Brown of the Goldkette Band. And John Kirby and Elmer James, both originally tuba players, who became fine string-bassists practically overnight".

Haggart worked scores of local gigs during the early 1930s, still managing to hear top class jazz performers whenever he could; on one trip to Princeton in May 1931 he heard Bix Beiderbecke play in an all-star pick-up band. Not long after this event drummer Ray McKinley took Haggart to an apartment that belonged to pianiste, Gladys Mosher, who was then Artie Shaw's girl friend, Gladys pulled out some recordings by Louis Armstrong's Hot Five and put them on the phonograph's turntable. When the music started it provided Haggart with a traumatic experience, "I had heard plenty of Louis Armstrong Big Band recordings, but that first hearing of the Hot Five's *Heebie Jeebies, Georgia Grind,* etc., opened up a whole new world for me". This inspiration was to play its part in Bob's later career.

During the early part of January 1933 Haggart met up with an old friend, Bill Sperling, who asked him if he could play a ten week season at the British Colonial Club, at Nassau in the Bahamas. Hag checked with his mother, then packed his bags and sailed with the band three days later. During the voyage to Nassau rough seas caused the piano to roll into, and smash, Haggart's double bass, fortunately he was able to borrow a three-string model in Nassau to work the season. "It was a great experience, playing all sorts of music. The light music concerts gave me plenty of opportunity to work at my bowing technique". The Nassau season lasted until March 17th; Bob remained with the same band when they returned to Long Island, and played a spring season with them at the Blue Hills Plantation near Princeton. When summer came he worked during July and August with violinist Mitchell Ayers' Band in Jackson, New Hampshire.

A similar itinerary filled the next three years of Haggart's life, seasons close to home, followed by a January trip to Nassau with Bill and Bob Sperling, returning to the USA each March. During Haggart's 1935 jaunt to the Bahamas he received a cabled offer to join the Dorsey Brothers' Orchestra, (having been recommended to Tommy Dorsey by Ray McKinley), but Hag didn't feel ready for that big step and declined the offer. Soon afterwards Benny Goodman expressed an interest in signing Haggart for his band, but again the bassist chose not to follow up the opportunity.

After Bob's March 1935 return from the Caribbean he followed his usual pattern and worked a season with the Sperling Brothers at the Blue Hills Plantation Club. Whilst there he received a telephone call from the Bob Crosby band's major domo, Gil Rodin. Bob recalls that the conversation began with Rodin saying "You're a hard guy to get hold of. We're looking for a bass player and you've been recommended by several people including Glenn Miller and Ray McKinley". Hag liked the sound of the job, and went along to audition at a rehearsal room at 799 7th Avenue, New York. He passed with flying colours.

The Crosby band took to the six-footer-plus with the infectious grin, and to his highly effective way of playing the double-bass, later they were to underline their approval by making him the only non-Pollack musician in the band's corporation. "After the audition, Rodin asked if I could join straight away, and I said 'I guess I can'. My first dates with the band were on recording sessions, then I was in at the deep end playing at the Roseland Ballroom with them. There were hardly any written bass parts, and I just had to find my way through head arrangements of things like *Pagan Love Song, Tin Roof Blues,* etc".

Bob vastly enjoyed the band's first spate of touring which took them into the Carolinas and Georgia. During their memorable season at Tybee Beach in Georgia, the band were taken to Desfusky, one of the many sea islands around the Savannah area, and there, under age-old oak trees heavy with spanish moss, the Crosby musicians were entertained in the open air by local black musicians and gospel singers. The setting and the sounds made a lasting impression on Haggart.

By the time Bob Haggart had served his first year with the Crosby band he had gained a national reputation, both with his fellow musicians, and with the growing number of people who were taking an avid interest in big band music during the mid-1930s. In January 1937, Haggart won the *Metronome* popularity poll on his instrument (and this was to be only the first of his many top placings), but unlike most of the other poll winners who acknowledged their victory by adding their name to a "ghosted" article of thanks, usually written in the current killer-diller jargon, Bob responded to his success with a feature that detailed his love of the blues, which he said should be "played softly, and from the heart without any attempt to make an impression", and went on to describe them as "the best medium of self-expression in jazz".

This obvious sincerity also shone through all of the various instrumental advice columns that Bob wrote for music magazines during this period.

Whilst other players were only recommending the latest trends, and restricting their advice to new developments, Haggart stressed both old and new approaches, and pointed out that there was no crime in occasionally slapping the bass to produce the right effect in a vigorous ensemble.

All the while during the time that Haggart was gaining his masterly technique on the bass he was also absorbing and practicing the finer points of big band arranging. Haggart's scores during the late 1930s were amongst the finest arrangements ever written for big bands, he was able to combine the intensity of the jazz recordings that had inspired him with an ingenious concept of voicing and a superb use of thematic development. He liked Deane Kincaide's approach to arranging, and he worshipped Duke Ellington's skills, but there are no direct debts to either man in Haggart's work, he was truly original. Deane Kincaide himself summarised this when he said "He would have attained greatness without me, or anyone else". Haggart's powers of visualising and adapting unusual material was exemplified in his treatment of the Mitchell Christian Singers gospel song *I'm Prayin' Humble*. The anecdote about him finding the 78 rpm recording, has been mentioned earlier, but the original inspiration for adapting such material had been born as Bob sat listening to the live performances by black singers during the Crosby band's 1935 tour of Georgia and South Carolina.

The turning point in Bob's personal life came in 1937 when he met Helen Frey at one of the band's gigs (the couple recently celebrated 45 years of marriage). Helen, who was a step-daughter of the band's celebrated benefactress, Mrs Celeste Le Brosi, didn't immediately go overboard for Bob, she remembers thinking of him as "A conceited ass". Bob for his part was also cagey, after Mrs. Le Brosi had said "Have I got a girl for you!"; the couple's first meeting was unpromising. But at a re-introduction soon afterward they became mutually enamoured; they were married in March 1938.

Amongst his Crosby band colleagues, Haggart developed something of a reputation for absent-mindedness, simply because he was usually pondering on his next arrangement, or catching up with sleep whilst the band journeyed on to the next gig. He was always a great one for slumber, and used to dive along the band-bus gangway so as to reserve the back-seat in order to stretch out his lanky frame in something approaching comfort. On railroad journeys he was quite happy to moon out of the window deep in thought, which led Bob Crosby to describe him as "the foggiest character I've ever met". All of the band were greatly amused by a Haggart travelling routine which involved talking to a little green man called Fred.

Bob's dry sense of humour won him many friends within the Crosby band, the musicians also got constant pleasure from the cartoons that Haggart drew. With a few deft lines he could encapsulate the idiosyncrasies of anyone in the band, and when he chose to illustrate an anecdote in pictorial form even the most uncollectorish members of the band begged for a copy. Art ran music a close second during Bob's early life, and he has never lost his interest in painting. He showed considerable promise, and studied at the Art Students League, but he decided to divert his time to practising music. Never-the-less, he has produced some interesting paintings over the years, and has been exhibited in various galleries. His principle interest has been in the impressionists, and recently he has resumed studying under various teachers in New York and in Mexico where he and his wife usually spend part of each winter.

After a year or two on the road with the Crosby band, Haggart developed into what might euphemistically called "a steady drinker", happily for his health he was also something of a trencherman, able to down lots of booze and huge meals in easy rotation. In the easy going system of room sharing that existed when the Crosby band were on the road, Bob usually split the expenses of a double room with road manager, Joe 'Red' Kearney, or with Deane Kincaide during the early years. Later on, sharing might involve Matty Matlock, or almost anyone in the travelling party. On one tour Bob shared with Bob Crosby who suggested effective ways of dispelling a hangover, all of them involving an intake of alcohol. For a brief time in 1936, Bob lived in hotel rooms with Joe Sullivan who always had a bottle or two clinking away in his luggage.

Haggart, who had always enjoyed Sullivan's early recordings with Billy Banks, was proud to work with Joe. Later on Hag also played alongside Jess Stacy who had also paid his dues on many historic sessions, but overall his favourite pianist amongst the Crosby band's keyboard players was Bob Zurke. "Zurke's contrapuntal sense made things interesting for a bassist, and whereas the others played heavy tenths with their left hand, which tended to block out my bass line, Zurke's small hands meant he had to work on a different principle, and this allowed me more freedom. Zurke was certainly a schooled musician, and he read music like a snake, but you could have been fooled by physical appearances. He always seemed to wear the same suit, winter or summer, and there was always perspiration on his face. He felt he couldn't play a note unless he'd had a drink, so we decided to play a practical joke on him at one of the band's lunch-time sessions at the Blackhawk. We put cold tea in the bottle of Three Roses whisky that he kept in a locker in the bandroom. Zurke dashed in, sweating as usual, poured out a shot, added some coke to the glass, and gulped the lot down. He wiped his mouth, uttered a Polish salutation, and said 'Boy, did I need that!'. Then he went down to the ballroom and played fine piano".

Bob Haggart rarely got involved in band politics, he says he was simply too engrossed in his music. Years later, when the rest of the long-time corporation members look back on the band's various business crises, Bob, whose memory is excellent, invariably asks "Gee, was I there?", simply because he paid no attention at the time to a raging dispute.

The natural charm that Bob displays in everyday situations moves with him easily when he goes on stage. The twinkling blue eyes provoke a warm response from an audience, and, as if by magic, Hag is able to shed years the moment he picks up his bass. On tour during the 1930s, Haggart was definitely one of the fans' favourites, and was usually besieged by autograph hunters when a gig had ended. The tall, bashful-looking member of the fan dance routine was guaranteed to pluck at the heart strings of girls in the audiences, and listening males realised that the charmer was also a superb musician.

Bob Haggart's arrangements played an invaluable part in the success of Bob Crosby's band, a large percentage of their outstanding recordings were based on his orchestrations. Besides *South Rampart Street Parade, Dogtown Blues, Diga Diga Doo, Between the Devil and the Deep Blue Sea,* etc, he also added delightful touches to tunes that didn't deserve the artistry he bestowed on them. As a composer, Bob enjoyed several successes in the late 1930s, one can only surmise how prolific he would have been if his arranging schedules had not been so time consuming.

After the band's final theatre tour in late 1942, Bob didn't make the move to California like most of his colleagues, he decided to remain on the east coast, his home, and his draft examining board were there. But even after the Army Medical examiners had turned him down, Bob showed to inclination move to California. He was virtually inundated with commissions to arrange for various big bands, and his services as a bassist were in constant demand at radio and recording studios. During the 1940s, Haggart recorded with many jazz immortals, including Duke Ellington, Louis Armstrong and Billie Holiday. He also spent time, lucratively, in various radio bands, and for one period had the plum job of playing, live, a broadcast signature tune that lasted less than a minute - that was all the gig entailed. Bob also enjoyed considerable success writing and producing advertising jingles. The advent of bop didn't panic Haggart into changing his style of playing, he had always possessed a fine harmonic sense, and over the years he gained a vast knowledge of all styles of music. Like many other highly schooled musicians of his era he realised that there was nothing threatening about jazz musicians exploring harmonies that had long been used by Classical composers. Bob half contemplated changing to a five-stringed bass in the mid-1940s after being presented with one by a manufacturer, but the change never materialised. Bob was approached by a sailor in uniform who said he desperately needed to borrow a bass to play a much-needed gig, he loaned the newly acquired five string bass, and never saw the instrument or the sailor again.

Decca, stimulated by the revival of interest in traditional jazz that took place in the early 1950s, asked Bob Haggart and his ex-Crosby colleague, Yank Lawson, to record an album of old jazz favourites. Hag sketched out the arrangements by copying out the melody lines from old recordings. The Lawson-Haggart band was a long-lasting success, which produced a series of albums that sold well over a period of many years. The project offered fascinations for both men, they enjoyed the musical freedom that the sessions offered, and they liked tackling some of the rarely heard material. For Haggart the transcribing of the tunes was sometimes a welcome trip down memory lane, and sometimes a revelation, as in the case of the band's Jelly Roll Morton tribute, when Haggart encountered some of Morton's rarer tunes for the first time.

The 14 year period following the 1942 break-up of the original Crosby band was for Haggart a period of intense activity and rigorous work schedules, mainly in the exacting studio world. Bob's defence against the wear and tear of the ultra-busy itinerary was alcohol, but by 1956 he knew that drinking was wrecking his life, and that of his wife Helen, both of them vowed to stop drinking, and they have maintained their abstinence ever since.

Throughout the 1950s and 1960s, Bob Haggart often took part in various reunions of Bob Crosby alumni, but his closest musical contact was with Yank Lawson, with whom he worked in various studio bands, notably on long-running television shows. In 1966, Bob and Yank were part of the ex-Crosbyites get-together at the Rainbow Grill in New York, and they also shared the bandstand for a series of annual jazz parties organised (since 1963) by the wealthy jazz lover Dick Gibson, in Colorado. The sets that featured Hag and Yank were ecstatically received, not only by the audiences who thronged the Trocadero Ballroom, but also by those who heard the sessions on issued albums. The musical approach engendered by Yank and Bob's group was like an enlarged, up-to-date version of the old Bob Cats.

The success of these informal groups inspired Dick Gibson to suggest that a similar unit could become a highly successful touring unit. Thus the group that came to be known as "The World's Geatest Jazz Band, was born. Neither Bob nor Yank were in favour of the billing, but Gibson's superior knowledge of marketing won them over, and they agreed to the bold name. Opinions vary as to which was the most star-studded version of the W.G.J.B., but whatever the personnel, the band never failed to produce music that was skilful and invigorating.

For a decade the World's Greatest Jazz Band enjoyed a high degree of international success, playing to delighted audiences in Europe, in South America, in Australia and all over the United States (one of their many prestigious bookings was at the White House in 1976). The group made a series of excellent albums, gained a whole army of fans, underwent a managerial crisis or two, and finally disbanded. Bob's eyes don't have their usual twinkle when he summarises the W.G.J.B. era, one gets the impression that he feels the band was never quite able to capitalise on a success that was very close at hand. "We had some wonderful times, no doubt about that, and some of the recordings match up to the *Porgy and Bess* session of which I am still proud of, but perhaps we didn't quite scale the heights that we could have done. Maybe we should have only used Yank on trumpet from the beginning, and not the two trumpets. Billy and Yank worked wonderfully well together, but the two trumpets seemed to need two trombones, and we sometimes fell into an area that didn't have the advantages of a big band, nor the mobility of a small band".

During the 1980s, Bob and Yank were able to resume their own small band using the trade mark that had been on so many successful recordings - the Lawson-Haggart Jazz Band. With this group the two men further strengthened their reputations for always presenting spirited small band jazz in an admirably professional way. Sometimes, during the W.G.J.B. period this professionalism was vital, because for a while the two men did not enjoy the smoothest of personal relationships. Both Bob and Yank share many of the same friends, and aspirations, but to some onlookers it seemed as if their partnership would never survive the 1970s, happily it did, and in recent years both men have moved back toward the easy-going relationship they shared during their days in the Bob Crosby band.

As Haggart nears 70, he is able to enjoy a more relaxed schedule than previously. The royalties from his various compositions have cushioned him from any financial hardship, and both he and his wife are able to spend part of each year in the warm climate of Mexico. They share a common interest in seeing the world's art treasure, and each of them continues to study, Bob painting, and "Windy" sculpture, both are well on the way to mastering the Spanish language.

On a recent trip to Italy, Bob, in order to keep his fingers tough, sat in with an orchestra playing in the San Marco Square in Venice. The group soon discovered who their "guest" was, and he was besieged by admiring musicians, in describing the scene he said, "before I was merely a fair New York bass player on vacation". Such modesty is typical of Haggart, and blends beautifully with his droll humour. He was a vital factor in the success of Bob Crosby's band, but to hear him reminisce you would never guess it.

Hilton 'Nappy' Lamare

Chapter 18
Nappy Lamare

Almost all of the original Bob Crosby sidemen came from musical families, the notable exception was Hilton 'Nappy' Lamare, whose guitar work and vocals played an important, albeit under-publicised, part in the success of the band. Nappy rarely took solos, but his vocals, - usually delivered in a light-hearted drawl - always pleased the listeners, and his amiable personality won him many friends.

He was born on Dumaine Street, New Orleans, on the 14th June 1907, the son of a printer whose ancestors had journeyed to the New World from France; Hilton's mother was of German origin. As Hilton entered his teens it seemed to go without saying that he too would be a printer, like his father, and his father before him. The young man had no aversion to following the craft, and happily spent school vacations learning all he could about type faces, proofing and paper sizes. But, one day, whilst strolling idly along a New Orleans street, Hilton saw and heard a black marching band, within its ranks was a shortish, broad-shouldered young trumpeter, who was creating what seemed to Hilton Lamare the most marvellous music he'd ever heard. It was like a happy dream to the young schoolboy, and looking back over sixty years later, Lamare still can't believe his luck, because those first responses toward jazz were evoked by a musician who was soon to turn the music world upside down. The young man whose sound had flown out of the marching ensemble like a golden arrow was, bizarrely enough, Louis Armstrong.

No printer's ink was as indelible as the memory of that sound, and Hilton spent as much time as he could listening to Louis, and to Kid Rena and Punch Miller. There seemed nothing in the world so important as getting himself a trumpet and trying to play the music that these giants were creating. His parents gave him the money, he bought a horn and began practising loud and long.

Hilton was soon in the midst of other young musical New Orleanians, all of them doing their best to recreate the jazz sounds that were part of their heritage. Hilton made fair progress, but one boy, banjoist Emmett Durel teased Lamare about every aspect of his trumpet playing. Finally Hilton's patience snapped and he angrily told his tormentor, "It would only take me a month to learn to play the banjo better than you do". Durel laughed at what he took to be an idle boast, but there and then Lamare decided to make the drastic change, he abandoned the trumpet for the banjo. He began taking banjo lessons from one of the finest young musicians in the area, Jules Bauduc

Jr. Lamare made swift progress, and within the month was playing the banjo in a local band, he was still only 13.

Gradually, the best of the local young musicians drifted together to form up a small band called *The Midnight Serenaders*. The group took any sort of engagement that was offered, one of their first paid gigs was playing as accompanists for a silent movie, at a dollar apiece. It all seemed pretty glamorous to Hilton who was still a pupil at the Warren Easton School.

Hilton struck up a friendship with Jules Bauduc's brother Ray, who was just starting to find work as a drummer. When Hilton hadn't got a gig he helped Bauduc carry his drums to various engagements, "Ray wasn't fully grown, and he had a huge bass drum that was so big he couldn't sit behind it and be seen, so he used to stand up to play, until he grew taller". Hilton also studied with a fine black guitarist, Narvin Kimball, Kimball and another riverboat player called "Sunny" were Lamare's two particular favourites when it came to playing with what he calls "a good beat".

During the early 1920s, Lamare chummed up with a younger musician, Eddie Miller, who was making excellent progress on saxophone and clarinet. Lamare's middle name is Napoleon, and as he often slept in late, Miller began calling Hilton, "Nappy", and the nickname has remained with him ever since. As a teenager, Nappy gigged with many bandleaders in New Orleans, both on banjo and guitar, working with musicians like Sharkey Bonano, Monk Hazel, and Johnny Wiggs made learning an enjoyable process.

Lamare was impressed by the playing of Lew Black, banjoist on recordings made by the New Orleans Rhythm Kings, but, as a young man, his favourite discs were those recently made in Chicago by Louis Armstrong's Hot Five. "I bought all of those records by Louis. I used to try and sing like him on *Heebie Jeebies* and *Big Butter and Eggman*. Louis was my idol, even though I was playing guitar and banjo". Nappy's cheerful singing became a feature of his work, and he was usually called on to provide a few vocals on all the gigs he took.

Nappy's boyhood friend, drummer Ray Bauduc, returned to New Orleans after touring with trumpeter Johnny Bayersdorffer's Band, and asked Nappy if he wanted to join the group. Nappy readily agreed, and during the summer of 1925 worked with the band at the Spanish Fort, then left New Orleans with them, to make the long road trip to California. The band were away for several months, on the West Coast, and in Indianapolis, then they returned to New Orleans to find that work was very scarce.

Bayersdorffer and violinist Billy Lustig became the co-leaders of a new band, and Lamare and Bauduc left with them to play in Chicago. After a month in the windy city things began to look extremely bleak and Nappy went to New York to look for work, there he met up with Billy Burton, a violinist from New Orleans, who had a contract to take a band to Atlantic City. Nappy jumped at the job, and never regretted it, for whilst working in Atlantic City he met his wife Alice, who was then singing in *The Ryan Sisters,* a vocal duo.

Nappy returned to New Orleans, and began working with the New Orleans Owls, (with whom he recorded in 1927), and also with trumpeter Tony Fougerat, but it was increasingly difficult to earn a living wage playing music in New Orleans. Even one of the top bandleaders like George "Happy" Shilling could only afford to pay his musicians three dollars per engagement, his advice to Lamare was forthright and well-intentioned: "Go back up north, and stay there". Nappy took the hint and went back to New York and contacted Ray Bauduc who was working in Ben Pollack's Band. Pollack's guitarist, Dick Morgan, was planning to leave the band, and Bauduc recommended Lamare for the vacancy. Pollack auditioned Lamare in July 1930, and asked him to start work with the band in September, after they had finished playing a season in Saratoga, New York. Nappy stayed around New York and took in the music scene, not always with pleasure, "All the bands around New York at that time were so stiff, nobody ever relaxed. I heard plenty of real 'Mickey Mouse' stuff".

After the Pollack band had completed their Saratoga booking, several of its members decided to leave, amongst the new recruits was Nappy's buddy from New Orleans, Eddie Miller, like Lamare he joined in September 1930. Nappy soon settled in, and was delighted to oblige when Pollack called him out front to sing a comedy song, he also worked out some effective vocal duets with Jack Teagarden, including one called *Bend Down Sister,* which according to other band members was so well performed it should have been recorded.

Lamare played in many cities with Pollack's Band, including Cleveland, Detroit, Chicago and New Orleans, but the residency that stands out for him was the 1933 booking at the Casino De Paree in New York. By then, Lamare had emerged as one of the personalities of the group, he could easily make an audience smile, and this meant that was often called on to assist various cabaret acts with whom the Pollack band worked. An uncharming dancer insisted that he had to have a guitarist on stage with him for his act, one who could play seated at the top of a ladder, whilst wearing a sombrero. Nappy cheerfully obliged, and raised no objection when asked to smoke a cheroot whilst strumming. The stage was dimmed and only Lamare's silhouette was seen by the audience, that was until he began puffing away at his cheroot with a ferocity that turned it into what Eddie Miller describes as "a fiery roman candle". The band became convulsed with laughter, and so too did the audience. The only person not amused was the egotistical cabaret artiste. From then on he managed without a guitarist up aloft. Lamare was philosophical about the debacle, "Those damned cheroots were a lousy smoke, give me my Picayune brand of cigarettes any day".

After the exodus from Ben Pollack's Band took place in late 1934, Lamare paid a brief visit to New Orleans before linking up with the rest of his colleagues in New York. He became a founder-member of the Bob Crosby Band, and remained until the December 1942 break up. His only absence took place in 1938, when he entered a Chicago hospital for an appendectomy, his place in the band was taken temporarily by Len Esterdahl.

Nappy was one of several golf "fanatics" within the Bob Crosby Band, he also had a keen interest in photography, and was always snapping away at the rest of the band, sometimes when they least expected to be photographed. Some of his work was published, and one shot of saxophonist Doc Rando's young daughter was used by the Adohr Farms company in their dairy produce advertisements. Nappy and his wife Alice had three sons, Hilton Jr, Barry and Jimmy, all of whom were regularly photographed by their proud father.

Nappy enjoyed the Blackhawk, Chicago residency more than any other that the Crosby Band played. The collegiate crowd there loved Lamare's slightly whacky singing, and the venue, was, probably more than any other place, the "home" of the Bob Cats. Nappy enjoyed the big band numbers, but at heart he was most interested in the small band's jazz routines. Like all the other New Orleans musicians in the band, he was openly proud of his Crescent City heritage, "You don't have to start an investigation to learn where the music of the Crosby band was conceived. It's strictly New Orleans in character and not without reason. Back home you are exposed to good jazz when you're still a little shaver, and you grow up absorbing the right kind of music".

After the Crosby Band disbanded in late 1942, Lamare worked regularly with Eddie Miller's Band in California. Eddie could foresee that he would soon be called up for the services, so he asked Nappy to continue leading the band whilst he was away. After Eddie had been drafted in 1944, Nappy took over the personnel that had been working with Miller and played engagements along the Californian coast, but because of draft intakes and travel restrictions it became an impossible task and Nappy soon cut down the line-up into a small band which worked mainly around the Los Angeles area.

When Eddie Miller was released from the Army Air Force he resumed leading a big band for a while, which featured Nappy on guitar and vocals, but he disbanded to enter a film studio orchestra. The two men remained firm friends, they often met socially and played many casual small band dates together during the 1940s. They were also part of the Capitol recording studios 'pool' of musicians, and played on scores of dates as accompanists to various artistes. Nappy continued to lead his own small band, and for a brief period in 1946 co-led a sextet with his old colleague, drummer Ray Bauduc.

Lamare kept in close contact with other ex-Crosby musicians who lived in the Los Angeles area, and early in 1947 formed up a business partnership with two of the band's ex-saxophonists, Doc Rando, and Noni Bernardi. The three men purchased what had been Earl Handson's night club on Ventura Boulevard in Studio City, Los Angeles, they renovated the place, got the necessary licences to serve drinks and provide music then opened up their own night spot called "Club 47" (in honour of their musicians' union, Local

47).
Besides taking an active part in the club's administration and in the general toil the three partners took turns in providing the music, playing alongside a pianist and drummer (usually Lee Countryman and Zutty Singleton). Sitters-in were welcome and some star-studded line-ups assembled there to play jam sessions that Lamare remembers with nostalgic affection. The lively atmosphere of the club attracted many film stars, and some of them (with a little persuasion) got up and sang with the band. Bob Mitchum's croaky but expressive blues singing was often heard there, and many famous big band leaders, including Benny Goodman, Harry James and Ray Anthony graced the small bandstand at various times.

Except for a spell in 1948 when he worked with Jimmy Dorsey's Band, Nappy was on hand to help with the running of the club, dovetailing his activities there with the playing of freelance gigs, both as a sideman and as a leader. But, by early 1950, Lamare thought it wiser to redevelop his own band on a more permanent basis, they began playing at the Beverly Cavern, in Los Angeles, filling-in on the nights that the resident Kid Ory Band were absent. The group soon achieved an attractive cohesion and were chosen to be the resident band on a KTLA television show called *Dixie Showboat.*

In 1950, when Nappy Lamare's Straw Hat Strutters began their regular appearances, television was only just beginning to establish itself. Its appeal developed with an astounding rapidity, and so too did the reputation of Nappy's Band. An appearance in the film *Hollywood Rhythm* also helped to increase their popularity. They played many prestigious bookings in Los Angeles, including the Palladium, Sardi's, and the Astor, they also did a riotous season at the Hangover in San Francisco.

Nappy retained his interest in Club 47, but with Doc Rando often absent, playing regularly in theatre and radio bands, it was left to Noni Bernardi to hold the fort. The three partners decided in 1951 that there were too many headaches in running the club, and they put it up for sale. By then KTLA's *Dixie Showboat* had gone national with the result that Nappy's group was offered work all over the States. The band toured regularly until 1954, most of its material consisted of traditional jazz favourites, and songs that featured what Nappy calls his "novelty voice", he also played many numbers on banjo - the instrument he affectionately refers to as "pork chop"

Lamare continued to lead the band during the mid-1950s, but by 1955 most of their dates were in the Los Angeles locale, which gave the leader a chance to resume his prolific freelance recordings. Nappy also took part in several re-unions of ex-Bob Crosby sidemen, and flew to the East Coast in 1955 to work with Bob.

In 1956, Lamare enjoyed another working re-union, this time with drummer Ray Bauduc, this get-together proved to be the start of a long musical partnership between the two musicians, whose co-led *Riverboat Dandies* worked consistently throughout the remainder of the 1950s. From the onset, the two co-leaders stressed that the "accent of the band will be placed on entertainment", and they lived up to that maxim, providing a light-hearted blend of dixieland favourites, speciality numbers and vocals. Nappy began doubling on Fender bass and was thus able to recreate Bob Haggart's role on the band's version of *Big Noise From Winnetka.*

By the early 1960s, both Nappy and Ray felt they'd had enough of the touring routine, they decided to bring the band off the road, both men stayed in Los Angeles for the next few years, but eventually Bauduc carried out his plan to move to Texas. In 1962, a severe auto crash almost ended Nappy's musical career, but slowly, through regular physio-therapy he was able to resume regular playing. By 1963 he was again leading a band locally, and also played a long residency in a banjo and piano duo with Bob Marquis, he also worked in Joe Darensbourg's Band.

For the next decade, Nappy continued to lead his own bands on a casual basis, mostly in California, but sometimes he took trips out of the state to play in reunion bands organised by Bob Crosby. He also guested at various jazz festivals, and was persuaded to make an occasional appearance with *The World's Greatest Jazz Band.* In 1975, he took part in the package show *A Night in New Orleans* which visited Europe; he returned to Europe to play the 1981 Nice Festival with Bob Crosby.

The great sadness of Nappy's later life came with the death of his wife Alice, he still keeps in close touch with his three sons, and during 1982 visited one of them in New Zealand. He continues to keep in practice on his instruments, and plays gigs as often as he wants to, his closest contact with the Bob Crosby gang is his life-long friend Eddie Miller, who lives close by, but all of the alumni keep him posted with their news; Yank Lawson recently sent him an ancient camera to add to his vast collection. Nappy has a good word for almost everyone in the music business, and the sentiments are heartily reciprocated.

Billy Butterfield and Eddie Miller, 1940.

Chapter 19

Billy Butterfield

Billy Butterfield's name inevitably enters any discussion about the Bob Crosby band, a fact that underlines the impact that his trumpet playing with Crosby made on jazz listeners. Billy wasn't with the Crosby band for any great length of time, slightly less than three years, but, even though he enjoyed many successes in other famous bands, including Artie Shaw's and Benny Goodman's, he is invariably referred to as "the-ex Bob Crosby sideman". Thus he has often been part of many of the Bob Crosby reunions that have taken place during the past 30 years; his ex-colleagues from that band revere his playing, and delight in his easy-going company.

A lover of subtle jokes, and off-beat anecdotes, Billy possesses a quiet charm and an innate friendliness. He is a thoughtful man, often retiring amongst strangers, but unfailingly courteous and friendly to well-wishers. He speaks in slow, soft sentences, occasionally hesitating in mid-phrase until he finds the exact word to make his meaning crystal clear. He can talk informatively on a wide range of subjects, and listens readily, but one can almost hear him groan when someone attempts to get him penned into a discussion about a discographical query concerning a recording he made many years ago. He never gets impatient, but sometimes those bright china-blue eyes lose their lustre as he is being remorselessly grilled about the name of an obscure third trombonist with whom he worked once on a session long ago.

Endless discussions about his own recordings would not figure high on a list of Butterfield's favourite activities, even so, he never bites a discographer, for, as he readily explains, he can still clearly remember his own days as an admiring, teenage jazz fan. His particular heroes were Louis Armstrong, Jack Teagarden, Bunny Berigan, and Eddie Miller - by the time he was 20 he was working alongside Miller in Bob Crosby's band.

Billy, born in Ohio in January 1917, comes from a musical family. His father, a keen amateur musician, had been at school with the American cornet virtuoso, Frank Simons, and it was arranged that Billy went to Simons for lessons. He stayed with the same teacher for almost two years before being offered a place at Transylvania College. There, Billy was persuaded to study medicine, but as the college had a good dance band, his chances of qualifying as a doctor diminished with each gig that he played. There just wasn't time to work with the college band and with local outfits and still get all the college's homework done, so Billy quit being a student and joined a band in Lexington, Kentucky led by Andy Anderson, a fairly non-musical ex-All American Basketball player. A trick of fate occurred whilst Billy was working with Anderson's Band, and it altered his whole life. In 1936, Bob Crosby, and bassist Bob Haggart, were travelling by car during a string of summer one-nighters when their automobile broke down in Lexington. Immediate repairs were out of the question, so they wired details of their predicament to the rest of the band, and settled down to take in the night-life of Lexington. At the local Joyland's Park bandstand they heard Butterfield's gorgeous tone ringing out loud and clear, and Haggart immediately realised that the young player would be an asset to the Crosby Band. He and Crosby approached Billy, who said he was only too willing to be considered for the job. All parties concerned celebrated this first meeting, and Bob Haggart can still remember the hardness of the Joyland Park bench on which he awoke some hours later.

Next day the two visitors moved on. Months passed and Billy came to the conclusion that he was no longer in the running for a place in Bob Crosby's Band. Early in 1937, together with several other musicians from Andy Anderson's Band, he joined Austin Wylie's Band in Pittsburgh. His outstanding work with Wylie's Band was heard on the radio by Bob Haggart and Matty Matlock and they persuaded Gil Rodin to increase the size of the trumpet section to a three man unit in order to accomodate the obvious talents of Billy Butterfield. A telegrammed offer was sent to Billy, who accepted the seventy five dollars a week salary, and packed his bags. The money involved was little more than Billy was already making, but he seized his opportunity to work alongside musicians whose playing he greatly admired.

Billy joined the Crosby Band during their residency at Billy Rose's Aquacade in Cleveland, Ohio. "What the band didn't realise was that I would have worked for less, I was that keen to join them". The new arrival, being an addition to the trumpet section, found that there were no third trumpet parts written, some were hastily commissioned from a freelance arranger named Bob Pierce, but they did not blend in easily with the other two trumpets, so Billy worked out harmonies and added his own parts. Soon Yank Lawson, Zeke Zarchy and Billy were all swopping the lead trumpet parts, and this practice continued when Charlie Spivak replaced Zarchy. Spivak was one of the few musicians with whom Billy didn't enjoy an easy relationship, and the two men rarely shared a social conversation.

"In general, the Crosby Band was a special gang of guys, a true fraternity" says Billy "several of them remain life-long friends of mine. Our official base was in New York City, but the touring schedule was coast-to-coast. When we had a long stay in a particular city everyone in the band brought along their wives and families, that happened when we played a long residency at the Blackhawk in Chicago. I took an apartment for my family for a hundred dollars a month, and we settled down for the entire run."

Whilst the Crosby band were in Chicago on one of their periodic stays,

Billy was featured on the celebrated recording of *I'm Free* (which later became *What's New*) "I nearly didn't get that one, Charlie Spivak made a grab for the melody part, but Bob Haggart had marked my name on it. I had to make a good job of it, so you can imagine my feelings when I heard Haggart play the first copy of the recording on the gramophone he kept at his hotel. It sounded lousy, woefully off-pitch, I couldn't believe it and went into the room to hear it more clearly. We then discovered that Haggart had got hold of a copy on which the record-hole was off-centre so it all sounded out of tune, fortunately all the rest were okay".

Billy has always had a soft spot for people who don't automatically toe the line of conformity, and within the ranks of the Crosby Band he found two ace deviants, Bob Zurke and Irving Fazola. "Occasionally Faz and I would share a room when we were on tour. He was a big drinker, but never any trouble to me. He just wanted fun, he was one of life's party-goers, and he was a marvellous player. Drinking heavily hardly affected his playing, it didn't show in his work, except maybe until the last set of the night. His weakness was he couldn't stand anyone to laugh at him, if they did he'd get as mad as hell. Zurke could also do his share of drinking. I nicknamed him "Lord Chesterfield" because in winter-time he wore an ancient overcoat with a velvet collar. He didn't go in for sartorial elegance, and on one occasion when we were asked to buy new dark shoes to blend in with our band uniforms Zurke simply said "Fuck that". He went into a nearby hotel, sat down at one of the writing desks they had, and began dipping his handkerchief in the inkstand and dabbing it on his off-white summer shoes turning them into the required navy blue colour, when he had completed his task, he took both shoes off with a great air of nonchalance and put them on the radiator to dry. Needless to say they looked a wreck on the bandstand".

"I was a non-corp member of the band, and so were Faz and Zurke, somehow it did make a difference, not in friendships between various members of the band, but in attitudes. Overall, it was a happy band, naturally there were minor rows, there has got to be when 14 guys live and work together for long periods, but nothing vicious, ever. We could all share a laugh, and we had plenty, and many good times, particularly when Mrs. Le Brosi was our guardian angel, laying on the finest food and the best drinks for all of us to enjoy at her expense". The veterans of the Crosby Band, in listing Mrs. Le Brosi's amazing generosity cite the occasion on which she 'bought Billy Butterfield a car'. But Billy sets the record straight on that one.

"Mrs. Le Brosi was a dear kind woman, but she did not buy me an automobile. One night she told me, in the course of conversation that she had put the deposit down on a new model, but having thought things over she realised that she hadn't any need of it. If I wanted it, I could pay the balance, I jumped at the offer and bought the car".

During his last year with the Crosby Band, Billy introduced two of his ex-Austin Wylie colleagues into the band, reedman Bill Stegmeyer and trumpeter

Bob Peck, both of these were assets to their particular sections being brilliant readers. Not everyone in the Crosby brass section was a perfect sight-reader, and this made Billy's job all the harder since it often meant he had to play the lead trumpet part on an arrangement, and also play the solos. "Muggsy had his own individuality, but he wasn't much of a reader in the section, whereas Sterling Bose could play nice jazz, but could also read well".

Billy feels that 1940 was the turning point for the Crosby Band as far as earnings, "Pay from theatre dates rose, and there were extras from recordings, and money from the sponsored radio shows, so there were bonuses on top of a basic rate". But all this activity meant that Billy was away from his wife and family more than ever. "Coming off the road was more my wife's idea than mine, but I did need a change and when I was offered a chance to stay in Chicago and work in Bob Strong's Band on radio I took it, I had a pal, Dick Maltby in that band and things worked out for a while, but when Bob took a band on the road that was much less successful. I got the chance to join Artie Shaw, originally to play for the movie *Second Chorus,* but it became a regular thing, and I guess I was there about five or six months, it was good while it lasted".

After leaving Shaw, Billy joined Benny Goodman's Band ("that was twice as loud as Artie Shaw's Band, or Bob Crosby's"), this move allowed Billy to compare, at close quarters, the respective merits of the two most famous clarinet-playing bandleaders of the era. I always get the impression that Billy would not like to be wrecked on a desert island with either of them, but as far as their musical company, Billy feels that Goodman was the superior improviser. He found both men to be enigmatic, but as he continued to work on-and-off with Benny Goodman for over thirty years he estimates that he was the least understandable of the two, "I always used to think that if I returned once more to work with Goodman I'd finally understand him as a person, but I never did. Of course, all of the famous bandleaders had to keep their distance from the sidemen, just so that discipline could be maintained, the leader might be employing musicians who were his old drinking buddies, and things change the more successful people become".

Billy's first stint with Benny Goodman lasted for almost a year, he left early in 1942 to join the up-and-coming Les Brown Band. "That was really Joe Glaser's idea. He had signed Les Brown and was trying to build the band up, it was Glaser who actually paid my salary". Billy only spent a short while with Les Brown, he then felt that it was time to start taking up the offers he was receiving to work in various studio bands. His ability as a soloist, both sweet and hot, his sight-reading capabilities and his adaptability made him an ideal session musician. But, just as he was settling into a lucrative groove at CBS and NBC his draft papers arrived and he spent the next three years in the US Army.

For many musicians, conscription into the services meant immediate drafting into a big service band in which few military duties needed to be performed. For Billy things were very different, he was posted to an Infantry Regiment and did his full share of boot and rifle drill. Billy remembers it all philosphically, "There were consolations. I could carry my mouthpiece anywhere. I've always believed in pushing that into my chops when there were no facilities for practice. Even today, I'll be sitting watching television, and I'll be grinding that mouthpiece cup into my lips, and buzzing away".

In the immediate post-World War II period, many star soloists were tempted into becoming leaders of their own big bands. Billy Butterfield was amongst that large contingent of optimists, in 1945 he succumbed to what Rex Stewart once called "the dreaded complaint - leaderitis". To this day, Billy regards the experiment as one of the big mistakes of his life "I suppose it cost me about 35,000 dollars, which in the 1940s was a lot of money. I went into it full of hope. We set out as a fourteen piece band, I carefully selected the musicians and commissioned good arrangements from people like Bob Peck, and I had Bill Stegmeyer on hand as staff arranger. Everything was right except the period of time, because the bottom fell right out of the big band business just as we were getting started. I put every cent I had into it, hoping that the lack of business was only a temporary lull, but it wasn't".

"Our last tour ended fairly abruptly in Indiana. Being stranded without money is a bandleader's nightmare, and it happened to me, we had to wire to our record company, just to get enough money to make our way back to New York. I was forced to have all the arrangements in the library re-written for a smaller band, just to keep going. Out of it I learnt an important lesson: it's better to pay 25 per cent commission to an agent for regular, well-paid work than to pay 10 per cent on occasional dates. I also learnt who my friends were, some guys who I had known for years struck hard bargains when they knew I was down as low as I could be".

It took Billy many months of hard work, in the studios by day, and in the clubs at night, to straighten out his financial predicament. During this period, he joined the house-band at Nick's, the famous New York club named after its founder, Nick Rongetti, a jazz-loving restaurant owner, who only introduced a discord into the musicians' lives when he sat in on piano. Billy did countless nights as Nick's, sometimes working there for months on end, dovetailing this with daytime sessions in the studios. "After Nick died, his wife ran the place, and she really objected to our schedule of also playing at Eddie Condon's Club, but as she was only paying out around forty dollars a week, we used to shrug it off. For quite a while I played regularly, in turn, at Nick's, at Condon's, and at Ryan's. I think Jimmy Ryan's was one of the most tiring gigs ever, we had some good times there, but those long hours were tough. On Saturdays and Sundays there was live music from 5pm until 4am. Old Joe Grauso, the drummer, actually used to doze off to sleep whilst he was playing, he kept going right up to the moment of sound sleep, then we would have to nudge him to set him swinging again".

During this period, Billy often worked for the legendary band-leader Paul

Whiteman, who was then the musical director at the ABC studios in New York. Billy maintains that one of the most awesome binges of his life occurred on a night out with the portly conductor. "Paul would go for quite a while without having a drink, I don't think his wife liked him to even touch the stuff, but every now and then he'd burst out, but he never wanted to drink on his own, so he'd press-gang musicians into joining him. He was prepared to pick up the tab, but you had to keep up with him, drink for drink, then he'd be happy, and less guilty maybe. One night, he took me and Hank D'Amico, who was playing clarinet in the band, out for a taste. Many hours later he insisted that Hank and I went back to his place, which was way out of Manhattan, for a nightcap, he also insisted on driving us there. By this time, Hank and I didn't even know where we were, otherwise that nightride could have been a nightmare. Next morning, Paul's auto looked just as though it had been a battle, part of somebody else's bumper was still attached to Paul's fender. Hank was so ill he couldn't make the studio call that day, and Whiteman got so angry he fired him, but mercifully he relented and had him re-instated. Paul was always okay with me, but he had a mean streak in him which used to surface when he spoke to his old guitarist, Mike Pingitore. Mike looked after the music library, but he was disabled and couldn't move fast, so Paul used to bawl at him at the top of his voice "Speed up, speed up, you misshapen old devil".

"Time is money in a studio band, and everything works out fine as long as you do your job okay, and don't ask too many questions. You learn from experience how each particular musical-director wants things done. The clarinet player, Sal Franzella, was a good musician, but he couldn't stop pointing out his own mistakes to the guy he was working for, but this particular leader was a terrible musician, and he had no idea when Sal, or anyone else, had played a bad note. Sal apologized once too often, and found out that he was leaving the band, he could have been there forever if only he had kept quiet".

"There was nothing like that attitude in the Bob Crosby Band, guys there would shout out "Hold it, I want to get this right". Gil Rodin, wasn't a great saxophone player, so someone in the reed section would say 'Let's do it until we get it right', there was a feeling that we were all working together. Most of the other successful bands of that era had instrumentalist leaders, who were constantly being featured, the Dorseys, Goodman, Shaw, etc., but in the Crosby Band everybody had a chance, there was more scope for individualism".

Some of Billy's favourite memories concern the occasions when he was in studio bands that accompanied Louis Armstrong, his backing to Louis's vocal on the recording of *On Blueberry Hill* is exquisite, but Billy particularly remembers a series of broadcasts with Armstrong that were played live to the East Coast. Three hours later the band and guest star re-assembled and played another show that was beamed to the West Coast. Billy, Louis, and some of the other musicians spent the interlude between shows relaxing in

Hurley's Bar, Billy says the net result was that "the West got some of the swingingest shows ever".

Anyone attempting to compile a discography of Butterfield's freelance recordings would have the enormous task of tracking down the countless studio dates on which he played anonymously. Some of these sessions interested Billy, others were totally mundane, but as he points out, it isn't easy for a professional musician to find an ideal regular working environment. Occasionally, Billy played gigs for a well-known American 'society' bandleader who believed that 'the customer is always right'. At an inauguration ball, an eminent, but heavy customer accidentally stepped on the bandleader's tender big toe. The maestro turned a violent shade of purple and rose two feet in the air, on the descent he heard the heavyweight trampler apologize, choking back tears of pain, the leader gave a low, obsequious bow and said "It was my pleasure, Sir!".

Billy and the rest of the 'subs' in the band curled up with helpless laughter, but those musicians who were on the regular payroll looked stonily ahead. This, and dozens of other incidents, made Billy realize that there were more and more musicians in New York seeking fewer and fewer jobs. Butterfield had long wanted to get away from the clique-like atmosphere that pervades the New York freelance scene, so with his wife and two daughters he moved south, first to Maryland, then to Richmond, Virginia, then on to the Atlanta, Georgia. In each locale he organised his own territory band which toured the college circuits and played hotel ballroom residences. Billy's wife, Dottie, who had sung professionally with several name bands, often worked with her husband on these engagements. "Those ventures were quite satisfying, and they didn't cost me anything, unlike my earlier efforts at leading a band. I guess I might still be doing the same thing, but tastes change, and so do dancing styles, along came rock played by groups, and they got the bookings".

During the mid-1960s, Billy and his family were on the move again, this time to Florida, which has remained home ever since. From his base in Fort Lauderdale, Billy travels to jazz festivals all over the world, he has also taken part in many Bob Crosby re-unions, and was a pillar of strength in *The World's Greatest Jazz Band* for four years, doubling trumpet and flugel horn, alongside his good friend, Yank Lawson. Yank has always been one of Billy's biggest fans, another of Billy's long-time associates, clarinettist Matty Matlock said "I think Billy is the greatest all-around trumpeter in jazz, it's a close thing between him and Clark Terry but I think Billy has certain assets that I don't hear in Clark's playing". Trumpeter Manny Klein, who probably knows as much about brass-playing as anyone in the world, said "Billy Butterfield is one of the only jazz trumpeters who could have played and interpreted all of the great classical pieces".

Not long ago, I was privileged to attend a musical reunion in which Billy, and several of his old colleagues from the Bob Crosby band, played a date at

Carnegie Hall. At the rehearsals I was delighted to hear that Yank Lawson and Billy Butterfield in tandem hadn't lost their telepathic understanding, or their ability to produce music of great power and swing. I was also vastly impressed by Billy's fill-ins behind various vocalists, after one such bout of inventiveness, Eddie Miller leaned over and said "That was real tasty Billy". To hear the sincerity of this praise, given so spontaneously, was positive proof that Billy's lifetime colleagues are also his biggest admirers.

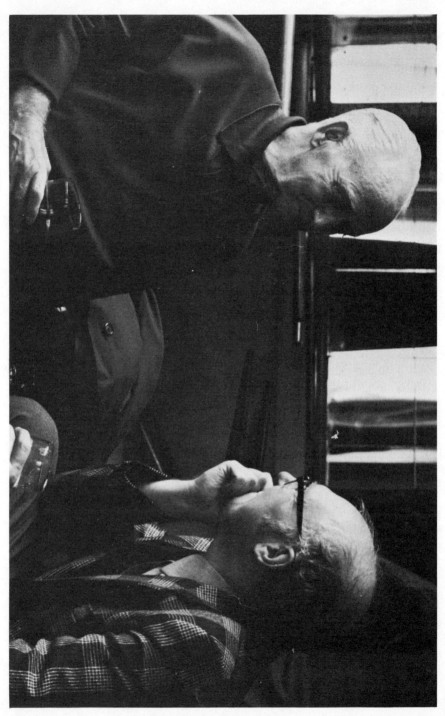

Matty Matlock and the author, 1972.
(photo courtesy of Reg Peerless)

Chapter 20

Matty Matlock

Few clarinettists have ever taken on a hotter seat than the one that Matty Matlock filled when he joined Ben Pollack's Band in 1929, for the previous incumbent was none other than Benny Goodman, already acclaimed by many of his fellow professionals as the finest jazz clarinet player in the world. Matty never aspired to that title, but with the first notes he blew with Pollack's Band he made everyone aware that they were listening to a very fine musician, one who could solo or play an accurate section role with equal ease.

Diligent practice and conscientious study were the basis of Matty's success as a musician (and later on as an arranger), but he never lost the enthusiasm for jazz that developed during his boyhood. Matty's passion for jazz was born almost at the same time as he first handled the clarinet that was loaned to him by the scout-master of his troupe, in Nashville, Tennessee. Matty was then around twelve years old, he had been born Julian Clifton Matlock on the 27th April 1907, in Paducah, Kentucky, but moved with his family to Nashville during infancy.

When school had finished for the day, Matty shared his time between the Boy Scouts' Band, and working in a local drug store. "My mind was on music most of the time, even when I was serving or helping to restock the shelves. The store sold Paramount records, but they didn't have anything to play them on, so I took them home to listen to them. They struck my fancy. There was something there that I liked". Matty also managed to hear Jean Goldkette's Band broadcasting from distant Detroit, and those sounds also inspired him.

Matty worked hard at mastering the clarinet and his newly acquired saxophone, during his teens he played in various local groups, then successfully auditioned for a band led by pianist Beasley Smith, which was then working at the Jackson Hotel, in Nashville, within the band was another young musician burning with jazz ambitions, drummer Ray McKinley.

In 1927, McKinley and Matlock went with Beasley Smith's Band to Lake Pau Pau, Michigan, to play a summer season, on their day off the two young musicians regularly travelled to Chicago to hear Ben Pollack's Band at the Blackhawk Restaurant, in the early hours they'd move across to the Sunset Cafe to listen to Louis Armstrong. "It was a fantastic experience, to hear so much music in one night. Benny Goodman being featured with Pollack, Louis and Earl Hines playing duets, unbelievably good".

Matlock's next bandleader was Jimmy Joy, whom he joined in the spring of 1928. Matlock who always regarded Joy as one of the nicest bandleaders he ever met, worked mainly around Louisville, Kentucky with the band, but also went with them to Chicago in May 1928 to make his recording debut. After a few months, work became scarce, Matlock moved back to his home town and rejoined Beasley Smith, but he was soon on the move again, this time to Pittsburgh to join a band co-led by tuba-player Frank Tracy and violinist and saxophonist Nelson Brown, which was billed as the Tracy-Brown Orchestra (its alumni included Ray McKinley, trumpeter Grady Watts, and arranger Lyle 'Spud' Murphy).

Benny Goodman and Ben Pollack never enjoyed the easiest of relationships, so it came as no suprise to fellow musicians to learn that Goodman had quit Pollack in the summer of 1929, his temporary replacement in the band was Joe Catalyne, but when trombonist Jack Teagarden was visiting his brother Charlie in Pittsburgh he heard Matlock playing in the Tracy-Brown Band, and realised that he had found a permanent clarinettist for Pollack. In October 1929, Matlock travelled to New York and joined one of America's leading bands, "I was in seventh heaven, but at the same time I was scared about taking Benny Goodman's place, it all worked out and I joined Pollack, who was really a grand person".

The move to New York enabled Matty to hear live performances by many of the bands, Fletcher Henderson's, Chick Webb's, and Don Redman's, that he had formerly listened to on the radio. In Harlem he also found places that cooked Southern style food, and provided memorable music, including cutting contests between the great stride pianists James P. Johnson and Willie 'The Lion' Smith.

Matlock had tried his hand at arranging before he joined Ben Pollack, but playing the Fud Livingston arrangements that he had listened to as a fan, gave him the inspiration to begin a devoted study of arranging methods, under various teachers including Otto Cesana. Soon he was writing well-received scores for Pollack's Band, his jazz playing also improved by leaps and bounds. When Matlock first joined Pollack he tended to try and follow too closely in Benny Goodman's stylistic footsteps, but with Pollack's encouragement, he developed his own way of playing.

In 1930, almost a year after Matlock had joined Pollack, an upheaval in the band brought in Eddie Miller and Nappy Lamare, both became life-long friends of Matlock's, the three musicians shared years together in Pollack's Band, and in Bob Crosby's Band, and also appeared together on countless recording dates (and golf courses) during the 1940s, 1950s and 1960s.

Matty provided his share of anecdotes during the Pollack Band days, but perhaps the one he is best remembered for occurred at the Casino De Paree in New York. One night, whilst the band were accompanying a cabaret artiste called "Cardini", Matty began to feel distinctly ill at ease. He had totally misjudged his bladder capacity during the previous intermission's drinking time, and now urgently felt a call of nature. He whisperingly asked his colleague, Eddie Miller, for advice, but Eddie couldn't suggest any course of action. Suddenly, Matlock had a brain wave, during a piano solo he called quietly to Billy McVea in the trombone section, "Say Billy, I was thinking of using that big mute of yours in an arrangement, would you mind passing it to me?". The trombonist obliged, and passed a receptacle that was soon to bring relief to Matlock, who laid his alto saxophone across his sap to shield his action. At the next intermission, one of the big plants in the night club was irrigated, the mute was washed out and handed back to the trombonist, who remained blissfully aware of his great humanitarian deed, but was always puzzled as to why an arranger should need to see a mute rather than hear it being played.

Matlock always retained a lasting degree of affection for Ben Pollack, but, like the rest of his colleagues in Pollack's Band, he was appalled at the way the leader neglected his duties to concentrate on Doris Robbin's career. When the 1934 mass exodus took place, Matlock moved from California with his wife Lura, and took up residence in the Electric Court apartments at Jackson Heights, Long Island.

Matty was kept extremely busy during his first few weeks in New York, for it fell on him to do the bulk of the arranging for the new band that had risen from the ashes of Pollack's group. Matty, Deane Kincaide and Glenn Miller all took their own scores to the Long Island band rehearsals, and, as was the rule of these gatherings, they conducted and directed their own arrangements, there was no band leader out front. At this stage of the band's history there was no official leader, Gil Rodin was the band manager, but Bob Crosby was soon to join the team.

Matty played on the Bob Crosby Band's debut at the Roseland Ballroom, and also worked on all of the residencies that the band did in 1935, including a tour of the south, but the band's need of new, suitable, arrangements was so great, Rodin and Matlock came to the conclusion that it would be more useful if Matty remained in New York to concentrate on writing for the band whilst they played a January 1936 season at the Biscayne Kennel Club in Florida; reedman Sid Stoneburn temporarily took Matty's place.

A year later, when the Crosby Band moved down to New Orleans to play a season at the Hotel Roosevelt, Matty again stayed in New York to concentrate on arranging for the band, and to be near his wife who was expecting their second child. Matty's deputy in the band this time was Johnny Mince. Matty and Johnny actually swopped jobs, Matty took over Mince's place in Ray Noble's Band at the Rainbow Room, New York for a while, then worked with Bunny Berigan's Band at a New Jersey road-house, both jobs allowed him to return home each night, and to work regularly on writing new arrangements. During this period, Matlock also played on early recordings by Bunny Berigan's newly formed band.

In the spring of 1937, Matty resumed his place in the Bob Crosby reed section, taking most of the clarinet solos, the rest of his waking hours were spent in devising arrangements. To lighten his burden, Rodin kept up a constant search for a jazz clarinettist who would be suitable for the Crosby Band. Irving Fazola seemed the ideal man for the job, but Rodin's attempts to sign him were thwarted again and again.

Meanwhile, Matty continued to play and arrange, taking on the additional task of providing musical sketches (introductions and endings mainly) for the newly featured Bobcats contingent. Under pressure, Matty produced a string of fine instrumentals for the full band, including *Panama* and *Wolverine Blues*. These were tailor-made for the Crosby Band, whereas some of Matty's earlier charts for them, like *Pagan Love Song* and *Woman On My Weary Mind* had been previously used by Ben Pollack's Band. After Pollack had threatened various bandleaders about the use of arrangements formerly played by his band, Gil Rodin thought it best not to feature any more ex-Pollack material on record. This move unfortunately deprived the jazz world of a studio recording of Matlock's arrangement of *Honeysuckle Rose*, which his colleague Bob Haggart thinks was one of the best scores that Matty ever did.

Haggart said "Matty was a very gifted arranger. First of all I think his main inspiration was Fud Livingston. He often used to say 'Fud would have done this, or that', then he began to develop his own individuality, which was inspired by Jack Teagarden's trombone playing, you'll often hear Jack's phrases forming part of a Matty arrangement". Jack Teagarden shared top place with Louis Armstrong in Matty's list of favourite musicians during the 1930s, later on, he developed a great liking for Bobby Hackett's playing. "My taste has always gone for cleaner playing", Matty used to say "in later years, I used a certain trumpet player a lot and Yank Lawson used to rib me when he saw me, and say 'that guy just can't play jazz', but I always thought he did a good clean job and sounded nice, so I used him". Matty, in common with most of his colleagues in the Crosby Band, loved to play and to listen to, the blues, citing Jack Teagarden and Louis Armstrong, again, as his favourite blues instrumentalists; his favourite blues singer was Bessie Smith.

Matty had to put up with a good deal of good natured 'country boy' banter from his city-born colleagues in the Crosby Band, who used to ask him how comfortable Davy Crockett hats were back home. On one tour, jokers arranged a hog-calling contest and made Matty the hot favourite to win. The band bus pulled up at a gate that led into a huge field, and the contestants were asked to holler one at a time to see who would muster the hogs quickest. Matty did his best, but had no more luck than those who went before him, then Ward Sillaway took his turn and let out a bellow so powerful he had every hog in the county roused and running.

Finally, in the spring of 1938, Irving Fazola joined the Crosby Band, and Matlock was able to hand over the job of clarinet soloist to the newcomer. Matty occasionally played on dates with the band, but officially he was now their full-time arranger. Sometimes long periods would elapse before Matlock was called on to sub with the band, and he became restless about not playing often. To keep his embouchure in shape, and his fingers nimble he'd play anywhere, and the Crosby musicians can remember him delighting various of their children by playing nursery songs to them as they all sat around a birthday celebration table. Matty also jumped at the chance to take part in jam sessions, and did so when the Crosby men shared an after-hours blow with the Count Basie Band at the Howard Theatre in Washington early in 1939.

Matlock greatly admired Fazola's clarinet playing, and scored several features for him, including the magnificent arrangement of *Sympathy,* never-the-less, he was delighted to return to the reed section not long after Fazola left in the summer of 1940. At that time, most of Fazola's solo work was re-allocated to Hank D'Amico, but when he left, Matty regained the position of featured clarinettist. Matty's skills as an arranger, plus his easy-going nature, had kept him in the background during the late 1930s, but he was never forgotten by fans of the Bob Crosby Band, and on his return received a warm welcome, and much applause whenever he was featured.

When the December 1942 break-up of the band occurred Matty and Lura decided to make their home permanently in California. There Matty was kept busy playing various studio dates, and working (and arranging) for Eddie Miller's Band. Matty, Eddie, and Nappy Lamare all lived fairly close to each other, and often shared a round of golf. Matty had no illusions about his golfing skills, and usually described himself as 'a scraper', never-the-less, he often felt that all traces of luck left him the moment he stepped on the course. During one match with 'his side-kick' as he called Eddie Miller, Matty sliced six balls into a lake that was situated nearly behind him. With some fury in his voice he asked Miller "What's par for this hole?". "Three" was the reply. "Well, they ought to be damn well ashamed of themselves for fixing it as low as that" said Matty, boiling over with frustrated anger. But, it wasn't long before he was back at his local course at Kirkwood, California, swishing the air with undiminished enthusiasm.

One of Matty's many illustrious regular studio dates involved playing for Bing Crosby's weekly radio shows in the 1940s and 1950s, this involvement led to him arranging Gary Crosby's hit record of *Sam's Song.* Matty also played on countless sessions organised by arranger-composer Paul Weston, who held Matty's talents in the highest esteem. In 1981 he wrote, "If called upon I can make a case (as can my wife Jo Stafford) that Matty Matlock was the best clarinet player who ever lived - much more versatile than some of his more famous peers". Matty was especially proud to have been featured on the recording of Paul Weston's *Crescent City Suite,* he was also delighted to have taken part in Billy May's *Sorta Dixie* album in 1955.

For a time it seemed as though Matty's talents as a clarinettist would keep him so busy that there would be no time for arranging, this was particularly the case after the widespread success of the radio, film, and television versions of *Pete Kelly's Blues,* which featured Matty's Band. The star of the series, Jack Webb, picked most of the tunes that were used, but Matty did all of the musical organisation. A spin-off from the series resulted in Matty leading his own band *The Paducah Patrol*, on a series of albums for Warner Brothers, the personnel usually featured jazzmen who were working in West Coast studio bands, including trumpeters John Best and Dick Cathcart, Abe Lincoln and Moe Schneider on trombones, and one of Matlock's all-time favourite percussionists, Nick Fatool, always referred to by Matty as "the listening drummer", Eddie Miller was a stalwart on all of the sessions.

Matty's participation in one 1957 session, gave him as much pleasure as any recording he ever made, this was the *Coast Concert* date, which featured two of his favourite musicians, Jack Teagarden and Bobby Hackett. "That date lasted for twelve hours, but it was so much fun, I could have done another twelve hours without blinking". Another particularly happy memory for Matty was recalling the time in the 1960s when he took his clarinet along to sub for his guitar-playing son, Buddy, on a trio gig in the San Fernando Valley area. A good deal of Matty's work outside the studios was with small bands, but he never lost his skill for big band arranging, and this is particularly obvious on the *Double Dixie* album he scored for Harry James, which included fine tributes to Louis Armstrong on *Weatherbird* and *Cornet Chop Suey*.

Matlock, like most of his Crosby Band colleagues, got to actively dislike the "Dixieland" tag that was somewhat condescendingly used to describe their music. Matty felt the word was restricting, and encouraged type-casting, "Some people think it means you can only play three tunes in two keys. It's really a put-down label". However, Matty never lost his love of loose, informal ensemble playing, particularly when the musicians involved understood each other's styles. He once said that playing in the front line of a jazz band meant "not grabbing all the space and filling it with your own notes, leave room for someone else to have some fun too".

Matty never lost his links with Bob Crosby, and continued to take part in band and Bobcats reunions, including a tour of the Orient in 1964 and New York bookings in 1966 which marked the emergence of "The World's Greatest Jazz Band", co-led by his ex-colleagues, Yank Lawson and Bob Haggart. He also took part in the W.G.J.B.'s embryo sessions at Dick Gibson's jazz parties in Colorado, but never considered joining the band on a regular basis, Matty felt his touring days were over. He did however make a pleasure trip to Britain, with his wife Lura, in spring 1972, he didn't take a clarinet with him, but played superbly on borrowed instruments.

Matty was not a man of lofty ambitions, he never entertained the idea of leading a band permanently, "Let someone else have the headaches", and he never went out of his way to cadge publicity, but on his trip to Britain he did achieve one ambition he'd held for a long time, he visited the town in Derbyshire that shared his name, Matlock. There were no direct descendants to call on, Matty just wanted to look around the place.

Not long after his return to California Matty began to encounter health problems, which turned out to be serious enough to cause him to restrict his work schedule. After a debilitating operation, he became a mere shadow of his former bright self. He was forced by ill health to give up playing in public, and soon he no longer had the strength to practice the clarinet or the flute, other pleasures like golf, swimming and walking proved too much for him, and he ended his days as an invalid. When he died in June 1978, tributes came from far and wide. The City of Los Angeles proclaimed a "Matty Matlock Day", his birth-state, Kentucky, honoured him, as did his home-town of Paducah, who posthumously bestowed its highest award, but none of these offerings were as heart-felt as the sense of loss that Matty's family and all of his ex-Crosby Band colleagues suffered so deeply.

Irving Fazola

Chapter 21
Irving Fazola

Listing all the great jazz clarinet players who were born in New Orleans would be a big task, but one certainty for inclusion in that compilation would be the late Irving Fazola, an immensely talented musician, who is still spoken of in his home city as being the finest of the white jazz clarinettists.

Despite the fact that Fazola's talents are widely acknowledged, very little has ever been written about him. This omission was partly of his own making, he usually avoided publicity like the plague, even during illustrious stays with famous bands, such as those led by Ben Pollack, Glenn Miller, Muggsy Spanier, Teddy Powell and Claude Thornhill. During a prestigious two year stay in Bob Crosby's Band, Fazola won the Down Beat clarinet poll two years in succession, but even those honours didn't induce self-advertisement. But, he was not, in any way, a precious artiste living only for his music, he was a bulky, rough-and-ready character who loved playing the clarinet, who also thought in double-portions about food, booze and women. Fazola didn't care whether the public knew anything about his history, he let his music speak eloquently for him, remaining disinterested in giving opinions or interviews to journalists.

He was born Irving Henry Prestopnik on the 10th of December 1912, in New Orleans, Louisiana. Fazola (often shortened to Faz) was a nickname given him in boyhood. The exact origin of the sobriquet still remains a controversy amongst old men who were boys the day the Prestopnik became Fazola. One thing is for certain, the re-naming was done by trumpeter Louis Prima. Some say that Prima teased Irving after he heard that he was playing in the Roma Band (a 29 piece ensemble that performed only from written music). "You one of those Fah-so-la guys now?" said Prima, and the three solfeggio notes stuck, and became the clarinettist's new name. Others suggest that Prima called the Roma Band's music, 'Fazola' music to connect it with the Italian 'Lucky Beans' that were placed on the St. Joseph altars in New Orleans as part of a religious ceremony.

Whatever its origins the nickname was immoveable. Fazola's boyhood friends still pronounce the name as 'Far-so-la', not 'Faz-o-la'. Irving himself preferred to be called simply 'Faz'.

Luke Schiro, one of those friends from the early days, said "Irving and I began playing music around 1928. Faz had a 'C' Melody saxophone, which he traded in for a Soprano sax, he studied this under the late Dan Sanderson. I was starting to play clarinet, so we were always talking about reeds, and mouthpieces, etc. At times, Faz studied hard, then he would get contrary and put his sax across his lap until the hour's lesson was up. Dan Sanderson summed up Faz's temperament, he didn't command him to pick the instrument up and play, he simply carried on instructing him".

Fazola's mule-like stubbornness, which stayed with him for the rest of his life, could well have exasperated a teacher with less foresight, but Sanderson chose the right tactics, as Luke Schiro explains, "One day, something snapped in Faz, he went through his method book from front to back in a breeze".

Jacob Sciambra, long a prominent attorney in New Orleans, but for many years an active musician, also remembered Faz as a teenager, "Fazola lived near Claiborne and Ursulina, I think he was born there. He attended a school close to his home, and never got beyond the 4th grade, he stayed in that grade for about 2 years, then they offered him a chance to leave, which he took with all haste". Fazola, Sciambra, and pianist Ewell Lamar all studied later at the Loyala School of Music in New Orleans.

"We were all young musicians together, and he took a liking to me, but in general his character was positively bovine, he developed his dislikes instinctively, and if he didn't like someone, he'd simply take a swipe at them without warning or apparent reason" says Sciambra. Another musician from this era, Wilfred 'Bill' Bourgeois (b. 1907), said Faz dealt in two emotions, warm liking and deep hatred.

Faz lived with his mother (who was Irish), his younger brother Louis and a sister. They were a working-class Catholic family. No one remembers Fazola talking about his father, who was an Austrian of Hungarian descent. Faz's childhood was full of normal boyish activities, he swam a lot, played ball games and joined the local Boy Scouts. He disinterestedly took a series of piano lessons, but was smitten by music after buying a cheap, second-hand saxophone.

From the age of sixteen, Fazola often visited the Schiro family home (their neighbour was, co-incidentally, the famous black clarinet-player Big Eye Louis Nelson). Luke Schiro, a year older than Faz, had a collection of jazz records, most of them by Louis Armstrong, others by the New Orleans Rhythm Kings (featuring clarinettist Leon Roppolo). "Faz loved listening to the records, he was overwhelmed by Rap's playing. He forthwith embraced Rap's style. I had an Albert system clarinet at that time, and taught Faz the fingering. Faz used my clarinet more than I did, within a week he was playing it. He then took lessons on clarinet from Professor Giuffre, who only taught the Albert system of fingering. I changed to Boehm system and took lessons from the late Jean Paquay".

The names of these two teachers crop up again and again in the reminiscences of white clarinet players from New Orleans. Jean Paquay, whose family were from Belgium, was a huge man who stood over six feet tall, and weighed about 230 pounds. He played clarinet in the French Opera

House Orchestra, and taught the Boehm system of clarinet to dozer of aspiring musicians. His chief teaching rival within the city was Santo Giuffre, from Milan, Italy. However, the two men rarely encroached on each other's 'territory' since Giuffre exclusively taught the Albert system.

Fazola never had trouble in reading music, so when he switched from saxophone to clarinet he was able to concentrate on acquiring technique, which he did rapidly. For one brief period he changed 'sides' and started to learn Boehm system from Paquay, but he soon reverted to the Albert styled clarinet and played that system for the rest of his life. During his teens he also took up the flute, he made amazingly rapid progress on it, then without explanation, never played it again.

Within months of beginning on the clarinet, Fazola was able to play complicated orchestrations on sight, and to transpose them into any key, but he had considerable difficulty in improvising. He had a good musical ear, and could learn other player's solos with ease, but when it came to extemporising his own ideas he was diffident. He became positively bellicose when the subject was raised. At a rehearsal of one of the first regular bands that he joined, John 'Candy' Candido's Little Collegians, he was asked by the leader to improvise a break, Fazola immediately became ruffled, got out of his chair and made for the door saying, "You can't do that, I can't variate".

Bill Bourgeois was one of the clique of young musicians who hung around the Fern Dance Hall in the French Quarter of New Orleans, he remembers Fazola during this period very clearly, "Many of us youngsters used to sit in with the band at the Fern. The hours were long there, and the musicians welcomed sitting-in, so they could take a rest, it was really a jitney dance-hall. Eventually I got the offer to join the band that was resident there, led by banjoist "Buzzy' Willox. Fazola, who was younger than me, came and sat by my side with his clarinet, but he was very shy about cutting loose with his own improvisations, so I would hum a musical idea to him, then gradually he realised what he had to do in the ensemble, and this led him into improvising a solo".

Fazola was also learning about life as he hung around the New Orleans dance halls. During his teen-years he developed three dominant interests that went with his passion for music, they were eating, drinking and finding girls. The plumpness that was to stay with him through adulthood was just beginning to shape his frame, it was encouraged by his vast appetite for food of all sorts - his greed was so indiscriminate that he became known to all his pals as 'The Goat'. By the age of seventeen he had already developed his life-long fondness for alcohol, at that age Luke Schiro remembers that Faz's favourite tipple was gin, with beer chasers. As to the ladies, Faz's first passionate affair was with 'Bebe' the midget hostess who worked at the Fern Dance Hall. The sight of the two shapes together, large and small, may have appeared incongruous to onlookers, but 'Bebe' stimulated within Faz an energetic interest in female company that never dwindled.

Gradually, Fazola became more confident about improvising and listening musicians realised that the clarinettist was developing a highly imaginative approach to jazz playing. At first, there were some uneasy moments when Faz's colleagues shouted out encouragement, he stopped playing immediately and gave them a very hard look to make sure that he wasn't being mocked, when he realised that the appreciation was genuine he resumed his warm-toned, intricate improvisations.

Some of the members of the Warren Easton High School Band formed up a small jazz group called the *Eastonites,* which was led by W.N. Marbut. Fazola accepted an offer to join them, a move that greatly increased his confidence as an improviser; his playing was well featured when the band did a prestigious date at the Palace Theatre. Faz's local reputation grew, and he was kept busy playing gigs with Candy Candido's Band, and with Pete Percino's Susquehanna Orchestra.

In the August 1929 issue of *Prelude,* the journal of the New Orleans Musicians' Union, it was noted that "Irving Prestopinik" (sic) saxophone and clarinet had been initiated into the Union local. By then, Fazola had struck up a friendship with trumpeter Louis Prima (born 1911), who lived nearby to Faz on St. Peter and Claiborne. Prima often used Faz on the many gigs he got playing for the Italian Community in New Orleans. Fazola and Prima, both errant spirits, easily fell in with each other's plans. Having received a nick-name from Prima, Faz obliged by re-christening him "Feet". The two youngsters' mutual interest in playing jazz went along with a shared hedonistic approach to life. Fazola soon adopted Prima's habit of calling all local straight musicians "Willies", thus any non-jazz opus was known simply as "willie music".

But despite the contemptuous assessment of reading bands, Fazola often played gigs (doubling clarinet and alto-saxophone) with groups that specialised in "willie music". His all-around musicianship was superb, and during the early 1930s he worked with many New Orleans bandleaders including, Ellis Stratakos, Johnny DeDroit, Roy Teal, Abbie Brunies and Wilbur Dinkel, he also played countless gigs aboard the Mississippi riverboats. During one of his first gigs (with Earl Dantin's band) on a steamer Fazola was heard by Verne Streckfus, whose family owned the line (which had employed numerous jazz musicians), he was not particularly impressed, but hearing him a couple of years later, Streckfus commented on the improvement, and observed that Fazola was building a formidable individual style based on Leon Roppolo's best work.

Up-and-coming jazz musicians like trumpeter Sharkey Bonano and pianist Armand Hug booked Fazola whenever they could. By the time the clarinettist was 21 he was a local musical celebrity, playing on radio in a sax section with Charlie Cordilla and Sal Franzella. Offers for Faz to join touring bands came with a monotonous regularity, but he remained uninterested. He found contentment in New Orleans, and declined offers of more money from travelling bands by saying "I can have as good a time here as any place". He loved the pace of New Orleans life, and its food meant a great deal to him. By now he realised that he was a fine player, but he had no ambitions to follow the path to New York that many of his musical contemporaries had already taken.

In a 1976 issue of *Second Line* magazine, Johnny DeDroit reminisced about the Fazola of this period. "He had the most beautiful tone. He played spots with Leslie George and me. We both wanted him in our bands, and when I landed the Jung Hotel job he came over to my band. He could play Spanish music like nothing you ever heard. He was not prepossessing in appearance. One job, we wore white linen suits. We had two - one on, and one at the cleaners. Only cost 25 cents a suit in those days and I insisted my men look well at all times. Well you know how Faz was, he'd go out after the job was over and he'd drink and show up on the job wearing the same, crumpled suit, and I'd go and get his other and pay for it myself. The man was such an eater. In a restaurant, Faz would look at the menu and say 'Give me two of everything but the soup. Some people don't know what an intelligent man Faz really was. They just know about his playing".

During the early 1930s, almost every jazz-orientated musician who visited New Orleans made a point of hearing Fazola's clarinet playing, all those that did were much impressed by his tone and technique and by his deeply-felt, expressive blues playing. The New Orleans contingent within Ben Pollack's Band made sure that all of their colleagues caught an earful of Faz's playing, during a 1932 visit to the city. Ben Pollack, an ace talent-spotter, was so impressed he offered him a job with the band after only hearing one number, but Faz repeated what he had told several other bandleaders, he wanted to stay home in New Orleans, and that's exactly what he did until September 1935 when Ben Pollack came back.

Pollack, still smarting from the effects of having his musicians walk out on him a year previously, brought a newly organised group to play a short season at the Hotel Roosevelt in 1935. One of his first off-duty tasks in New Orleans was to seek out Fazola and offer him double what he was getting locally, to come on the road with Pollack's Band. Even with those terms Fazola remained unimpressed, he said he would think things over, but he had not counted on Pollack's persistence. The drummer-leader realised that a player of Fazola's immense skills would be a useful card in his gamble to retrieve his previous fame, he simply wouldn't take a 'no' from Fazola, and eventually the clarinettist relented and decided to go on the road with Pollack, first stop Chicago.

National recognition came to Fazola whilst he was in Chicago with Pollack, *Down Beat* in its June 1936 issue said Fazola "plays the blues, with a tone like Roppolo, and plays with a lot of feeling", and a few months later John Hammond commenting on the arrival of Pollack's Band in New York wrote "Pollack has at least one great musician - the clarinettist Fazzola".

Journalists were uncertain about the clarinettist's spelling of his name, but they were unanimous in praising his talent, George Frazier wrote "Fazola is one of the outstanding artists of 1936".

As a member of Pollack's Band, Fazola made his record debut on that first trip to New York, the results reveal the importance that Pollack attached to Fazola's role within the band, he is literally the star of the proceedings, featured even more than Harry James. On the first two titles cut he is entrusted with establishing the melody, and he does so with tone, expression and various subtleties that are the work of a mature, thoughtful musician. Someone once said that if Fazola played *The Stars and Stripes* he would have given it a bluesy feeling, the clarinettist certainly imbues *Song of the Islands* with an attractively, mournful edge. This time an Hawaiian guitar plays the initial melody, before Fazola begins building a series of strong variations that turn a dull arrangement into an auspicious feature for jazz clarinet. The clarinettist is also well featured in the Pollack small group sides made a day or two later, on *Jimtown Blues* and on *Peckin'* he plays elegant solos that show his tone off to great advantage, both in the high and low registers. Pollack himself drums superbly on this set of small band recordings.

Considering that his stint with Pollack's Band was his first real taste of the touring life, and the hassles and hilarity of the one night stand game, Fazola settled in easily. He kept himself to himself for the first few weeks, but gradually began to beam approval at the good music that was going on around him. Pollack was no longer the leader of a top band, but the group wasn't scuffling, even so, there was no travelling luxury for any of the band, and for long periods of a tour, trumpeter Harry James would also act as driver for the bandbus. Discomfort rarely irked Fazola, providing he'd had a good time in the last venue, and was well topped-up with calories and booze he didn't care whether the road was bumpy or not.

Fazola was generally affable with his fellow musicians, providing they left him alone when he wanted to sit quietly. He seldom engaged in deep conversation with anyone, and was prone to grunting out mono-syllabic replies, but his skills as a musician more than made up for any social shortcomings. One sideman said, "For long periods he gave the impression of being simply an eating-and-farting machine, but when he started playing the clarinet it was obvious that he was a superb, sensitive artist".

Ben Pollack's Band settled in for a long stay on the West Coast that was scheduled to take up most of 1937, their first Californian residency of the year was at Pollack's old stamping ground, the Cotton Club in Culver City. Graually, homesickness gnawed away at Fazola, he wanted to see his mother again, and all his pals in New Orleans, he wanted to relax at a table piled high with gumbo and other local delicacies, eventually he went to Pollack and handed in his notice. The guile with which Pollack had induced Fazola to leave New Orleans wasn't enough to stop him returning there. Faz caught a train back home, and was soon doing the rounds and sitting in with various bands, he was fixed up with a regular job almost immediately, with drummer Augie Schellang's Roosevelt Rhythm Kings.

New Orlean's previously ultra-lively entertainment scene was slow to recover from the effects of the Depression, and throughout the 1930s, the musicians there averaged less wages than their counterparts in New York, Chicago or Los Angeles. Fazola still loved his home city, but a taste of the big-time had developed his musical ambitions. Alongside his love of jazz had developed a desire to be tested musically, and although Fazola never became sycophantic towards audiences, it was reassuring for him to hear a big crowd heaping generous applause on him. New Orleans in the mid-1930s was in something of a musical doldrum, as far as the local reading bands were concerned, and Fazola reasoned that if he had to spend most of his evenings playing written music for a living he might as well do it in skilful company for good money. So, when Gus Arnheim, a respected commercial bandleader invited Fazola to join his band in New York, the clarinettist accepted, and moved north in May 1937.

All of the ex-Ben Pollack sidemen within Bob Crosby's Band made it their business to listen to their ex-leader's 1936 recordings - the first he had made since the big walkout of 1934. Opinions varied as to the overall merits of the discs, but everyone was hugely impressed by Fazola's clarinet playing. When they had completed their summer 1937 tours, the Crosby Band went back to New York, where Rodin made it one of his first tasks to contact Fazola. Rodin saw Fazola and made him a definite offer to join the band, not much was said, but Rodin felt convinced that the clarinettist, in his taciturn way, had agreed to become a member of Bob Crosby's Band, accordingly he proudly told *Down Beat* magazine of his 'capture'.

The ink was scarcely dry on the music magazine's story when a news flash announced that Fazola had joined Glenn Miller's Orchestra. Miller had long been determined to employ Fazola, having worked alongside him on the 1936 Pollack Big Band dates. Miller rarely went out of his way to employ 'characters', but he chose to ignore any strictures he may have felt, if Fazola agreed to join his band. To everyone's suprise he did.

Actually, Glenn Miller developed a genuine liking for Fazola himself, which consolidated his enormous admiration of the man's clarinet playing. In his book "Glenn Miller", George T. Simon points out that Fazola became the fifth member of the reed section when he was added to the band, thus his glorious tone was able to implement Miller's developing ideas about a clarinet lead for the reed section. Faz was told he would be playing an important part in Miller's Band, and this encouraged him to take the offer, but the invitation was made all the more appealing by the fact that it meant he had to go back to New Orleans to join the band, which was then playing a residency at the Hotel Roosevelt.

After the New Orleans residency ended on 25th August 1937, the Miller Band moved off to resume their touring schedule by playing at the Adolphus

Hotel in Dallas. Fazola played superbly throughout his stay with Glenn Miller's Band, and off-stage he enjoyed himself at every possible opportunity. Writer George Simon recalls amazing drinking bouts between Faz and lead-trumpeter Bob Price. After they had finished work for the night, they'd sit on the edge of a bed and determindedly drink as much as they could, never allowing each other's glass to remain empty, the first one to fall off the bed lost the contest. Most of the band looked in on these suprisingly long duels, laughing at the two men's hilarious efforts to remain upright. Glenn Miller occasionally popped his head around the door to check progress, but as he had to fight the urge to join them in their 'bender' his chuckles at the antics always seemed to have a nervous edge.

In a 1937 letter to George Simon, Glenn Miller mentioned in passing that Fazola was the only clarinet player with a chance of establishing his own musical identity. Miller felt that Artie Shaw, Johnny Mince "and all of them" played like Benny Goodman, but "Faz, like Ol' Man River, keeps rolling along and he doesn't want to know from anyone. For me there is only one Faz". Fazola's exquisite tone graces several Miller recordings, its liquidity and expressiveness is near its best on *I'll Remember This Moment* and *Doin' The Jive*.

After a succession of ill-fortuned winter dates, Glenn Miller decided to take a temporary respite from the headaches of bandleading, easing himself out of a managerial dispute at the same time. The sidemen accepted their notices, played their last dates with the band then scattered far and wide. After Fazola's last date with Miller on the 2nd January 1938 he made immediately for New Orleans. Ben Pollack, who was playing a return date at the Hotel Roosevelt, heard on the grape-vine that Faz was back in town and instantly made a place for him in the band. Pollack wanted the clarinettist back permanently, but Gil Rodin had already been alerted by Glenn Miller that Faz's talents were again on the market. Rodin guaranteed to top any pay deal offered to the clarinettist, but this time he made sure that Fazola formally accepted the chance to join Bob Crosby's Band. *Tempo* magazine wryly remarked "Rumours are around again that Fazola will join Bob Crosby's band and by the law of averages it may really happen this time", in the same March 1938 issue, the magazine carried a lively story concerning Fazola's last days with Pollack:

"New Orleans: Irving ("Fazola") Prestopinik (sic), clarinet ace appearing here with Ben Pollack at Roosevelt Hotel, is displaying a lump on his head sustained in combat most foul, of which there are many versions. Fazola's version: A non-union trumpet man mistakenly picked up a trumpet case belonging to a Pollack band member in a local bistro, and Faz in reclaiming the trumpet got a whack on the head with a piece of iron. No appreciable damage".

Fazola's noggin had healed by the time he joined Bob Crosby's Band in March 1938, and he was soon in action on recording dates. His sound blended superbly with that of the reed section, and he had no problems in sight-reading the arrangements. He quickly settled in socially, all of the New Orleans contingent knew him, and the other members of the band soon lost the apprehension they had acquired by hearing stories of Faz's temperament. Eddie Miller says "He was a sweetheart, a great guy", and Yank Lawson stresses, "I never saw him hit anyone". Billy Butterfield said "Faz was a fun guy, he loved having a swell time, and he was a superb player. I got along fine with him". Faz's colleague in the sax section, Joey Kearns, was also full of praise "He had a beautiful tone, and although he had good technique he always played with restraint. He and Bob Zurke were the only musicians I knew who could drink heavily, and still keep command on their instruments. Fazola's favourite drink was gin, which he referred to as "Big Mouth". He was always ' a fun guy' and it was always pleasant to be with him".

Fazola didn't undergo a drastic change of character when he joined Bob Crosby's Band, he simply reacted to the spirit of camaraderie that existed around him, but if he didn't like anyone he was still likely to show his feelings physically. The contrast between the man and his music was enormous. His playing was always articulate, and his amazing breath control allowed him to create long ingenious phrases couched in a tone that was mellow, but never flaccid.

Bob Haggart got on well with Fazola, and greatly respected his musicianship, "To look at him you would never think he could play such beautiful music. He could turn the air blue with his swearing, every other word was an oath, but he couldn't stop himself, and if band wives were in the company he'd usually sit silent, knowing that if he started to talk, it would be mother-fucking this, and mother-fucking that".

Fazola liked Chicago, next to New Orleans it was probably his favourite city, and during the Crosby Band's residencies at The Blackhawk he soon got into a routine of revelry. But, no matter how much booze he had drunk or how little sleep he'd had, Fazola was always punctual on the bandstand, as indeed was the band's other most consistent funster, Bob Zurke.

Faz never quite looked elegant even when he put on a brand new tailor-made suit, clothes meant little to him, and he was likely to sleep off a hangover without as much as shedding a garment. After a few months with the Crosby Band, Fazola set out to improve his sartorial appearance, and at the same time rid himself of inconveniences like organising laundry lists. The answer he felt was to get a valet. Accordingly he engaged a Damon Runyon type character called "Square Deal Davis", whose dubious history was a direct contradiction of his nick-name. Square Deal's job was to make sure that everything irksome was taken care of, and that a regular supply of booze was always ready at hand. The arrangement didn't last long, Faz soon got weary of the valet's smooth-running schedules.

One of Faz's favouirte haunts in Chicago was Paul Mares's New Orleans Barbeque. The ex-New Orleans Rhythm Kings' trumpet player let Faz eat all he could (a fearsome quantity at most times) as long as he played some clarinet for the customers. Down Beat's George Hoefer, a fan of Fazola's, vowed that this was where the clarinettist played at his very best. Hoefer, a keen record collector, got to know Fazola in Chicago during the late 1930s, and soon learnt that Faz was not the man to ply with discographical queries, "Fazola couldn't understand record collectors - they non-plussed him because they didn't play. One night I was in his room at the Eastgate, and Faz pointed to a small pile of Dixieland records, (Olivers, Armstrongs, New Orleans Rhythm Kings) saying 'Take them with you, if they'll do you any good, but leave the hillbilly sides, my chicks like them'."

Fazola wasn't an exuberant, natural showman, but he had the gift shared by most superb performers of making people listen to his playing, the mellowness and emotion made contact. He tended to look rather surly and intense on stage, and became decidely grumpy if the band was playing badly, but if all the sections were swinging, Fazola would curve his arms up to his neck and roll his head by way of approbation. But, no matter how dark his mood was, it would disappear if the next number called was a blues; Faz loved playing on a 12 bar blues more than on any other sequence, and his solos in that format were usually sublime. Ray Bauduc, not given to wild acclaim, said "Fazola's clarinet is the closest thing to perfect blues instrumentally I've ever heard".

The celebrated bout of fisticuffs between Fazola and Ray Conniff which ended the clarinettist's stay with the Crosby Band is described elsewhere in this book. It's probable that the confrontation wasn't the sole reason for Faz's departure, some of his colleagues felt that Faz's interest in the Crosby Band was waning. He had never stayed for two years with the same band in his life. After the fracas with Ray Conniff, Fazola immediately handed in his notice to Gil Rodin, when that expired he left, coincidentally on the same day, 1st June 1940, as Billy Butterfield departed. This time, instead of moving back to New Orleans, Faz decided to remain in Chicago for a while, but after working in Jimmy McPartland's Band for a couple of months he decided it was time to return home.

In September 1940 he again did his rounds in New Orleans, and picked up the chance to join trumpeter Tony Almerico's nine piece band at the Casino Ballroom, the band relied heavily on printed arrangements, but occasionally Almerico, trombonist Julian Lane and Fazola cut loose with some inspired jazz. Fazola also played some riverboat jobs not long after his return, and on one of these he was surrounded by musicians who admired his playing, amongst them reed-man John Reininger, who later worked in Fazola's band. "The listeners called out for *March of the Bobcats* because they all knew the Crosby recording that featured Faz's wonderful solo. The band obliged and played the number, but Faz improvised a totally different chorus. Disappointment registered on a number of faces, and someone later asked Faz why he hadn't played 'his' solo. 'Shit' he said 'who do you think was playing the solo, the man in the moon? that was my solo'. The listener explained that the crowd wanted to hear the solo that Faz had recorded with Bob Crosby's Bobcats, reluctantly, Faz saw what they wanted, and thereafter obliged whenever he played the tune, but he always followed it with a totally improvised chorus".

A restlessness for faster musical company again overtook Fazola, his problem was solved by a letter from New York, sent by clarinettist Jack Ferrier (who had worked with Faz in Bob Crosby's Band). Ferrier advised Faz that Claude Thornhill was looking for a top class clarinettist to play a prominent part in a new series of arrangements. This was exactly the sort of testing role that Faz was looking for, he contacted Thornhill and immediately got the job.

Several of Thornhill's recordings are graced with short, brilliant performances by Fazola, and his tone has rarely been heard to better advantage. He became engrossed by the musical approach that Thornhill was taking and in order to play a fuller part in the orchestrations he began playing bassoon and oboe.

Claude Thornhill was delighted to have Fazola in his band, at the time he said "Wonderful, isn't it? Fine guy too, just sits there and takes it easy and blows". Fazola's placidity even allowed him to share a viewpoint with a journalist, he told George Simon about his admiration for Benny Goodman's clarinet playing, "Put Benny above everybody else. Man, you know he gets better with age. I don't know how he does it". Faz added that his two other favourites were Louis Armstrong and Jack Teagarden.

Thornhill trombonist, Tasso Harris, told writer Ian Crosbie, "Faz and the rest of us stayed in a boarding house together, also taking our meals there. Faz was a warm guy with a fine sense of humour, and easy to be with, except when he'd drink too much, then look out!". Another sidemen, George Pausen said "He was truly great. He was some drinker, too. He would order 6 crates of gin at a time. He would sleep most of the day, get up about 4pm, pour a large waterglass full of gin and drink the lot, prior to eating a huge bowl of salad. He used to perspire profusely on the stand, one time, when the sweat was running out, soaking his shirt and jacket, he leaned over to me and said "Man, look at all that good gin going to waste. Whenever Faz was being tempermental, and Claude had to solve some problem with him, he would have me act as intermediary. He had a fierce temper and when he first arrived he was wearing a huge, wide-brimmed cap of a type never seen in the East. Some of the guys made remarks about it and Faz vented his spleen on them".

Claude Thornhill's brilliant arranger, Gil Evans, shared his memories of Fazola's stay in that band with Charles Fox. "He had the most beautiful liquid sound; a very special player. He hated Glenn Miller. We were working Glen Island Casino and on Sunday nights Glenn would come out to hear the band, and as soon as he walked in the door, Fazola would put his horn down and go downstairs to the bar and stay there until he left. That would infuriate Glenn, because Glenn was, about punctuality and all that, a martinet. Faz knew that, he just wanted to needle him. Faz would be downstairs, and he'd say to the bartender, 'Give me nine shots of gin', but he didn't want them in one glass, he wanted them in nine, in a row".

"Faz cooked his own food in his apartment, where we lived. He cooked only New Orleans food. It used to be a problem in the band, the four saxophones would be in the front row, and the baritone sax and Fazola behind them, on a hot night Faz would reek from the garlic, the ochre and the gin. The players, they'd say it's your turn to play on that chair tonight". Faz never explained why he so disliked Glenn Miller, but cornetist Bobby Hackett once said that Faz had tried to rejoin Miller and Miller had declined the offer.

Once Fazola had mastered the intricacies of the Thornhill arrangements, his fingers began to itch for more solo space, he played some happy sets, just with the rhythm section, during periods when business was quiet, but gradually he became more restless. For a change of pace, Fazola got up early some mornings during the Thornhill Band's Glen Island Casino residency, and went into Manhattan to rehearse with Muggsy Spanier's newly organised big band. Muggsy, an old colleague from Ben Pollack's Band, had been badgering Fazola for weeks to join the band, Faz pondered, aware that Thornhill was soon to leave Glen Island to start touring, a prospect that didn't please Faz. He handed in his notice to Thornhill, who fixed ex-Glenn Miller sideman, Jimmy Abato, as the replacement, then Fazola dithered about leaving, and Thornhill very considerately paid wages to both Abato and Fazola. Abato was greatly impressed by Fazola's playing and said "That son-of-a-bitch, without any formal training, does things I can't do with all my years of study".

Eventually, Fazola left Thornhill and joined Muggsy Spanier's Big Band at the Arcadia Ballroom, N.Y. (on the 1st of January 1942). Faz was to be an ace factor in Spanier's attempts to move into the prestigious area that Bob Crosby's Band was occupying. With arrangements by Deane Kincaide and Fud Livingston, and good soloists, Spanier felt confident that the band would soon make progress. Faz made his record debut with the band only days after joining them, and, as ever, sounds superb, particularly on *Hesitating Blues*.

Spanier's trombonist, Vernon Brown, told Ian Crosbie that the band were elated about Fazola joining them. Muggsy's star tenor player, Nick Caiazza was also delighted to play alongside the newcomer, "His flawless technique, his pure sound and ideas made his as near perfect as can be. All this far outweighed his drinking habits, two fifths of gin a day, and at times, his hard-to-put-up-with attitude. One night at a rehearsal he and Fud Livingston had a helluva fight".

Deane Kincaide, a vastly experienced musician and arranger, was just as enthusiastic about Fazola's playing. "He just sat there and made all the other clarinet players look like pikers. The Arcadia was packed every night and yet at the back of the room Faz's sound carried over the band like a bull-horn. As a man he was formidable, nobody messed with Faz! But when he liked you, you had a friend and benefactor for life".

Spanier's big band got itself into shape at the Arcadia Ballroom, and the leader began to look forward to tackling some lucrative tour dates. He announced to the musical press that he had signed the weighty trombonist Ford Leary to balance Faz's poundage aboard the band bus, but that balancing act was never tested, when all seemed set for the band's first tour Fazola decided he had seen enough of life on the road and gave in his notice to a startled Spanier, peeved at unexpectedly losing his finest soloist.

To the great surprise of the musical press, Fazola suddenly surfaced in Teddy Powell's reed section at the Log Cabin, Armonk, New York, in March 1942. As usual, Fazola immediately made his talents obvious and many musicians began making a point of listening to Powell's broadcasts from the Log Cabin. Saxist Marty Berman, told Ian Crosbie, "I joined Powell in 1942, and one of the reasons was Faz had joined and suggested I come on. He was totally uneducated, coarse and sometimes hostile, especially when really drunk, but he was the dearest, sweetest, most lovable man when you knew him. He was a total musician with great knowledge, exceptional facility, a tone as big as his belly soul to match. Many a night he would play the blues, or a lament like *Summertime* and there would be tears on the stand".

Saxist George Bohn used to drive Faz out to the gig each night from his hotel in Manhattan, most times he remained quiet throughout the journey as though in deep thought. The toll of heavy drinking, indiscriminate eating, late nights and fast company was having an effect on Fazola, who was often breathless and feeling unwell. He went for a medical check-up and was told that he had to take things easy, he left Teddy Powell's Band in June 1943 and played some dates at the Famous Door club in New York with fellow New Orleanian George Brunies, all the while casting out for a job that wouldn't tax his health too much. As a result, he received an offer from the ultra-commercial bandleader Horace Heidt. He wanted Fazola to play an occasional feature as one of the Musical Knights in his Lawrence Welk-like stage productions. So for most of the summer of 1943 Faz sat unobtrusively in Heidt's saxophone section, doubling clarinet and alto, making the most of his feature spot on the *One O'Clock Jump,* on which he played choruses on clarinet and alto (one of the only times in later years that he played improvised solos on saxophone).

This strange sojourn with Heidt was to be Fazola's last taste of working away from New Orleans. Despite the easier working schedule, Faz's blood pressure remained alarmingly high and he was advised to take a rest. In October 1943, Faz left Heidt's Band whilst they were playing in California and moved home to New Orleans. The visit was intended to be a vacation to allow Fazola to recuperate, when a few weeks had passed, Heidt made contact with the clarinettist and asked for an assessment of the situation. Fazola, just about to tuck into a bucket of oysters, affably told the bandleader that he was in New Orleans to stay, which turned out to be a prophetic forecast. Heidt well aware he was losing a considerable musical asset announced that he was "bitterly disappointed" that Fazola had decided not to rejoin.

Fazola was happy to seek out his boyhood friends once more, including attorney, Jacob Sciambra. By then Faz was grossly overweight, the 250 pound load on his 5ft 8 inch frame did nothing to alleviate his blood pressure problems. The clarinettist told Sciambra that he was suffering a good deal from the painful treatment he was receiving for a disease he had contracted a few years earlier. In spite of these ailments, Faz stayed cheerful, jocularly informing friends that he had come home to die.

Fazola remained a fearsomely heavy drinker, and his collosal intake of alcohol was causing the early symptoms of cirrhosis of the liver, his compulsive eating was also adding to his health problems. David Weinstein, now President of the New Orleans Musicians' Union, said "Faz just couldn't do anything in moderation, if he had a fifth of whisky in front of him he'd drink it all, and I've seen him sit down and eat four dozen oysters. One big 'poorboy' sandwich, which would have been a lunch for anyone else, wasn't even a snack for Faz, he'd have to order another, and then another".

During the mid-1940s, Faz worked regularly in *The Dambusters,* a big band that David Weinstein led at the local radio station; for most of his stay with the band Faz played baritone saxophone, doubling clarinet. The 13 piece group played a live radio show from 5.15 am until 9 am on six mornings a week, they also did private engagements. Weinstein recalls "Faz always made the gig, despite his health problems. There wasn't too much jazz involved, so Faz's main task was playing the baritone sax in the section, but he was regularly featured on clarinet. He hadn't been married too long at this time, and was quite congenial, except to one of the trumpeters, named Marion Suter, he and Faz had what could be called a clash of personalities. One of the other trumpeters was Al Hirt".

Besides his radio work, Fazola also did a good deal of freelance work (he was featured on the Esquire National Jazz Foundation Concert in April 1945), and also led his own band for various residencies in-and-around New Orleans. In 1945, after working with Leon Prima, Faz led his own band at the Plaza Club in Kenneria, Louisiana. With a 7 piece contingent from that band he resumed recording in 1945, cutting sides for the Keynote label, which showed that he had lost none of his inspiration or finesse. Tony Demado, the trumpeter with that band, spoke of working with Fazola, "I have nothing but beautiful memories of this great artist, to me was the greatest of the greats. His health was very poor at this particular time, he wasn't supposed to drink or over-eat, but disregarded both rules completely. He was playing both alto and clarinet at the Plaza Club, but hated playing alto. His brother, Louis 'Blue' Prestopnik, was also playing alto and clarinet in that band. Faz was not married at this time. When he got married it was to Joe Rotis's sister.

Joe Rotis was an old trombone-playing pal of Fazola's, after a brief courtship, Joe's sister Helen married Faz. The marriage had many happy moments, and when Fazola met up again with Eddie Miller, who was visiting New Orleans, he said "Why didn't you guys let me in on the secret that this marriage deal was good. I wish I'd have done it years ago". For a time Faz was sharply dressed, sporting a buttonhole flower, and a crisp handkerchief in his top pocket.

In October 1946, Faz formed up a new band to begin a residency at the Marine Room on Canal Boulevard. John Reininger played tenor saxophone in that band, and has never forgotten the night that Faz turned to him nonchalantly and said, "If I die tomorrow, I've lived as much life as people who get to be 70". Faz was then only 33.

Fazola saw no reason what-so-ever to move from New Orleans. In 1945, Eddie Miller begged him to join his big band in California, and a little later Ray Bauduc did his utmost to induce Faz to work on the West Coast, but nothing would make the clarinettist budge, Bauduc cheerfully accepted defeat "He gets homesick. He's got to be where there's gumbo handy". The residency at the Marine Room was one of the several spots at which Faz led his own band during the period 1946-48. Most often his bands were dixieland-orientated, occasionally Faz himself wrote out impressive arrangements, but usually his band worked without music, concentrating on what Faz called "real good tunes". He believed in avoiding, whenever possible, any tunes that were in the Hit Parade. At the time of the success of Pee Wee Hunt's version of *Twelfth Street Rag,* youngster Pete Fountain, went up to the bandstand at "Two Tony's Club" and asked Faz to play his version of the hit, he was told, unceremoniously, "Get lost, kid".

Now a jazz celebrity, Fountain was then just a beginner on clarinet, undeterred by the brush-off, Fountain went to hear Fazola whenever he could and developed into one of his staunchest fans. Eventually, Faz repaid the compliment and went to hear his devotee play at The Parisian Room one Sunday afternoon, in the Junior Dixie Band (who had recently guested on Horace Heidt's popular show). Faz approached Fountain, unaware that they had ever spoken together, and said "You're the one my mother keeps talking about. She heard you on the Horace Heidt Show".

Fazola was always close to his mother, Camille, and for a time heeded her advice on ways to improve his health. David Weinstein remembers, "Faz's mother insisted that he go to her doctor for medical advice, the doctor stressed that Faz must adopt a regime of simple living, but Faz got tired of being good, he consulted another doctor who said 'You go ahead and have a drink if you want one', and that was all Fazola wanted to hear. All his old excesses started, and his health began to fail".

Throughout most of 1948, Fazola continued to work regularly on radio with pianist Ogden Lafaye's Trio, and during the evenings at club jobs, often in the growing number of 'strip' joints' that were sprouting along the French Quarter streets. Faz's last regular job (in early 1949) was at the Mardi Gras Lounge, where he was heard by critic Leonard Feather, in New Orleans on a visit. Feather had been told of Faz's serious health problems, so was totally suprised when the irrepressible clarinettist turned up to play at the Hotel Roosevelt's Sunday afternoon jam session. Faz was still playing superbly. Another visitor to New Orleans, Vic Schuler, also heard Fazola at the Mardi Gras Lounge, less than three weeks before the clarinettist's death. He too reported that Fazola was playing 'swell clarinet'. Faz's old sidekick, trombonist Julian Lane was on that gig, these two, and the rest of the band, were delighted when Jack Teagarden dropped into the club one night to jam with them. Fazola's brother-in-law Joe Rotis arrived with his trombone and Faz was soon turning in a superb performance soaring majestically over the trombone choir.

Even on that last residency, Faz refused to change his life style, often he'd sit down with Julian Laine after the club had closed, and with bottle close at hand he'd ask Julian to recite a monologue called *Digby O'Dell - The Friendly Undertaker,* the hearing of which always greatly pleased him. But Faz never became docile. One evening he gave a young trumpeter a lift home in his car, after they had gone a block the youngster began knocking Dixieland music in general, and some of Fazola's favourites in particular. Faz leant over, opened the passenger-side door, swung his ample frame against the infidel and pitched him straight on to the street.

Eventually Faz had to pay the price for ignoring the repeated warnings about his health. In March 1949 he died in his sleep, at his home, 812 Bordeaux Street, New Orleans. Faz was 36, but looked years older. None of the New Orleans musicians were suprised by the news of his death, but all were saddened. He is still warmly remembered in his home city, and his reputation stands as high as ever. Veteran reed-player, Charlie Cordilla, who worked alongside both Roppolo and Fazola has said categorically that Faz was the greatest player of them all.

In September 1960, Fazola's mother gave his clarinet to the New Orleans Jazz Museum, the fine Selmer Albert model is a prize item in the collection of great jazz musicians' intruments. The fact that his clarinet became a museum exhibit would have baffled, and amused Fazola no end.

Yank Lawson, with Doc Rando and Max Herman, 1942.

Chapter 22

Yank Lawson

Even in moments of the utmost seriousness it would seem unnatural for anyone who knows John Rhea Lawson to call him anything but Yank - rarely can a nick-name have stuck so tight. Certainly he was never John to any of his Crosby Band colleagues, or one suspects to anyone outside of his home town of Trenton, Missouri, where he was born on the 3rd May 1911. It has often been said that the correct spelling of the surname is Lausen, but this is not so, the mistake arose initially because a union official at the Local 802 American Federation of Musicians, misread Yank's handwriting. A powerful figure, Yank stands 6 feet 4 inches, and is of Scottish and Irish ancestry. He tends to be formally polite on first introductions, and terse in disagreement, but most times he is full of good humour, and excessively generous.

Lawson's long-held nick-name was given to him during his musical childhood. By the age of eleven he was playing saxophone, and as one of the leading local saxmen was called Yank Smith, John's schoolboy pals complimented his efforts by saying he sounded to them like 'Yank'. Yank Lawson's musical tuition started when he began piano lessons at the age of five, his mother, a pianiste herself, encouraged Yank's obvious musical aptitude. But, neither the piano nor the saxophone (on which he played local gigs in the mid-1920s) seemed to satisfy Yank's powers of musical expression, and it wasn't until he began fooling around with a cornet, during his early teens, that he found his destiny.

Yank was a natural brass player and made rapid progress on the cornet, he switched to trumpet and took lessons from a fine teacher, Carl Webb (who later became a Professor at the University of Missouri). Yank, a bright school pupil, went on to augment his knowledge at the University of Missouri, doing well on a Liberal Arts Course. He played in a college dance band, which allowed him to have free food on the campus (a great help in tough times). The band also played gigs away from the college at weekends, and this provided Yank with a steady supply of spending money.

When the college group played a shared date alongside a visiting band, the travelling musicians took away with them a good impression of Yank's musical skills, and other bandleaders soon got to hear about the tall young man who blew as hot an improvised lead as anyone in the Middle West.

Slatz Randall, himself an ex-University musician, out of North Carolina, offered Yank a job in his band, accordingly Yank quit college and took up the life of a professional musician. Also in Randall's band was saxophonist

Deane Kincaide, who became a long-time friend of Yank Lawson. In 1932, Yank made his record debut with Randall in Chicago, and during that same year, whilst visiting Minneapolis, met Harriet, the girl who became his wife. After a series of wide-ranging tours throughout the Mid West, business for Randall declined drastically, and Yank left to join a band led by the one-armed trumpeting character from New Orleans, Joseph 'Wingy' Manone. Yank worked in many small Louisiana towns with Wingy's band, but his most indelible memories come from the time that the band hit rock bottom in Shreveport. "Things looked good whilst we were playing at the Youree Hotel, but then suddenly there was no work, and no money, and we were literally close to starving. Things got so tough we put bird-seed in some old mousetraps, caught birds and ate them. Wingy sailed through the crisis, seemingly oblivious. I guess he deserved to be, he was walking along the street smoking reefers that were nearly a foot long, and blowing smoke all over the policemen standing on the corner. One day, one of them got suspicious and said to Wingy 'You smoking some of that muggles', No, I ain't said Wingy, 'but, I know who is, that Bubber Broyle who runs the music store'. He'd say anything that Wingy, a strange, strange character".

Yank had always been taught by his father to look after himself, but this kind of scuffling just wasn't any fun, so Yank cashed in an endownment policy that his grandmother had taken out for him, and, with the sixty dollars realised, struck North. "That sixty bucks was all I had in the world, I got on a bus and rode the 3,000 mile journey up to Minneapolis to see Harriet".

After a happy re-union with his girl friend, Yank visited nearby St. Paul to hear Ben Pollack's Band playing at the Hotel Lowery, Pollack's staff arranger at this time was Yank's friend, Deane Kincaide. On the night of Yank's visit, Pollack's trumpeter, Sterling Bose, had gone off on one of his periodic 'benders', and after Kincaide had introduced Yank to members of the band, several of them suggested he bring his trumpet along to a rehearsal the band were holding the next day. Yank turned up, read everything that was put in front of him, did some impressive improvising, and joined in the head arrangements as though he had been with the band for years, he got the job there and then.

Yank was overjoyed to be playing alongside such fine musicians as Eddie Miller, Matty Matlock, Ray Bauduc, Nappy Lamare and the rest of the men whose work he had heard many times on the radio. Here at last was a bunch of musicians who could play supremely well, and who were keen enough on jazz to spend hours talking about recordings by Louis Armstrong and Bix Beiderbecke, the two trumpet players whose work Yank admired most.

In 1933, Yank, by now firmly entrenched in the Pollack Band, married Harriet, his best man was the band's bassist, Jerry Johnson. Later that year, Yank and his wife, made their first ever trip to New York. "Gil Rodin, Harriet and I drove from Chicago to New York. We got there just as prohibition was ending, and our booking was to play at a deluxe night spot - Billy Rose's

Casino De Paree. We played for the show (under a guest conductor) then Ben Pollack would return out front, and we'd play for dancing. You'd look around the dance floor, which was actually the stage, and see all sorts of celebrities. We made some records soon after we got to New York, then the Musicians' Union realised that I hadn't got an 802 card, which meant I couldn't record in New York until I'd effected a transfer from my own local. Our trombonist Joe Harris was in the same boat. I continued to play the residency, but Stew Pletcher came in for the next recordings".

Eddie Miller introduced Yank to the regulars at Plunkett's Bar on West 53rd Street, and gradually Yank got to know most of the jazz musicians who were based in New York. He sat in at various places, and on one notable occasion found himself on a bandstand with the legendary Sidney Bechet. After they had played a very lively *Jazz Me Blues* together, the famous New Orleans reedman turned slowly to Yank and said, with great dignity, "Very good young man, but you beat it in too fucking fast".

After a highly successful stay in New York, Pollack's Band played a string of one-night stands before beginning a month's residency at the Hollywood Dinner Club in Galveston, Texas, starting in late June 1934. Whilst the band were there the town underwent terrible flooding, and water several feet deep swept through the streets. The deluge suddenly hit the Hollywood Dinner Club and everyone ran to find higher ground, everyone except Connee Boswell (who, together with her sisters, was guesting with Pollack's Band). Connee crippled since childhood was unable to move, and Yank went through the water and carried her to safety. Yank has never mentioned this heroism, but all those present have never forgotten his bravery.

By the time the band had reached Galveston, Ben Pollack was totally absorbed in promoting the career of his singer, Doris Robbins, and seemed disinterested in getting bookings for the band, this meant that when the Texas engagement ended there were no immediate dates in the book. All of the regulars in Pollack's Band were used to their leader's mode of operations, in the past, there had been other lean times, devoid of bookings, but usually the musicians found casual work with local bands until Pollack sent details of a forthcoming engagement. But the chances of travelling musicians finding freelance gigs in the Galveston area were extremely slim. So, during the enforced lay-off that followed the Texas booking, most of the New Orleans contingent in the band made their way home, as did other members of the group. But Yank's wife, Harriet, who had travelled with him to Galveston, was in the late stages of pregnancy, by the time the booking ended, the birth was imminent, so Yank remained in Galveston, and soon he and his wife were proud parents of a baby daughter.

Ben Pollack told Yank to sit tight in Galveston until he heard from him, this meant that a long period during which Yank had to disconsolately kick his heels waiting for news from the bandleader. Just as the last of Yank's money was running out, a telegram from Pollack arrived saying "Come to Culver

City, California, Hall of Fame program in the bag".

"Pollack's promise about the 'Hall of Fame', which was then a big radio show, became something of a band joke, since when we got to the Coast we found out that we were definitely not on the program. However, we did have a residency at the Cotton Club in Culver City, which was just across the street from the M.G.M. studios, it was something of a landmark because it had a fake Elizabethan facade. To get to California I had to catch a rail day-coach all the way from Galveston, Texas, and for some reason or another I had to take the dog along with me. I arrived nearly flat broke, but got a taxi from the station, a few seconds before I got out to meet Pollack the dog was sick all over me".

"The movie crowds came into the Cotton Club regularly. We played in one hall, and in another part of the club there was a band featuring Lionel Hampton, whose duties included accompanying a spectacular floor show that had some excellent dancers. There was some beautiful girls amongst the troupe, and one of our band had a fling with one of them, next morning he realised all her body make-up had come off on the sheets, and he had a nut-brown bed".

"There was still no sign of the 'Hall of Fame' and ever after when someone made a false promise it became known amongst the band as a 'Hall of Fame' deal. The big problem was that Pollack kept cutting our money so that he could spend more on promoting Doris Robbins, he took her from one film agent to another. Finally we'd had enough, the writing was on the wall, and Gil Rodin could see that all his and our previous efforts were being wasted, so around Thanksgiving we decided to move en bloc to the East Coast".

Yank has always retained considerable respect for Pollack despite the traumas. "He was a wonderful drummer, and basically he was a tolerant guy. Too bad he let other things mess up his life. After we left him in California in 1934, I didn't see him for years, but then one morning, around 4 am, I bumped into him at Nick's in New York, and he was as friendly as could be".

Yank certainly wasn't loaded with money when he arrived in New York early in 1935. "Actually, I was flat arsed broke. I moved into the Chesterfield Hotel and took the cheapest room they had, no bath. Later, when things began to settle down, Harriet and I shared an apartment with Ray Bauduc and Edna". Yank still hadn't qualified for an 802 Union Card, and found to his dismay that the months he had spent working with Pollack in New York didn't count as a probationary period for the transfer, as officially he shouldn't have been there at all, so whilst the rest of the Pollack 'Orphans' played in Red Nichols' "College Prom" radio show, Yank had to find gigs as and when he could.

During Yank's first months in New York he played a wide variety of dates, working with Smith Ballew at the Hollywood Cabaret on Broadway, and 48th Street, (he also accompanied Sophie Tucker at the same venue), and played casual jobs with Harry Richman, and Will Osborne. Finally the union transfer period was completed and Yank was able to play on all of the record dates that Gil Rodin organised, he also took part in Mound City Blue Blower's sessions with Red McKenzie.

There were no union restrictions on Yank rehearsing with his ex-Pollack colleagues in the band that was soon to come under Bob Crosby's aegis. Though Yank has always preferred to play loose, informal jazz, he went along happily with all the various styles that the early Crosby Band was expected to present, ranging from the softly-muted role that he was required to play for hotel dinner music, through to the fiercely blown ride-outs that usually brought an evening's music to a close. Yank's natural musical ability was never shackled down; his playing was always rhythmically strong, his tone hot, and his improvisations completely unfrivolous. This direct, powerful way of playing the trumpet is highly reminiscent of the man himself.

During the early stages of its career, the Crosby brass section never achieved a dynamic blend, this was partly due to frequent personnel changes, but the main reason was that the musicians who were excellent section players were not attracted by the sort of money that the Crosby band could afford to pay in those early days. Yank explains, "In the mid-1930s, top-class lead trumpet players were at a premium, they could earn hundreds of dollars every week, playing radio shows and doing studio work. They didn't go through the hassle of playing one-night stands and travelling for about a quarter of the money they were used to earning. Andy Ferretti was a first class lead-trumpet player, and a great guy too, he enjoyed playing in the Crosby Band, but all the time he was with us he could have been earning more money elsewhere, eventually he was tempted away. It was the right move, because Andy became one of the most respected trumpet men in New York, second only, I think, to Charlie Margulis. Andy sure could drink, he went to the doctor for a check-up, and the doctor asked him 'Do you drink more than a pint of spirits a day?', Andy said 'Good God, I spill more than that'.

Ferretti always remained a good friend of Yank's so too did another member of the Crosby brass section, Ward Sillaway. "Ward was an orphan, he later married our singer, Kay Weber. He was a marvellous guy, he and I used to play tennis together, we had lots of fun, but during one game with Ward at the Harvard University Courts in Cambridge, Mass., I stretched up and pulled a big muscle in my back and had to be strapped up for weeks which made playing the trumpet kind of awkward. We used to call Ward 'the blonde Chinaman', which fitted his facial expression".

"After I left Crosby to join Tommy Dorsey, Ward followed on and made the same move. Tommy used to tease Ward, on a hotel job he'd pass his own trombone parts to Ward, and then go and sit out front to listen, knowing that the parts were extremely difficult, he'd order up a plate of crullers, a sort of doughnut, and when Ward hit a bad note Tommy would get the waiter to take a single cruller up to the bandstand, Ward got one served every time he hit a clinker".

Tommy Dorsey, who could be something of a tyrant, had a great liking for Yank, and for his trumpet playing, and in the summer of 1938 Yank eventually accepted Tommy's repeated invitation and joined the trombonist's band. "The money was a big factor, Tommy literally let me write out my own cheque, but the music was of a high standard, and I found the team spirit within the band was excellent, certainly as high as the Crosby Band, we had a lot of fun. I didn't row with Gil Rodin before I left the Crosby Band, nothing like that, but I was just so weary of the way the corporation deal had worked out. We only had two share-outs in my time, and when anyone questioned the financial structure there was a great deal of talk about re-investing our gains back into the corporation, but I had a growing family. To this day, I've never quite understood, or unravelled the financial tangle that the corporation got itself into, we were doing great business everywhere, but this was never reflected in the money that reached us. The first agency presented us with some preposterous charges and expenses, but even taking all that into account I felt pretty dissatisfied. I got on fine with Tommy, always did, so I made up my mind to leave Crosby. I still feel it was the sensible thing to do, and Tommy soon proved how considerate he could be. Not long after I joined him, I developed Bell's Palsy down one side of my face, (from falling asleep against a cold window I think), I had to quit playing the trumpet for a while, but Tommy paid my full wages until I was able to return to the band. You just don't forget things like that".

"Tommy demanded certain musical standards, and if you met them he was okay, he'd even laugh at situations that other bandleaders might not accept. Shortly after Charlie Spivak and I joined Tommy, he said to the two of us, and to Moe Zudecoff (who later became Buddy Morrow), 'Say fellows why don't you three come down with me to hear my brother's band tonight?'. 'No thanks', said Moe 'I don't ever socialize with leaders'. Some bandleaders might have got mad at that sort of response, but Tommy let out a genuine chuckle".

Eventually, Yank felt the need to quit touring in order to spend more time with his family in New York. Abe Lyman said to him, "Work with my band at the Strand theatre for a month, and I'll use you on two regular radio shows". Assured by the security Lyman offered, Yank quit the touring life, temporarily, as it turned out. Early in 1940, Yank worked with Richard Himber, then joined the theatre orchestra that was playing for the Broadway show *Louisiana Purchase*. Yank, who had never had any difficulties in reading music, thought that playing for a show would be an interesting change, to make sure he didn't encounter any difficulties he took some tuition from the cornet ace, Del Staigers, on the art of orchestral work, a move that was to pay rich dividends later.

But after playing the *Louisiana Purchase* for some months, Yank began to feel decidedly restless, as if by telepathy Gil Rodin contacted Yank with a lucrative offer to rejoin the Crosby Band. "Harriet and myself talked it over at length. The money was excellent, and this time I had no need to bother my head with the problems of the corporation, I'd be on a salary. I couldn't leave the show immediately, I had what was called a run-of-the-show contract, but after I worked out my notice I got into a big Chrysler that I'd just bought and drove off to rejoin the Crosby Band in Arkansas. We then played places like Dallas, and San Antonio, gradually moving over to California for a season on Catalina Island".

"That summer at Catalina was near perfect. I took Zane Grey's old apartment which was on a hill overlooking the harbour. The work schedule wasn't too arduous and we had plenty of time to relax, it was there that I finally got around to playing Bob Crosby at tennis. Bob had played a lot of tennis since he was a kid, and so had I, but it took us years to actually get around to playing each other. I'm pleased to say I picked up the twenty dollar bet we had on the match, I think nearly everyone in the band turned out to watch".

"The trumpet team we had there was a good one, Max Herman and Lyman Vunk used to swop the lead parts. I didn't care for some of the arrangements that had been added, they certainly didn't do anything to establish a new style for the band, rather, they tended to make us sound like most of the other bands who were around at that time". Yank, like Eddie Miller, has never been interested in becoming an arranger, "For a while I lived next door to Bill Challis, who was a renowned arranger. He began to coach me informally about scoring, and voicings, but I couldn't work up any enthusiasm, so we dropped the idea. I've always preferred small groups to big ones, they offer the musicians so much more freedom".

After the Crosby Band's final theatre tour in the fall of 1942, Yank made his way back to his family in New York. "almost everyone in the band except Bob Haggart and me, went back to California, but I lived on the East Coast, and that's where my draft board was. It so happened that I was being continually deferred because by then I had four young children, so I didn't go into the services after all".

By late 1942, Yank was working in Benny Goodman's Band at the Paramount Theatre in New York, but this was only a temporary berth, within weeks he was fulfilling dates with various studio bands. Yank's reliability, temperament and talent made him an ideal musician for the demands of studio work, and during the 1940s and 1950s he played on countless recordings, and radio programs, undertaking engagements that ranged from blowing a few bars on a jingle to participating in a full concert orchestra under Toscanini's baton. Yank worked with just about every famous vocalist in America during this period, including Bing Crosby and Frank Sinatra. "Bing was always friendly toward me, but then I never had occasion to need him. He always had a gag ready, but I think he was really a loner, who hated to think people were trying to use him". Yank's work with Frank Sinatra includ- ed a superb recording of *Stormy Weather,* on which his plunger playing is unsurpassable; even Yank likes that one.

In 1951, Yank and his long-time colleague Bob Haggart began recording a series of small band items that paid tribute to the jazz pioneers. The series was conceived, and produced by the ex-owner of the famous Commodore Record Shop, Milt Gabler. The billing used: The Lawson Haggart Jazz Band, became a bye word with discerning record collectors who were delighted to hear two of their favourite ex-Bob Crosby sidemen in such musically congenial circumstances, playing such worthwhile material. The melodies for some of the more obscure numbers were transcribed by Bob Haggart from old recordings, Haggart always paid homage to the originals, but there were innumerable deft individual touches within the loosely organised ensembles. Yank has rarely sounded more dynamic than on this series of recordings, adding a continual vitality to the free-wheeling ensembles. The basic personnel for the Decca series was Yank, Bob Haggart, Bill Stegmeyer on clarinet, Cliff Leeman on drums, Lou Stein on piano, and Lou McGarity on trombone, occasionally the band was aumented. Over several years, the star studded group paid tribute to numbers previously recorded by King Oliver, Jelly Roll Morton, Bix Beiderbecke and Louis Armstrong, and did so in superb style. The series began in the last part of the 78 rpm era, and are still being re-issued today.

Another great recording project that both Yank and Bob Haggart got involved in during the mid-1950s was the Louis Armstrong *Musical Autobiography* sessions, on which Louis recreated many of his earlier triumphs. Few things have given Yank more pleasure than being chosen by Louis to play the trumpet parts originally recorded by King Oliver in the remakes of the Creole Jazz Band's tunes. Yank was also delighted to share a double trumpet session with Louis at the Newport Jazz Festival.

Dream gigs like those were undertaken during the brief periods in which Yank wasn't busily engaged with his work in the studios. His self-imposed discipline sounds daunting, "I hardly left New York during the years 1942 to 1968, and for one period I hardly took a day off for three years. My kids were in college and I needed the work".

Yank was one of the first radio-studio men to transfer to a television band, he became a staffman at NBC and remained there for many years, working on the Tonight show regularly, he also played on programs hosted by Milton Berle, Perry Como, Steve Allen, and took part in the *Show of Shows, Hit Parade* plus numerous other spectaculars. Throughout this period he was a constant inspiration to the younger members of the studio brass teams, and trumpeter Mel Davis still recalls the awe he felt in observing Yank sight-read a supremely difficult piece of music without uncrossing his legs. During his years in the television studios, Yank never lost touch with the New York club scene, often dropping in to see old friends from the jazz world, and ending up by sitting in to play a few numbers with them. In 1966 Yank played a regular stint at Eddie Condon's Club.

To a casual questioner, Yank tends to give the impression that he regards his career in music, as being nothing worth dwelling on, "I just did the best I could, that's all. No use worrying about what you were supposed to have done, no use practising after the event, time to do that is beforehand" is a typical reflection, delivered in a matter-of-fact way. Yank rarely wallows in nostalgia, nor does he believe in lengthy musical post-mortems, however, he knows when things have gone right for him or for any of the band that he is working with - after one session he got off the stand, and said "If you thought that was lousy, you've got good taste".

Yank certainly wouldn't claim to have total recall, but his memory has an off-beat brilliance. When several of his old pals have totally forgotten a name, or a situation from the past, Yank suddenly begins pouring out details. As when he unexpectedly recalled all of the words of a song that a former Olympic swimmer, Eleanor Holm, sang in a 1937 Aquacade show, though he hadn't thought about the ditty for over forty years.

Yank took part in several reunions of the Bob Crosby Bob Cats during the late 1950s and 1960s, the highlight of which was the visit to Japan and Australia in 1964. "The receptions were amazing, we played to over 15,000 people at a concert in Japan. We played Manilla in the Phillipines as well, but the open friendliness of the people of Australia really got to us, so many people seemed to know all about every Bob Cats' record".

The other momentous reunion of the Bob Crosby alumni occurred in late 1966 when Yank and Bob Haggart persuaded Bob Crosby, Eddie Miller, and Matty Matlock to come over from the West Coast to play at the Rainbow Grill in New York, there they linked up with trombonist Lou McGarity, pianist Ralph Sutton and drummer Morey Feld, later replaced by Cliff Leeman; the band (with Don Lamond on drums) cut two superb live albums, which led many jazz fans around the world to express a hope that such an illustrious and productive musical ensemble could become a regular working unit. The seeds of such an idea began to grow in the minds of Yank Lawson and Bob Haggart, and their vague plans were stimulated by an offer from Tony Cabot, who wanted to book a Bob Cats type of band for his Longchamps chain of restaurants. Inspired sessions at Dick Gibson's jazz parties in Colorado caused Yank and Bob to make definite plans to form a super group. Gibson, a long-time jazz fan and highly successful business man, became the entrepreneur of the new group, which became known as *The World's Greatest Jazz Band*.

In order to concentrate entirely on the new band, Yank and Bob Haggart decided to leave their long-held berths at the NBC studios; at the time both were working regularly on the *Johnny Carson Show*. Neither of the co-leaders were enamoured by the name that Dick Gibson had bestowed on the group, but both bowed to Gibson's superior knowledge of marketing techniques.

The group did its first recording in December 1968, and within a few months offers of work for the band were coming from all parts of the world.

Billy Butterfield on trumpet and flugel horn, Bud Freeman on tenor saxophone, and Bob Wilber on soprano sax and clarinet became long-time stalwarts of the *World's Greatest Jazz Band's* illustrious front line. The mini-section of two trombonists, underwent a number of changes during the band's career, utilising the services of several magnificent players including, Lou McGarity, Carl Fontana, Eddie Hubble, Vic Dickenson, Sonny Russo, Benny Morton, Kai Winding and George Masso. Ralph Sutton, the band's original pianist, stayed with the group for several years, as did drummer Gus Johnson, who took Morey Feld's place in the band soon after its inception. Maxine Sullivan, whose singing fitted in perfectly with Yank and Bob's concepts when they all worked together at a 1968 Dick Gibson party, became the W.G.J.B.'s vocaliste.

For almost ten years this super group toured with great success all over the world. As one star musician dropped out he was replaced by someone of equal eminence. The band seemed imperishable and sailed imperturbably through a change of management that saw Texan Bark Hickox take Dick Gibson's place. The group made several superb albums, blending tunes old and new, and presenting them in a unique, bold sounding way, which always swung.

Both co-leaders shared the pleasure, and the headaches of band-leading. There was rarely anything wrong with the music, but occasionally the band encountered promoters who either skipped with the admission money, or used it to settle previous debts. The unit reverted to a one trumpet set-up when Billy Butterfield left to spend more time at his home in Florida, though cornetist Bobby Hackett later occasionally guested with the group. Gradually the two co-leaders came to think that they too would like to spend less of their lives packing and unpacking suitcases, and worrying about travel problems. After a long consultation the two men decided to revert to their Lawson-Haggart Jazz Band billing, and as such they have continued to play many eminently successful engagements during the 1980s.

The new set-up has given more freedom to both men, enabling both of them to undertake solo tours of Europe in recent years. They also continue to play in some of the Bob Cats' reunions. The camaraderie still holds strong, and occasionally Yank will tease Eddie Miller after they've finished a reunion date "pass me that saxophone, I'll show you how it's done", says the trumpeter, pretending to make a serious attempt to relive his days as a saxophone player. Eddie always obliges cheerfully, and keeps up a smile as Yank seemingly attempts to blow the sax into a new shape. When the sound of this powerful barrage has ended, Eddie usually says, with some diplomacy "Gee, I wish I could play as loud as that".

In between well-spaced tours, Yank is happy to relax at his home in Maine, with his wife Harriet. He plays golf regularly, and loves walking. He delights in browsing amongst the large number of books (on many subjects) that he's collected over the years, and he likes cooking, preparing with skill and flamboyance, elaborate, exotic menus.

After undergoing a serious ulcer operation during the summer of 1981, Yank decided to give up drinking. He feels he is now a much mellower person. Nowadays all his fire is channelled into his trumpet playing. Yank still uses the same trumpet mouthpiece he first blew 40 years ago, and even after a long layoff from his horn he can still pick it up and blow with power and authority, "It's just that I use the dry lip method of blowing", says Yank modestly. He celebrated his 72nd birthday hopping across the Swiss-German borders to play yet another one-night stand. One of his favourite expressions is "It's been a lot of fun", and happily the pleasure shows no signs of diminishing.

"Thank God that Fazola never wanted to do this." Lt. Bob Crosby (US Marine Corps) and his travelling troupe at a Pacific base, 1945.
(photo courtesy of US Defense Dept.)

Chapter 23

Bob Crosby

Having a famous relative, particularly if they share the same surname, always brings a little extra attention, even to those who do not seek it. Reflected glory may provide a pleasant light to bask in, but when the shadows of a famous kinsman loom extra large it is sometimes difficult for the individualism of various members of the family to be noticed. Most people find their way out of the dilemma by choosing an area of enterprise that is totally different from that of their distinguished relative, but a minority risk the hazard of continual comparison and follow close in famous footsteps.

To do this in the entertainment world requires a special sort of courage, because once the public have sampled the curiosity value of the situation they tend to develop an attitude that makes progress more difficult than it would be for someone with an ordinary background. However, a blend of talent and persistence can overcome the problem, and the living proof of this has been provided by Bob Crosby's success.

Bing Crosby was undoubtedly one of the most famous singers who ever lived, his fame transcended the "crooning" era of the 1930s, and looks like being everlasting. Even now, years after his death, no posthumous revelation is too extravagant, or too insubstantial, to be ignored by various newspapers. During all the time that Bing's name made headlines, his younger brother Bob achieved his own durable success, as a singer, a bandleader, and a renowned master of ceremonies.

A ten year gap seperated the births of Bing, (b. 1903), and Bob (b. 1913), they were the sons of Harry Crosby and Catherine "Kate" Crosby, whose other children were Larry (b. 1895), Everett (b. 1896), Ted (b. 1900), Catherine (b. 1904) and Mary Rose (b. 1906). Both parents could trace eminence in their lineage, but by the time the Crosby household moved to Spokane, Washington in July 1906, family pride could be more firmly placed on heritage than it could on financial assets. None of the Crosby children suffered hardship through poverty, but none were cosseted, and each was made aware of the value of the wages that their accountant father brought home each week.

Bing's early successes as a professional singer in the late 1920s made little difference to the life style of the Crosby family in Spokane, and Bob's education took place in topsy-turvy fashion, whose changing patterns were shaped by the fluctuating amounts that the local Inland Products Canning Company paid to his father. Bob's education was gleaned partly at Webster

High School, partly at North Central High, and at Gonzaga - a Jesuit place of learning that had a high school and a college within its complex. Thus Bob's schooling was similar to Bing's.

Two weeks after his birth on the 25th of August 1913, George Robert Crosby was baptized at a local Roman Catholic church, St. Aloysius. He became known as Bob during childhod, as a sort of tribute to his mother's favourite brother, George Robert Harrigan. At school, and at college, Bob remained an average student, but early on in life he distinguished himself as an athlete, playing football, baseball and tennis with considerable skill, (he later became a fine golfer). The prospects of becoming a professional sportsman were not too remote to be ignored, but from childhood onwards Bob always had a yen to perform in show business. Neither Larry, Everett nor Ted had ever felt the desire to be paid entertainers, but Bob's restless ambition led him to sing in public whenever he could.

None of Bob's juvenile concert appearances in Spokane (then a town of about 40,000 inhabitants), were a sensational success, but he battled on, listening with diligence to the gramophone records that Bing sent home, and spending hours trying to find good music on distant radio stations. At 15, his show business hopes suffered a set-back, whilst playing baseball he removed the catcher's mask and accidentally took the full force of a swinging bat. The accident cost him his front teeth, he quit singing until he was fitted with a dental plate, even then he suffered a temporary loss of confidence, which Bob feels affected his vocal progress through his formative years. Eventually, he began to feel more sure of himself and resumed singing local dates, which included a stint at a walkathon.

Economically things were still restricted at home during the early 1930s, and in order to pay for his sophomore fees Bob took a part-time job working as a picker for the same canning company that employed his father. One day, Bob's work in the company fields at a place appropriately called Opportunity was dramatically interrupted by the arrival of his father waving a telegram that had been sent by bandleader Anson Weeks. The cable contained an offer for Bob to sing with Weeks' band for a hundred dollars a week, a much better pay deal than the 25 cents an hour he was getting for picking cucumbers.

"Apparently, Bing and Anson Weeks had a few drinks together one night, and Weeks asked Bing 'Are there any more at home like you?'. Bing said 'Sure, my kid brother'. So Anson got the idea of featuring me with his band, but the problem was he hadn't heard me sing. It was arranged he listen to me over our local radio station KFPW, but the laugh was that when he came to tune in from San Francisco he couldn't pick up the station at that distance, so he signed me unheard".

To maximise the publicity advantages of the situation it was stipulated that Bob had to visit Bing in Los Angeles before journeying on to San Francisco. It has been suggested that Bing virtually ignored Bob during the visit, but Bob denies this "Bing gave me lots of advice on phrasing, and particularly showed me how to bring out certain words in a lyric, he'd underline the important words in the song's lyric, and emphasis them when he sang, Just One More **Chance**, things like that. He also got me fitted out with a good tuxedo. On the morning I was due to leave, Bing was lying down, suffering from a king-size hangover, all he could muster as parting advice was, 'Make sure you keep your nose clean'. I told a writer about this once, and it became a dramatic issue, as though that's all Bing could be bothered to say to me. It wasn't like that, and I got mad about the way the story had been angled".

Bob made his recording debut with Anson Weeks singing in a style that was quite understandably like Bing's. He moved in to a hotel not far from the Mark Hopkins Hotel, which had long been the home residency for Anson Weeks' 15 piece band. After a shaky start, which led to a despairing return home, Bob returned to settle down and work amongst Weeks' experienced professionals, the personnel included Xavier Cugat amongst its 3 violinists. "I learnt a lot from Anson, who was a nice guy, but his style of music was definitely not what I liked. It had what we used to call a 'Mickey Mouse' approach".

Bob became distinctly restless in California, and a romantic attachment that had gone awry added to his discontent. When the Week's band went on tour in 1934, Bob let everyone in his family know that he would like to move East for a while. Bing Crosby's East Coast agent at the time was Tommy Rockwell, who with his partner Cork O'Keefe, handled several bands, including a new unit that was taking shape under the leadership of the Dorsey Brothers, Jimmy and Tommy. Rockwell, who had formerly been based in Chicago, as the manager of the Okeh recording company, was revisiting the city when Weeks' Band played the Aragon Ballroom. On Larry Crosby's advice (Larry was then Bing's personal manager), Rockwell listened intently to Bob then pronounced that he would do all he could to find him work on the East Coast.

This offer delighted Bob Crosby, who still regards Rockwell as one of the most memorable characters who ever worked in the music business. "He was a dynamic guy, with a wonderful capacity for recognizing talent. He'd not only helped Bing, and the Casa Loma Band, and the Mills Brothers, he was also able to sell a band to people, even though they'd never heard it. In one case, he sold Ray Noble's American Band to the Rainbow Room in New York before Ray had even formed it".

Tommy Rockwell invited Bob to stay at his summer home on Southern Long Island until he found a suitable place to live. Meanwhile, the new band organised by the Dorsey Brothers was holding regular rehearsals at the Manhattan office from which Rockwell and O'Keefe ran their booking agency. To fill in time for Bob Crosby, who was slated to join the new band, the agency got him a booking at the Paramount Theatre in July 1934, where he was hired to sing duets with vocaliste Lee Wiley, Bob's billing was "Living

Up To A Singing Name". It was only a temporary partnership, which Bob, thinking of Lee Wiley's feelings, says was just as well. "It was supposed to be a romantic duo, but I think my inexperience made it into more of a comedy interlude. My mind was really more on joining the Dorsey Brothers' Band. I had some of their records, including *Dr. Heckle and Mr. Jive* and I was looking forward to working with them.".

By 1934, Tommy Dorsey had already established a reputation for irascibility. He was a superb musician, and a man of decidedly fixed opinions, if he liked someone he could be generous and affable, but if he bore ill feelings toward anyone he made sure they knew it, both by word and deed. He and Bob Crosby were destined never to get on. Cork O'Keefe, whose agency represented both Bob and the Dorsey Brothers, said "Tommy Dorsey didn't like Bob for some reason, but we pointed out to him that the name would be good for the band, and so he grudgingly went along with the idea. It never did work into a smooth running arrangement, and when it ended it would be hard to say who was the more delighted, Tommy or Bob".

Bob's brother, Everett, hardly paved the way for Bob to make a smooth entry into the Dorsey Brothers' Band, and unwittingly ensured that the young singer would never experience the warmer side of Tommy Dorsey's personality. Recounting the words of advice he gave to Tommy Dorsey, just before Bob joined, Everett told a journalist, "I said 'You can have him if you knock some of the swell-head out of him. Tell him every night he stinks, and maybe he'll get the right sense of values".

Tommy Dorsey certainly took Everett Crosby at his word. He confronted Bob as soon as he had joined the band and said, "Look, I've got the best damn band in the land, why haven't I got the best Crosby?". This was only one of many spiteful remarks that Tommy made to Bob during his first few weeks with the band, for the first few days he refused to even let him sing. "Tommy Dorsey was a completely unpleasant person as far as I am concerned. Very difficult to get along with. He had no concept of other people's feelings, and seemed to be devoid of any true emotion, yet, he could pick up the trombone, and play beautifully, it wasn't great jazz but the tone was remarkable. His brother Jimmy was a pleasanter man, and he had a kinder approach, but even he, when he was drunk, could get nasty, and then he'd start picking on me".

Bob first worked with the Dorseys at the Sands Point Bath Club at Great Neck on Long Island, where they played the 1934 summer season. The band's guitarist was Roc Hillman, who recalls Bob's arrival, "I remember that it was with reticence that Tommy Dorsey agreed to take him on as vocalist, as they had Kay Weber, our vocal trio and also trombonist Don Matteson doing vocals. When we started at the Sands Point Club, Bob was with the band but only sang a few songs. Tommy (who was the front man) didn't speak to Bob very often, and when he did he was usually critical of Bob's work. I recall many intermissions finding Bob alone out by the balcony railing overlooking the water, in a very despondent mood, wondering if things were going to work out".

Drummer Ray McKinley, later to lead his own highly successful band, was with the Dorsey Brothers at the time, "Bob kept pretty much to himself, and was rather shy. Tommy didn't think much of him, either as a singer or as a person. At that time I was hooked on tennis, Bob could beat me, we played once or twice. Of course, Bob was working under the awesome image of Bing who was skyrocketing at the time, which may account, at least in part, for his shyness".

After the Dorsey Brothers Band had completed a season at the Sands Club, it began another residency in New Jersey, at Ben Marden's Riviera Club at Fort Lee. By then, Bob had made his first recording with the band, singing the song that Tommy Dorsey was later to adopt as his signature tune, *I'm Getting Sentimental Over You.* He continued to record with the band throughout the winter, and moved with them on to the next residency, which was at another of Ben Marden's clubs, this time the Palais Royale on Broadway.

Socially things were no smoother between Tommy Dorsey and Bob during the Palais Royale residency, but at least the enmity was mostly silent, much to Bob's relief. Roc Hillman observed from the rhythm section, "I believe that things were going more smoothly than with T.D. and Bob, and I recall a luke-warm affair between Martha Raye and Bob, she was working at a night club a couple of blocks away and would come over after the last show to see Bob, whose singing was improving, by the way. It was during this engagement that Bob and I met a pharmacist from Baltimore who thought he had the embryo of a hit song, which became *It's a Small World.* We helped him develop it, but couldn't get anyone worthwhile to perform it". Later Roc and Bob co-composed *You're a Double Lovely* which Bing Crosby featured, and a novelty *I Don't Write and Nobody Answers* which Ish Kabbible sang with Kay Kyser's Band.

Despite outward appearances, Bob still found Tommy Dorsey's general behaviour reprehensible. "At the Palais Royale I witnessed an amazing scene. One night Benny Maier brought in a new arrangement and delivered it to Tommy, who handed the parts out there and then, in front of the audience, saying 'Okay, we'll try this one now'. Jimmy Dorsey made a strong protest saying 'Look Mac, I'd sooner we check this out at a rehearsal', but Tommy was insistent, he said 'These guys are getting paid to be musicians, let's hear them prove that they are'. Tommy counted the band in, and they began playing the new chart, but either because of tenseness, or faults in the copying, there was a series of bum notes. Tommy screamed at the band 'Any musician worth his salt better get his part right this time'. The next run through was even more disastrous, and the embarrassed audience looked on aghast at what was happening".

Bob's painful tenure with the Dorsey Brothers was soon to end. Both Tommy Rockwell and Cork O'Keefe were all too aware of the considerable

261

ill feeling that existed between Tommy Dorsey and Bob, they wanted to solve the problem by finding a new berth for the singer. Gil Rodin, who already had a well-rehearsed band comprised of ex-Ben Pollack sidemen, called in to the Rockwell-O'Keefe agency seeking a front man for the group. His visit took place at a very opportune time, and O'Keefe was able to bring Rodin and Crosby together with the minimum of problems.

Bob Crosby, who has admitted that he was so disenchanted with Tommy Dorsey that he would have moved in any direction to get away from him, liked the idea of joining a newly formed band. He was even more enthusiastic when he heard some of the recordings that the group had already made. Gil Rodin was undoubtedly aware that the Crosby name would stimulate box-office interest, even if it wasn't stressed, and he liked the idea that he would be able to give guidance and advice to someone who was relatively inexperienced in the ways of the music world. Happily, Gil and Bob Crosby got on well at their first meeting, and this initial rapport grew into a happy partnership in which Bob took on the job fronting the band, whilst Gil managed the band's business, its discipline and its musical policy.

Years later, Rodin summed up Bob's co-operative approach, "His genial nature and his willingness to let some of the more technical problems be handled by others in the band better qualified has been the biggest factor in the success". The first thing about Bob Crosby that struck the ex-Pollack musicians was his sense of humour, he quickly joined in with the band's style of light-hearted ribbing, and he was soon as enthusiastic about good jazz as they were. One of the band's main areas of concern revolved around the inconsistency that Bob showed in his vocalising, another was whether he could appear less shy when he stepped out to front the band. The second of these worries quickly evaporated, Bob soon developed an attractive stage presence, and a flowing, relaxed - sounding line of patter, which won praise from Matty Matlock, "He could handle a show. He communicated with the audience". The quality of Bob's vocals always remained variable, but, to his credit, he readily acquiesced when Gil Rodin suggested that an instrumental should replace a vocal in the band's programme. But no one in the Crosby outfit thought that Bob was a softie, those who played sport with him knew that he was a determined character, with no fondness for losing, and when he held a strong viewpoint on a particular issue no one could shake him off it.

The biggest problem that Bob had to contend with during his early days with the band was in establishing his own individuality, he was always being introduced as Bing's brother, even by the men he worked with. It took Bob years to see the issue in perspective, but looking back he said "Psychologically, maybe, in the back of my head I never did get over the feeling that it was tough being Bing's brother, but I can't ever remember thinking of myself as being in the shadow of Bing. Once the customers were in I had to win them over".

The people who came to hear the band often let their curiosity get the better of them, and they'd begin asking direct questions about Bing. Bob lost count of the number of people each week who asked him if he was taller than Bing (he was), he could answer that one with a well-worn chuckle, but when the more aggressive customers demanded that Bob sing one of Bing's songs "just like Bing", he sometimes, understandably, felt dejected. Bing himself showed no direct interest in Bob's progress with the band, or so the younger brother thought. Years later he found out that a badly needed thousand dollars that had been loaned to the band by music publisher, Rocco Vocco, was actually donated by Bing, who had heard the band needed financial support via his links with the Rockwell-O'Keefe office.

The inherent quality of most of the Crosby family in those days was shyness, and Bing, for all his success, never specialised in extrovert presentations. Bob feels that Bing would have been appalled if news of his help for the band had ever been made public, he saw his brother as an extremely sentimental man, who tried to present a devil-may-care image to the music world. The Crosby children grew up in a reserved atmosphere, one in which Bob feels his parents shared a great deal of love, "But it was not exhibited in public. I don't think I ever saw my father kiss my mother. It just wasn't done". Harry Lowe Crosby was lively company, and liked joking, but his wife Kate, has been described by someone who knew the family as "the kingpin of the whole family, she was set in her ways, and strongly disapproved of any monkeying around by her sons, she was much respected by all of the children. She was the decision maker".

Bing and Bob's elder brother, Everett, "an affable extrovert" was probably the most outgoing member of the family. Analysing the difference between his two singing brothers he said "Bing just gets up there and doesn't care. He takes it easy, and if they don't like it he doesn't mind. But Bob works harder, smiles at everybody, knows most of the customers by their first names. Different personality altogether".

Gil Rodin and the rest of the band corporation were delighted that Bob was keen to be on good terms with the customers. In retrospect, Bob confesses that his affableness on the bandstand was often harder work than it seemed. "The hotel location jobs were definitely not my favourites. Often the people didn't want to listen or to dance, they just wanted to find out 'who was there'. There was a lot of snobbery, and the standard of footwork on the floor was of the 'businessman's bounce' variety".

In looking back to the 1930s, Bob feels that the most appreciative audiences that the band had were in the North Eastern states, "I always felt that the crowds in Boston, and in Maine responded very warmly at exactly the right moment. They were discerning, but if something was really good they were quick to respond, their reactions to jazz seemed more advanced. Whereas the crowds in Chicago cheered louder, they sometimes cheered regardless of the merits of a particular performance".

Bob Crosby soon learned how to handle every type of audience, and if he ever felt irked by the disinterest that some of the musicians displayed when

263

backing him on slow ballads he never let it show on stage. There was rarely any serious acrimony between Bob and the rest of the band, but, inevitably when the "honeymoon" period of the association ended there were a few ups-and-downs. Bob joined in the general badinage on tour, and had no qualms about sharing a hotel room with various sidemen, at times he liked to keep his distance and the musicians learnt to respect his moods, realising that he was something of a loner. He was inclined to become demoralised by what the critics said about him, and brooded over a bad performance, sitting silently for long periods, twirling the front of his hair fitfully. He liked to gamble, but treated any betting losses as a personal insult, but he never felt low enough not to be able to get pleasure from telling, with considerable skill, very amusing jokes.

For a period, Bob was disenchanted by the attitude of the music magazines' critics who hinted that this vocals were taking up valuable time in which they could be listening to the work of the jazz soloists within the band. Bob's vocal performances were usually either disparaged or ignored by jazz writers, the effects of his treatment touched the nerve of his inborn sense of insecurity, and as a result he built up a resentment that manifested itself in his brusque and sometimes off-hand treatment of certain journalists. They in turn retaliated, one paper commented that Bob showed "A dissatisfaction with the rewards of his labour" it suggested that Bob's personality "if wrongly applied, would obscure the talent and undoubted charm he possesses. He should be more tolerant". One writer who dealt with Bob over a period of many years describes him as "moody . . . but with a great sense of humour", another journalist wrote that Bob was "charming one moment and dour the next".

Eventually, Bob realised that the jazz-loving writers weren't gunning for him personally, any other vocalist working with a band packed with interesting instrumentalists would have received the same treatment. As a result, he became more co-operative with journalists, usually giving interviews that are frank and charming, albeit with a tendency to move on the defensive if he feels any questions are too probing.

There is no doubt that Bob became a more relaxed person after his marriage, in 1938, to June Audrey Kuhn, they are still together, and this long-lasting marriage is in stark contrast to Bob's brief first marriage to Marie. June, the daughter of Dr. LeRoy Kuhn, a Chicago surgeon, met Bob whilst the band were playing at the Congress Hotel in Chicago, she was then on Easter vacation from the Sarah Lawrence School in New York. The couple were soon deeply involved in a romance, and were married in Bob's home town, Spokane, on the 22nd September 1938. June was then 19, and Bob 25.

During the late 1930s, Bob's relationship with Bing neither improved nor deteriorated. Bing made several recordings with Bob's Band, and an occasional live appearance. The two wives, Dixie Lee and June enjoyed each other's company, but Bob was in a different position from his brothers, Everett and Larry, in regard to his dealings with Bing. Both Everett and Larry worked within Bing's considerable business empire, as did their father, Harry (he and Kate had moved to California). Bob steadfastly maintained his independence which seemed at times to the others in the family to be rather perverse behaviour. However, by 1940, Larry and Bob's father were taken on to the Bob Crosby Band payroll to assist with administration.

Almost from the first day that Bob ever began fronting his band rumours hinted that he was about to begin a career as a film star. Early on, Bob had appeared in musical one-reelers with Anson Weeks' Band, and later when he moved East in 1934, negotiations took place that led to screen tests, but no contracts were forthcoming. The Crosby Band made a short film in 1937, which featured them playing two numbers, but nothing more prestigious came up until they were in California in 1940. With Bob close at hand, the studios took another look at his acting potential, and as a result he appeared in a whole series of films during the early 1940s, the band also appeared in several of them.

Bob prepared himself for the screen roles by adopting a suggestion that he trim off 15 pounds in weight, he learnt his lines diligently and listened willingly to advice from fellow actors. Altogether, Bob estimates that he made 22 films (spread over three decades), in several of these made in the early 1940s he played light comedy roles, singing the occasional song, in others he was type-cast as a famous bandleader. One movie, a 1943 epic called *The Singing Sheriff* (in which Bob takes the title role), is always singled out for special mention when Bob is asked to comment on his Hollywood days. "It only took ten days to make, but it set Westerns back three years", and "The Western that almost made a success out of Easterns" are his standard quips on the subject.

The brilliant writer Nathaniel West, did the screen play for Bob and the band's first Hollywood film, *Let's Make Music,* but moments of distinguished artistry were few and far between in many of the early 1940s low budget films, and Bob was too much of a realist to see that there was any great future for him in movies. He looks back on his experiences in the film world with wry amusement, but enjoyed some of the brief, cameo roles he played in musicals during the 1950s.

One of the Bob Crosby Band's lasting successes in the film world was in providing part of the soundtrack for the 1942 film *Holiday Inn,* which featured Bing Crosby and Fred Astaire. Bob recalls the background, "It's a funny thing, but Bing fixed that up for us at a time when the columnists were saying, once again, that there had been a rift between us. Believe me, if Bing hadn't wanted us to get the job he would have just gazed out of the window and begun whistling when someone raised the question, instead he rooted for us. It was also at Bing's suggestion that I took his place for 13 weeks on the Kraft radio show, and I was always invited to play in the Golf Tournament that he organised (I usually partnered Dai Rees), and that would never have happened if we had been enemies. We didn't see one another often, but we were still brothers".

In 1943, Bob resumed leading a big band mainly to play dates on the West Coast, most of the personnel was culled from freelance musicians, throughout this period he was on call for any contractual commitments to the film studios, but he was soon to start playing a role in World War II. In 1944, he joined the US Marines.

At the very time that Bob was undergoing his basic training a minor scandal about a famous film actress's husband being on seemingly endless furlough broke in the California newspapers, apparently the husband's Marine Station Wagon was seen parked outside the couple's Hollywood home for weeks on end. A hasty tightening up of privileged treatment was made obvious to the American public by the immediate posting overseas of several famous personalities, Bob Crosby was amongst them. He recalls the decision, "Someone in Washington said 'Don't let the public get the idea that anyone in the Marines spends time at home on a soft number", so Lt. G.R. Crosby U.S.M.C. was speedily posted to the Pacific War Zone.

People who have known Bob for most of his adult life feel that his service in the US Marines played a huge part in developing his character. Out on a small island in the Pacific there was no hope for anyone unless they stood on their own two feet, and Bob did this firmly and capably. He was given the job of running a 29 piece entertainment unit, based in Honolulu, whose working territory covered many thousands of square miles. The troupe, which included musicians, a hypnotist, a comedian, and a juggler, flew (sometimes in hazardous conditions) in two transport planes, often stretching the fuel limits of those aircraft to the utmost as they travelled vast distances between one night stands.

Bob remembers Christmas 1944 as being one of the big occasions of his life. He assembled his band on Ulithi atoll and played a show that was relayed to the assembled 5th and 7th Fleets. He still re-lives, with visible pride, the moment when Admiral Bill Halsey, following on after the band's transmission, addressed the vast array of warships, delivering what Bob considers to be the most moving oratory he has ever heard.

Bob is always delighted when ex-servicemen who met him in some remote part of the Pacific during World War II come up and share poignant memories of those days. "We had a fine band out there, with excellent musicians in it, Al Caiola on guitar, and Bruce Turrell on tenor sax, Tubby Oliver played trumpet and sang. We weren't a total jazz group, we played all sorts of musical styles, whatever the homesick men wanted to hear, but we sure had to improvise on occasions, fixing up make-shift bandstands in rough country. We pitched out own tents, and stood in chow lines like everyone else. Sometimes we did eight shows a day, some of the stops at places like Peleliu we played to a hundred men and 150 islanders".

Lt. Crosby's powers of leadership came to the fore under these trying conditions, and his merits didn't go unnoticed by superiors. "In early 1945, I got secret orders to return to Washington. I was not to discuss the matter with anyone. I got on a service plane and sat next to Eddie Duchin. I found out later that he too was on a secret mission, the same one as mine, but each of us sat there making small talk, as cagey as could be. When I got to Washington I was asked to go on a War Bond Rally. So, accompanied by a US Navy Band, I did a short tour in the States, and took time off to make some V-Discs with various old buddies, then I was sent back to the Pacific until it was my time to return home".

During World War II, many famous bandleaders played for service audiences, but some accepted only those dates that were highly convenient, and highly publicised, and few chose to go to overseas war zones. Bob Crosby felt there was a good deal of feet dragging involved, and said so in print as he concluded his 1945 War Bonds Tour, criticising the excuses given by bandleaders about commitments, personnel, transportation and money.

In the fall of 1945, Bob Crosby was posted back to California to complete the last weeks of his service career compering the Armed Forces Radio Show *Swingtime*. He was already a vastly experienced broadcaster, but this period polished up his radio technique and gave him a good insight into the production aspects of radio. With his demobilisation imminent, Bob toyed with the idea of going into radio work full time, but his decision was delayed by a demand from the government for income tax on money he had earned during pre-service years. He decided the most lucrative course open to him at that time was to reform a big band.

As soon as Bob was released from the US Marines in late 1945 he contacted arranger Van Alexander to ask if he would like to resume the successful collaboration they had enjoyed on the East Coast in 1943. The new partnership started off well, but didn't last. Van Alexander explains, "Crosby and I hit it off very well, and he asked me if I would come to California to arrange and organize a new band for him. I packed up my family and headed west. After working with Bob for about 10 weeks, we had a falling out, due to a conflict of personality, and what he expected of me, so I was fired, and out of work in a strange town, where no-one knew me. It was quite a trauma at the time, but it turned out to be a blessing in disguise, as I had gotten to California, and to date (1982) have scored 22 motion pictures, had 6 albums of my own, etc".

The new band, with Van Alexander and trumpeter-vocalist Herb "Quig" Quigley, acting as straw-boss, made its official debut in late 1945 at the Pacific Square Ballroom in San Diego. Within weeks it was signed to appear regularly on the important *Fords Out Front* CBS radio show. The basis of the band was comprised of leading West Coast freelance musicians, including Gus Bivona (clarinet), Murray McEachern, (trombone), and Frank Carlson (drums).

In early February 1946, the band following Gene Krupa's Orchestra into the Hollywood Palladium. By then, Van Alexander had left and his place as chief arranger was taken, temporarily as it turned out, by pianist Tommy Todd. Gil Rodin joined the organisation as manager and chief administrator, having quit regular playing after the demise of the band he co-led with Ray Bauduc. Things began to develop for the band, and they left California to play dates in Detroit and New York. *Down Beat* magazine reported that New York musicians were "raving about Bob Crosby's Band at the Strand engagement".

Whilst on the east coast, Bob gave his views on the new band, comparing to the pre-war unit. "It's much more precise, and it's more consistent. Dixieland depends a lot upon individual inspiration, and look out for those nights when the guys in the band aren't inspired. And that old band played ballads so badly. This one does everything well, I think". When the band swung its way back to California to play a November 1946 residency at the Avodon, they had a new staff arranger, Nelson Riddle, who had met Bob casually in a New York dentist's waiting-room. Riddle accepted an offer to move to California and supply the band with two new arrangements a week for the sum of 75 dollars, it was a decision that led him on to many subsequent successes. Looking back Bob says "I was proud of that band, it had talented players and outstanding arrangements. It deserved to succeed, and it did, I soon got myself straight financially and sorted out the tax problems".

Bob's original intention of only returning to bandleading as a temporary expedient went by the board. With a new big line-up (which now featured Ray Bauduc on drums) Bob did widespread touring during the spring of 1947, prior to settling down in Los Angeles to take up the role of compere on the Campbell Soup's radio series *Club 15,* which was transmitted nationally throughout the USA and Canada. The programme, which was on the air Monday thru Friday regularly featured Margaret Whiting, the Andrew Sisters, and Hal Dickinson's Modernaires, it rapidly achieved huge listening figures, and proved to be a successful berth for Bob Crosby during the next few years.

Things were, in general, going smoothly for Bob, the main area of resentment for him during this period, was the treatment afforded him, (and other veterans he felt) by record companies. In 1946, he said "I had one helluva time when I first got back. Decca didn't want me back and I signed with ARA, where I made some lousy records. Finally Decca took me back, and what have they done - they've given me one record in four months". In October 1947, Bob, still disheartened by Decca's apparent lack of interest didn't seek a renewal of his recording contract, pointing out that Decca had only released a couple of recordings in over a year. Bing Crosby, described at the time as a "financial pillar" of Decca, made no statement. The two brothers rarely met except at family re-unions such as their mother's February birthday get-togethers, where Kate caught up with all the news about her twenty grandchildren. Kate and Harry (until his death in 1950) dwelt in comfort at Holmby Hills, Los Angeles.

During the *Club 15's* summer break, Bob (with the help of the show's musical director Jerry Gray) usually formed up a big band for extended tours that often took him to the East Coast. His strategy was one that was becoming increasingly popular with big band leaders, faced with enormous transport bills, it involved taking a few key sidemen from California, such as Johnny Best (trumpet), Ted Nash (tenor sax) and Murray McEachern (trombone) and recruiting the rest of the personnel in the various cities on their itinerary.

Bob's radio career thrived during the early 1950s, not only was he the star of *Club 15,* he also had an ABC network show as a Saturday night disc jockey, and worked as a singing master-of-ceremonies on his own NBC Sunday show. Subsequently he changed his weekend routine and commuted to New York to broadcast NBC's *Pet Milk Show,* returning to his Beverly Hills home briefly before starting off for the *Club 15* transmission. Bob still found time to occasionally round-up many of the original Bobcats to play at various festivals, and to take part in a couple of films with him *(When You're Smiling* and *Two Tickets to Broadway).* By then, Bob was doing his own musical administration, Gil Rodin having decided to devote all his time to radio and television production.

The rapid escalation of interest in television during the early 1950s soon persuaded Bob to concentrate on establishing himself in the new medium. By 1953 he was appearing five days a week on CBS, flying regularly, often with little time to spare, between Las Vegas and Los Angeles. All this activity was fitted in with his other commitments, which included his occasional appearances in feature films, working as a guest star on other television programmes, and often re-assembling the Bob Cats. Whenever there was time to relax, Bob, June and the family flew over to their apartment in Honolulu.

For one Bob Cats' re-union, held in 1955 on the East Coast, Bob managed to assemble most of the original gang, including Yank Lawson, Billy Butterfield, Matty Matlock, Eddie Miller, Nappy Lamare, Bob Haggart and Ray Bauduc. Even the band's former road manager-cum-music copyist, Hix Bluett attended, the reunion, which was for a CBS television show *America's Great Bands.* Later that same year many of the old team took part in a dramatised tribute to their former pianist, Joe Sullivan, which was televised as part of CBS's *Climax* series.

By the late 1950s, Bob Crosby was positively established as a national television personality in his own right, sans band, sans vocals, and even sans brother's shadow. Bob had always enjoyed a reputation for skilfully embroidering anecdotes, "Bob's Bullshit", as it was known to his sidemen in the band, and this skill came in particularly useful on television. Bob had also always excelled at delivering "gags", and this also made him popular with viewers, many of whom felt that he was even better at this particular art than his renowned brother. When the two men, Bing and Bob, got together professionally they always indulged in trading contrived insults.

Offstage, both brothers sometimes had occasions to brood over the other's behaviour, Bob was always declaring that he did not want to be called Bing's brother, and at one time considered having a contractual clause that forbade the use of Bing's name in connection with the band's activities. This struck Bing as odd, and he remarked "I didn't know I was something to be ashamed of". Bob, for his part, was displeased when Bing, in his 1953 auto-biography, *Call Me Lucky,* listed his favourite jazz groups without mentioning Bob's band (although he had done so on previous occasions), thirty years later that omission still puzzled Bob.

In May 1958, Bob flew to Britain to make an appearance at the London Palladium, as part of a British television spectacular. Whilst in London he also assembled a contingent from pianist Ronnie Aldrich's *Squadronaires* to play a BBC "Jazz Club" broadcast as the *Squadcats.* Throughout his stay in Britain, Bob Crosby was besieged by questions about his former sidemen, in answer he said he would be delighted to tour Europe with a re-assembled Bob Cats. He also aired his beliefs on the durability of various jazz styles. "Through all the musical fads, you can still find a cellar somewhere in every American city where someone is playing Dixieland. It will never become the rage again, but there will always be someone playing it".

Bob returned to the States, and took over the hosting of Perry Como's NBC television show for 13 weeks, whilst Como took an extended summer break. When that run was over, Bob resumed his own diverse television activities, which included commentating on a *World Championship Golf* series. But around this time, Bob developed the feeling that he had taken one turn too many on a roundabout that seemed to be gathering speed. He began looking around for business propositions that would allow him more time to spend with his growing family, by then he and June had five children.

After playing a season in Australia in 1961, headlining the *Hollywood Bandbox* show, Bob (and June) decided to move permanently to Honolulu, where both were soon busily involved in new enterprises. June whose first short story had been published whilst she was still a teenager, loved, and excelled at, cooking. She decided to combine both talents and in March 1962 began writing a culinary column for the *Honolulu Star-Bulletin.* Whilst working on this regular project she also completed the first of her books on cooking recipes.

Bob's new venture was as a partner in a Waikiki executive car rental company. He said at the time that he wanted a complete break from entertaining, and a lull from the tax headaches that had begun to plague him again. "I've made $400,000 a year doing a television show. I paid 83% in taxes plus expenses, including agent's fee, manager's fees, and so on. I ended up with what a man earning $30,000 a year would have in the bank". Unfortunately, Bob Crosby's Executive Rent-a-Car agency, and its fleet of 63 vehicles couldn't find enough customers. Bob estimates that in 8 months he lost $75,000 on the deal.

Whilst Bob was sorting out the debris of the car-rental company he commuted between Hawaii and Nevada to play a season with his band at the New Frontier in Las Vegas. Over the years he has played numerous seasons at the gambling mecca. For the Las Vegas gigs Bob often used musicians from his "old gang", such as Eddie Miller and Matty Matlock. In 1964, he organised a spectacular version of the Bobcats for a four week tour of the Orient and Australia. Miller and Matlock were part of the all-star line-up as were Yank Lawson and Johnny Best. The two trombonists were Lou McGarity and Moe Schneider, and the three piece rhythm section, Al Pelegrini (piano), Ray Leatherwood (string-bass) and Nick Fatool (drums).

Bob moved back from Hawaii to the mainland, and began to pick up the threads of his television career, and his bandleading activities, then in 1965, he was offered his own television show on Australia's Channel 7. The Crosby family again moved home and flew off to Sydney in January 1966. Bob did two one-and-a-quarter hour shows each week, one transmitted from Sydney, and one from Melbourne. The shows began in February 1966, and ended 13 weeks later, a steady stream of brickbats were aimed at the program throughout the run.

Recalling the venture, Bob says "The bad reviews were deserved. Initially, the show was promising, then they took away the writers, the production improved, but I was given ridiculously poor material. The schedules were crazy, I did one show on a Monday from Sydney, with the minimum of rehearsals, then flew to Melbourne to hastily get together a long show that was trasmitted live on Tuesday nights. We made good friends in Australia, but we weren't sorry to leave, a mass of little things just weren't right, and I nearly had a rebellion on my hands, the children hated the school unifoms, with long woollen socks, which they were forced to wear until late in their teens. I don't regret the trip, I learnt from the experience".

Before leaving Australia in June 1966, Bob aired his general feelings about his work in television, and his manner of interviewing guests, "I'm not interested in finding out whether a person's a pervert or a drunk. I just want to have an interesting chat with interesting people. When the critics said my nice-guy approach was too relaxed, well, I took that as a compliment. I am shy, and I don't find anything to be ashamed about that. I'm a sentimentalist. I'm a square. And again I don't apologise".

Bob flew back to the States and began leading a band for a residency at Lake Tahoe, Nevada. Later that year, there was an important residency at the Rainbow Grill, in New York's Rockefeller Centre. Live albums featuring inspired proceedings were issued on Monmouth-Evergreen; they not only feature expressive and exuberant jazz, but also capture the quiet complimentary asides that the musicians pay each other on the bandstand.

Domestically, 1966 was an important one, it featured two house moves, first to Carmel, California. Bob hated the fog that descended there with monotonous regularity "Too bad even for me to play golf, our stay there was mercifully brief". The family's next trek took them to La Jolla, close to San

Diego, in California, and there, at last, after over 20 moves, Bob and June have remained ever since.

The Crosby's 11th floor condominium became a lasting home, and a base from which Bob could plan his ever increasing band work schedules, happy in the knowledge that when there was time he could relax at his ranch. All of the children, Cathleen, Christopher, Robert Jr., Stephen and Malia have made their own mark in the world, and June has been kept busy with widely syndicated cookery features, her books on the culinary arts have been well received - *Serve It Cold* was on the best selling lists for many weeks.

Besides numerous residencies in California (including many bookings at Disneyland) and long stays in Nevada, Bob's bands have also played many East Coast engagements during the past decade, including a May 1981 sell-out at the Roseland Ballroom (where he had made his debut as a bandleader back in 1935). He has also organised dozens of reunions of the Bobcats for concerts and television shows, In 1981 he took many of the originals to Europe for engagements at the Nice Jazz Festival.

Even when his big band doesn't contain any of the original musicians, Bob still pays homage to his pre-war band by including its big hits like *South Rampart Street Parade* and *Big Noise From Winnetka*. Nowadays, Bob's big bands are formed up for specific engagements, he knows which musicians will be suitable in every city that he plays, and books them in advance. "People who say 'Bring back the Big Bands', don't take into account the transportation costs of getting 15 men and their equipment and instruments from one place to another. That's why I have key men throughout the country who I can call on, and who'll do a superb job. With the old band we wouldn't dream of playing polkas and waltzes, but we do them now, never-the less I always make sure that I've got men who can blow the truth when called on, who can play Dixieland numbers authentically. The main instrument for the small band numbers is the trumpet, if he understands the idiom everything tends to fall into place".

The problems of being Bing's brother had long been surmounted by the time of Bing's death in 1977. The brothers were not in close rapport during the last decade of Bing's life, there was no enmity, but Bob could never avoid feeling hurt when he learnt, quite often, that Bing had passed through San Diego without bothering to call. However, Bob was not at all distressed that Bing left him out of his will, "Actually I respected him for that, it was his way of saying 'You're independent, you can take care of yourself'."Bob was less than pleased with the spate of lurid revelations about Bing that have been published over the past few years, "Seems to me it's dangerous to die if you're a celebrity", and he was positively furious when Bing's widow, Kathryn, arranged an auction sale of her late husband's personal possessions.

Bob revered Bing's first wife, Dixie Lee, "a helluva woman", but never enjoyed the same rapport with Bing's second wife. "Bing hated phoneys, yet he married one. That woman was planning to sell my mother's family bible, but I put a stop to that. The big thing lacking in Bing's later life was friends, not just guys with whom he had a joke, but close buddies, something in his nature prevented him from expressing the affection that I'm sure he felt. He developed an image that was really a protective device against the world, he made himself a cellophane bag from which he could view the outside, but no-one could get close to him."

One of Bob's standard summaries of his contribution to the entertainment world is "I'm the only guy in the band business who made it without talent", and although this is often said for effect, he does genuinely feel that the original band might have fared better if their first choice as leader, Jack Teagarden, had been available. Admittedly the early band would have benefitted from Teagarden's superb trombone artistry, but it is difficult to imagine, Jack, affable as he was, permanently adapting to the self-imposed disciplines that made the Crosby Band such a successful team.

Bob became much more than just a figurehead for the band, he made the public aware of the individual improvising talents that existed within the group by compering so adroitly that even non-jazz fans listened eagerly to the soloists. The fact that Bob, as leader, didn't play an instrument himself, encouraged the soloists to project their talents with panache, unworried that they were attracting too much attention. Bob's singing of ballads was alarmingly variable, but some of his performances have a light hearted charm, and on up-tempo numbers he rarely failed to swing. He remains a pivot in the lives of the musicians from the original band, bringing them together from time to time, always getting genuine pleasure out of hearing them play what he still so lovingly calls "the truth".

Bob Crosby's sidemen
1935 — 1942

(Note: those marked with an asterisk * have individual chapters)

BARONE, Joe (trumpet)
> Born: c. 1906. Deceased. Briefly with Bob Crosby in early 1936.

*BAUDUC, Ray (drums)
> Born: New Orleans, Louisiana, 18th June 1906. With Bob Crosby from June 1935 until September 1942.

BEAN, Floyd R. (piano)
> Born: Grinnell, Iowa, 30th August 1904. Died: 1974 Briefly with Bob Crosby in 1939.

BENNETT, Mark (trombone)
> Born: Newark, New Jersey. c. 1912 With Rudy Vallee, Fred Waring, Isham Jones and Artie Shaw before joining Bob Crosby in 1936. Left early in 1937, later worked with Frank Dailey (1937), Buddy Rogers (1938), Jack Teagarden (1939), etc.

BERGMAN, Eddie (violin)
> Born: New York. c. 1908. Deceased. Worked with Ben Pollack in late 1920s and early 1930s. With Bob Crosby from June 1935 until summer 1937. With Henry King (1938), Freddy Martin (1941) etc., before becoming musical director for various hotels.

BERNARDI 'Noni' Ernani (alto sax/clt/flute/arranger)
> Born: Standard, Illinois. 29th October 1911. Father and uncle were musicians. Played high school dances before turning professional in 1928 to work with Hank Biagini, subsequently with Casa Loma Band (1931), Joe Haymes (1934), Tommy Dorsey (1934-35). Joined Bob Crosby early 1936, forced by ill health to leave in May 1937. After recovery worked briefly with Paul Leash's Band on Station WWJ and with Red Norvo. Joined Jimmy Dorsey (1937). With Benny Goodman (1938), studio work in New York (1939) - including recordings with Bob Zurke. To California with Kay Kyser (1940), with Kyser as musical director until 1945. Briefly led own band at Aragon Ballroom, Los Angeles, then entered building industry and achieved considerable success. Became a member of Los Angeles City Council in 1961, and served on the Council for over 20 years. Arranged for many recording bands, including Tommy Dorsey, Ziggy Elman, Toots

Mondello, Benny Goodman, Jimmy Dorsey, etc.

BEST, John McClanian 'Johnny' (trumpet)
Born: Shelby, N. Carolina, 20th October 1913. With Bob Crosby from September until December 1942.

BOSE, Sterling Belmont (trumpet)
Born: Florence, Alabama, 23rd February 1906. Died: St. Petersburg, Florida, June 1958. With Bob Crosby Band from August 1938 until early 1939.

BOWERS, Gilbert 'Gil' (piano)
Born: Iowa, c. 1908. Attended Drake University. As a teenager worked in trio with Rod Cless (clarinet) and Carl Bean (sax). With Ben Pollack (1930-34), with Bob Crosby (1935-36). Worked with Abe Lyman, etc., before moving to California in the early 1940s. Musical director for film studios during the 1940s and 1950s. Worked as accompanist for singer Dorothy Dandridge during early 1960s, including tour of Australia (1961), then became musical director for various touring shows. Lived in Majorca during 1970s, then moved back to USA and made home in St. Louis, Missouri.

*BUTTERFIELD, Charles William 'Billy' (trumpet)
Born: Middleton, Ohio. 14th January 1917. With Bob Crosby from September 1937 until June 1940.

CARPENTER, Clarence 'Pete' (trombone)
Born: Fredonia, Kansas. 1914. Raised in California. Played high school dances in Torrance, California (1928-30). First pro. job with pianist Bob Millar's Band, Los Angeles (1934). With Gil Evans (1936), Jimmy Dorsey (1936), Skinnay Ennis, (1938-40), Ozzie Nelson (1940). With Bob Crosby during summer of 1942. With Kay Kyser (1943). Radio work, then Republic studios from 1944-55. Concentrated on arranging in mid-1950s, quit playing in 1965, has enjoyed widespread success as composer for films and television shows.

CLAIRE, Dorothy (vocals)
Born: La Porte, Indiana c. 1920. Died: Indiana, 4th September 1982. Her sisters Betty, Judy and Debbie were all professional singers. Worked with Joaquin Grill's Band in Pittsburgh then joined Bob Crosby's Band from spring of 1939 until summer of 1940, subsequently with Glenn Miller, Bobby Byrne, Boyd Raeburn, etc. Featured on Broadway in Finian's Rainbow, then toured in double act with husband, tenor saxist Emmett Karls.

CONNIFF, Ray (trombone/arranger)
Born: Attleboro, Massachusetts. 6th November 1916. Left Bunny Berigan to join Bob Crosby's Band in June 1939, left in

December 1940 to work with Artie Shaw.

D'AMICO, Henry 'Hank' (clarinet/alto sax)
Born: Rochester, N.Y. 21st March 1915. Died: Queens, New York. 3rd December 1965. With Bob Crosby from May 1940 until July 1941.

DAY, Doris (r.n. Kappelhoff) (vocals)
Born: Cincinnati, Ohio. 3rd April 1922? Worked with Barney Rapp's Band prior to brief spell with Bob Crosby's Band during summer of 1939, left to work with Les Brown's Band, and subsequently enjoyed highly successful film career.

DE HAVEN, Gloria (vocals)
Born: c. 1922. With Bob Crosby in 1941.

DEPEW, William 'Billy' (alto sax/clarinet/flute/piccolo)
Born: Pittsburgh, Pennsylvania. 14th October 1914. Died: Pittsburgh, Pennsylvania. 29th November 1971. Began playing with local bands whilst still in high school, worked regularly with Sid Dickler's Band (1933-35). With Benny Goodman from July 1935 until January 1937. Joined Bob Crosby in May 1937, left four months later. Moved to California, worked with Lyle 'Spud' Murphy (1938), Wingy Mannone (1938), Earl Carroll (1939). Led own band in the early 1940s, then joined Spike Jones (playing and arranging). With Spike Jones throughout the 1950s, moved back to Pittsburgh in 1964. Joined resident band at Holiday House, Monroeville; played regularly until suffering fatal heart attack.

DESMOND, Johnny (r.n. Giovanni Desimons) (vocals)
Born: Detroit, Michigan. 14th November 1920. Attended Detroit Conservatory of Music. Worked on local radio, then formed Downbeats vocal group, who became known as the Bob-o-Links when they joined Bob Crosby in summer of 1940. Desmond left in 1941 to join Gene Krupa, later worked with Glenn Miller before following solo career.

EMERT, Jimmy (trombone)
Born: Pittsburgh, c. 1910. Deceased. Worked with Lloyd Huntley, Dave Harmon, Steve Matthews, Jack Pettis, Ralph Bennett, Freddy Bergin, California Collegians and Henry Halstead before joining Bob Crosby in January 1939. Left in June 1939, worked with Bunny Berigan, Will Bradley (1939-40), Hal McIntyre (1942), Billy Robbins (1947), etc.

*FAZOLA, Irving (r.n. Irving Henry Prestopnik) (clarinet/alto sax)
Born: New Orleans, Louisiana. 10th December 1912 Died: New Orleans, Louisiana. 20th March 1949. With Bob Crosby from March 1938 until June 1940.

276

FERRETTI, Andy (trumpet)
Born: Revere, Massachusetts, 1912. Deceased. Often with Bob Crosby Band during 1935 and 1936, finally left the band in February 1937.

FERRIER, Jack (alto sax/clarinet)
Born: Springfield, Massachusetts, 1913. Ex-University of Oklahoma, played varsity football. With Woody Herman (1937-38). With Bob Crosby from late 1938 until February 1939. With Jan Savitt (1939-40), Claude Thornhill (1940-41), etc.

FOSTER, Artie (trombone)
Born: c. 1909. With Vic Berton (1935) prior to spending a year with Bob Crosby (1935-36). With Tommy Dorsey (1937), then long spell in studio bands.

GOODRICH, Robert 'Bob' (trumpet)
Born: Alpaugh, California 30th November 1914. Started playing at 12, later studied with Louis Maggio. Worked around Hermosa Beach area (1931). Joined Everett Hoagland (1934). With Ben Pollack (1934-35), Leon Belasco (1935). Rube Wolfe (1936), George Stoll (1937), Ben Pollack (1937-38), Ray Noble (1939-40), Bob Crosby (1941). Ray Noble (1942). Radio studio work (1943), Meredith Wilson's Armed Forces Orchestra (1944-46), then after services worked at Universal studios 1946-59. Worked with various bands in Las Vegas until retirement, 1976.

GRACE, Teddy (vocals)
Freelance recordings with Bob Crosby, 1939.

GRAHAM, Bill (trumpet)
Born: c. 1912. With Tommy Dorsey, Isham Jones, and Fred Waring before working for Bob Crosby from Feb-June 1939. With Lennie Hayton (1939-40), then long spell at CBS prior to moving to Florida.

GREEN, Charlie (violin)
Born: c. 1907. With Bob Crosby in 1935.

*HAGGART, Robert Sherwood 'Bob' (string bass/arranger)
Born: 13th March 1914. With Bob Crosby from June 1935 until December 1942.

HARRIS, Joe (trombone/vocals)
Born: Missouri, 1908. Died: California, 1952. With Bob Crosby in 1935.

HART, Phil (trumpet)
Born: c. 1904. With Lou Gold, Ben Bernie, California Ramblers, etc., before working with Bob Crosby in 1935.

HERMAN, Max (trumpet)
Born: North Providence, Rhode Island. 1st July 1914. Trumpeter from age of 7, first gig at 13. Whilst in high school played in Carnival Band (Bobby Hackett on banjo), also worked in Providence night club with drummer Nick Fatool. Worked in home area with Duke Bellis, Perry Borelli and Al Mitchell bands, then to New York in summer 1936 to join Joe Haymes, later worked with Gus Arnheim, Hudson-De Lange, George Hall, Larry Clinton, Mike Reilly, Jan Savitt and Les Brown before joining Bob Crosby from October 1939 until September 1942. After serving with US Coast Guards worked in Hollywood studio bands until becoming officer of Union Local 47 in January 1957, subsequently became President of Local 47.

KEARNS, Joseph V. 'Joe' (alto sax/clarinet)
Born: Mobile, Alabama 27th February 1911. Began playing 'C' melody sax at the age of 12. Joined Battle House Six on tenor sax. Left Mobile in 1928 to attend University of Pennsylvania in Philadelphia, majored in economics. Graduated in 1932, worked with Meyer Davis and Howard Lanin before changing to alto sax to work with Jan Savitt (also arranged and played clarinet with Savitt). Left Jan Savitt in September 1937 to join Bob Crosby, moved back to Philadelphia late 1938, but rejoined Bob Crosby during summer of 1939, left in late 1940 to lead own band on WCAU radio in Philadelphia. Served in Air Transport Command 1942-46, then resumed leading own band on WCAU until 1948. Moved to New Mexico in 1948, studied agriculture at New Mexico State University, and became Assistant Professor in Dairy Husbandry, retired in 1966.

KINCAIDE, Deane (saxes/clarinet/flute/trombone/guitar/arranger)
Born: Houston, Texas, 18th March 1911. Raised in Illinois, worked with Byron Hart (1927) and other local bands. Did very first arrangement in Green Bay, Wisconsin, February 1929. With Wingy Mannone (1932), Slatz Randall (1932). With Ralph Bennett prior to joining Ben Pollack in May 1933. Left in January 1934, rejoined Slatz Randall briefly, then moved to New York in 1934. Arranged for Benny Goodman, then joined ex-Ben Pollack musicians and thus became a founder-member of the Bob Crosby band in June 1935. Played saxophone in the band until June 1936, then became staff arranger until spring 1937. Worked with Lennie Hayton and Woody Herman before rejoining Bob Crosby as staff arranger from September 1937 until March 1938. Briefly with Wingy Mannone, then worked with Tommy Dorsey (1938-40). With Joe Marsala, Ray Noble (1940). Briefly with Glenn Miller then joined Muggsy Spanier's Big Band (1941). Served in US

Navy (1942-45). With Ray McKinley (1947-50). Worked on Kate Smith TV Show (1951-54), occasional dates with Ray McKinley and Lester Lanin during the 1950s. Arranged for many important television shows during the 1960s, including Johnny Carson's Tonight programme, and Jackie Gleason's show, continued to play engagements on sax and clarinet until January 1981.

KING, Al (trumpet)
Born: Italy. 27th October 1904. Worked with Ernie Golden (1919). During the 1920s with Paul Specht, California Ramblers, Red Nichols, Ross Gorman, Original Louisiana Five, etc. Worked with Ben Pollack, Benny Meroff, the Dorsey Brothers, Gus Arnheim, etc. Left Freddy Martin to join Bob Crosby during summer of 1940, left in 1941. Also worked with Skinnay Ennis, Alvino Rey, etc.

KING, Bonnie (vocals)
Born: c. 1920. With Bob Crosby 1940.

KOENIG, George (alto sax/clarinet)
Born: Cleveland, Ohio. 2nd December 1912 With Austin Wylie during the early 1930s. With Benny Goodman (1937-38), Artie Shaw (1938), Teddy Powell (1939). Joined Bob Crosby October 1939, left in May 1940, and joined Red Norvo. Prolific freelance work during 1940s and 1950s, ran own music store thereafter.

*LAMARE, Hilton 'Nappy' (guitar/banjo/vocals)
Born: New Orleans, Louisiana. 14th June 1907. With Bob Crosby from June 1935 until December 1942.

LANE, Kathleen 'Kitty' (vocals)
Born: Harrisburg, Pennsylvania c. 1918. Worked with Henry Okun in Newark before joining Charlie Barnet early in 1937. During the late 1930s and early 1940s worked with : Glenn Miller, Isham Jones, Bunny Berigan, Red Norvo, Bob Chester, etc. Briefly with Bob Crosby in 1939 and 1940.

*LAWSON, John Rhea 'Yank' (trumpet)
Born: Trenton, Missouri. 3rd May 1911 With Bob Crosby from June 1935 until August 1938, from August 1941 until December 1942.

LINK, Edward (r.n. Levine) (vocals)
Died: 18th June 1946. Member of Bob-o-Links vocal quartet.

McKAY, Ted (r.n. Klein) (alto sax/clarinet).
Died: 1944 Music copyist for Bob Crosby Band during the years 1941-42, played alto sax in section during this period.

MANN, Marion (vocals)

Born: c. 1918. Worked as Alice Marion with Richard Himber's Orchestra. With Bob Crosby from spring of 1938 until May 1940, except for brief absences.

MARIO, Bob (r.n. Mario Bobadilla) (baritone sax/clarinet)
With Bob Crosby during September-December 1942 tour.

*MATLOCK, Julian Clifton 'Matty' (clarinet/saxes/flute/arranger)
Born: Paducah, Kentucky, 27th April 1907. Died: Los Angeles, California, 14th June 1978. With Bob Crosby from June 1935 until December 1942, during which time he often specialised in arranging for the band, temporarily forsaking his place in the reed section.

MENDELSOHN, Arthur 'Art' (alto sax/clarinet)
Born: c. 1916. Worked with Will Bradley before joining Bob Crosby in summer of 1941, left 8 months later. Worked with Hal McIntyre in 1942.

*MILLER, Edward Raymond 'Eddie' (tenor sax/clarinet/bass clarinet/vocals)
Born: New Orleans, Louisiana, 23rd June 1911. With Bob Crosby from June 1935 until December 1942.

MORROW, 'Buddy' (r.n. Muni 'Moe' Zudekoff) (trombone)
Born: New Haven, Connecticut. 8th February 1919. With Bob Crosby for a year from summer of 1941.

O'BRIEN, Floyd (trombone)
Born: Chicago, Illinois, 7th May 1904. Died: Chicago, Illinois, 26th November 1968. With Bob Crosby from May 1940 until December 1942.

PARIS, Tony (vocals)
With Bob Crosby 1940-42.

PECK, Robert 'Bob' (trumpet)
Born: Cleveland, Ohio. 29th June 1917. Began playing trumpet at the age of 10. Attended Ohio State University 1935-37. With Austin Wylie (1937), Ted Mack (1937), Morey Brennan (1938), Glenn Miller (1938), Hank Biagini (1939), Bobby Byrne (1939). With Bob Crosby from early 1940 until June 1940. With Bob Chester from summer 1940 until drafted into Army February 1941. Left Army in September 1945. With Billy Butterfield (1946-47), Shorty Sherock (1947), Claude Thornhill (1948) Returned to Cleveland in 1948, resumed University studies, became a teacher until 1980, also played many freelance engagements in and around Cleveland through to early 1980s.

RANDO, Arthur J. 'Doc' (alto sax/clarinet/flute)
Born: New Orleans, Louisiana, 1910. Worked with many bandleaders in New Orleans during the late 1920s, including Jules

Bauduc, and Don Vorhees. With Augie Schellang's Roosevelt Rhythm Kings (1937). With Wingy Mannone, Red Norvo and Henry Busse before working with Bob Crosby from May 1940 until December 1942. Prolific freelance work in Los Angeles during 1940s and 1950s, also served as Local 47 union official. As a cardiologist, taught at University of Nuevo Leon, Mexico during the 1960s, also guested with local bands. Medical specialist in Las Vegas during the 1970s and 1980s, also played regularly in the "The Royal Dixie Jazz Band".

*RODIN, Gilbert A. 'Gil' (saxes/clarinet/flute)
Born: Russia, 9th December 1906. Died: California. 10th June 1974. With Bob Crosby from June 1935 until September 1942.

SANDIFER, Cody W. (drums)
Born: Texas, Toured with Bob Crosby from September until December 1942.

SHEROCK, 'Shorty' (r.n. Clarence Francis Cherock) (trumpet)
Born: Minnesota, 17th November 1915. Died: California, 19th February 1980. With Bob Crosby from June 1939 until January 1940.

SILLAWAY, Ward (trombone)
Born: 29th March 1909. Died: Chicago, Illinois 1st October 1965. With Bob Crosby from 1935 until December 1938. Was married to vocaliste Kay Weber.

SMITH, Warren Doyle 'Smitty' (trombone)
Born: West Virginia, 17th May 1908. Died: California, 28th August 1975. With Bob Crosby from early 1937 until May 1940.

SMITHERS, Elmer (trombone)
Born: Indiana, Pennsylvania. Graduated from State Teachers College and joined Ozzie Nelson's Band from 1934-38. With Tommy Dorsey 1938-40, moved to California, with Bob Crosby 1940-41, left to do prolific studio work, also played for 18 years with Los Angeles Civic Light Opera Orchestra.

SPANIER, Francis Joseph 'Muggsy' (cornet)
Born: Chicago, Illinois, 9th November 1906. Died: Sausalito, California, 12th February 1967. With Bob Crosby from May 1940 until January 1941.

SPIVAK, Charles 'Charlie' (trumpet)
Born: Kiev, Ukraine, 17th February 1907. Died: Carolina, 1st March 1982. With Bob Crosby from November 1937 until August 1938.

SQUIRES, Bruce (trombone)
Born: Berkeley, California, 21st January 1910. Died North

Hollywood, California, 8th May 1981. With Everett Hoagland 1932), Earl Burtnett (1933-35), Ben Pollack (1935-37), Jimmy Dorsey (1937), Gene Krupa (1938-39), Benny Goodman (1939), Harry James (1939-40), Freddy Slack (1940-41), Bob Crosby (1942). Air Forces Ferry Band (1943-44). After services did extensive studio work.

STACY, Jess Alexandria (piano)
Born: Cape Girardeau, Missouri, 4th August 1904. With Bob Crosby from September 1939 until December 1942.

STARR, Kay (r.n. Kathryn Starks) (vocals)
Briefly with Bob Crosby, June 1939.

STEGMEYER, William John 'Bill' (saxes/clarinet/arranger)
Born: Detroit, Michigan, 8th October 1916. Died: Long Island, New York, 19th August 1968. With Bob Crosby from June 1939 until May 1940.

STONEBURN, Sid (clarinet/saxes)
Born: c. 1912. Died: Missouri, 1970. Worked with Red Nichols, Smith Ballew, Joe Haymes and Tommy Dorsey, etc., before brief spell with Bob Crosby early in 1936. Later with Lennie Hayton and Richard Himber before working in studio bands and with NBC Symphony. Moved to Kansas City in 1948.

STREET, David (vocals)
Born: Los Angeles, California, 1918. Died: Los Angeles, California, 1971. With Bob Crosby in 1941 and 1942, then worked with Freddie Slack before leading own band.

SULLIVAN, Joe (r.n. Joseph Michael O'Sullivan) (piano)
Born: Chicago, Illinois, 4th November 1906. Died: California, 13th October 1971. With Bob Crosby from September until December 1936, and again from June until September 1939.

TENNILLE, Frank (vocals)
Born: Alabama, 1914. Attended Auburn University, sang with Auburn Knights College Band (and played guitar). Local radio work then worked with Mel Ruick's Orchestra at the Biltmore Hotel in Los Angeles before joining Ben Pollack. With Bob Crosby for a year from June 1935. Left full time music, and declined all offers to resume professional singing. Frank's daughter is vocaliste Toni, of "Captain and Tennille" fame.

TILTON, Elizabeth 'Liz' (vocals)
Born: c. 1920. Sister of Martha Tilton. With Gene Krupa, Buddy Rogers, Ray Noble and Larry Kent before working with Bob Crosby in 1941.

TURI, Blaise (trombone)
Born: 1924. Briefly with Bob Crosby in the fall of 1942.

UHLMAN, Harry L. (trombone)
Briefly with Bob Crosby, September 1942.

VIERA, 'Pete' Norman (piano)
Born: Jacksonville, Illinois, 1908. Died: 1960 Briefly with Bob Crosby during the summer of 1939.

VUNK, Lyman (trumpet)
Born: c. 1919. Worked with Charlie Barnet before joining Bob Crosby in August 1941, left in December 1942, rejoined Charlie Barnet, then became a studio musician.

WADE, Eddie (trumpet)
Born: San Diego, California, 1910. With Bill Brokow, Harry Reser, Paul Ash, Smith Ballew, Benny Goodman and Paul Whiteman before working briefly with Bob Crosby in early 1940. Later became a radar technician.

WALKER, Bob (r.n. Robert Wacker) (vocals)
Born: c. 1916. With Bob Crosby briefly in 1936.

WEBER, Kay (vocals)
Born: Ellingwood, Kansas, c. 1915. With Smith Ballew, and the Dorsey Brothers before working with Bob Crosby from late 1936 until April 1938. Married Crosby trombonist, Ward Sillaway on 21st June 1938. Mrs. Sillaway now lives in Texas, and is active as a teacher of music and singing.

WILDE, Lyn and Lee (r.n. Wild) (vocals)
Born: Missouri, c. 1924. The twins sang on radio KXOK before working with Ray Noble in 1941. Worked and recorded with Charlie Barnet before joining Bob Crosby in 1942. Later that year signed MGM film contract and appeared in many movies including: *Presenting Lily Mars, Reveille with Beverly, Andy Hardy's Blonde Trouble, Twice Blessed, Look For the Silver Lining* etc. The twins became sisters-in-law when they married the musical Cathcart brothers, Tom and Jim. Lee recorded an album *Wild and Wonderful* in the 1970s (with Doc Rando on clarinet), she continues to sing with various bands in and around Oregon.

ZARCHY, Rubin 'Zeke' (trumpet)
Born: New York, 12th June 1915. With Bob Crosby from February until November 1937, and again from August 1938 until October 1939.

ZURKE, Bob (r.n. Robert Albert Zukowski) (piano)
Born: Detroit, Michigan, 17th January 1912. Died: Los Angeles, California, 16th February 1944. Piano from age of 3, lessons from Professor Lewis; played for Paderewski in Detroit, 1922. During the mid-1920s appeared regularly at the Coliseum, Detroit, and at

the Martha Washington Theatre in Hamtramck. Became professional during early teens, worked with Oliver Naylor, Thelma Terry, Hank Biagini, Seymour Simons, Frank Sidney, Don Zell, etc, before joining Bob Crosby in December 1936. Left Crosby in May 1939, led own big band before becoming solo pianist, moved to California in 1941.

(FURTHER BIOGRAPHICAL INFORMATION ON MANY OF THE BOB CROSBY SIDEMEN LISTED HERE CAN BE FOUND IN THE AUTHOR'S *WHO'S WHO OF JAZZ*)